Railway Track Diagrams
Book 2: Eastern
Edited by Martyn Brailsford

Preface

Quail Track Diagrams have been published since 1988 and provide a reference to Enthusi. ... ...u industry alike. They contain information which may exist elsewhere and in other forms but are unique in making it all available in one easily portable volume. In 2004, TRACKmaps took over the updating and publication of these volumes.

The idea was not new at the outset but only when the late Gerald Jacobs, with his historical sources collected over 40 years with British Railways, joined forces with John Yonge of the Quail Map Co as cartographer and publisher did the principle find two people with the knowledge and the attention to detail to put it into full and effective practice. The result of this collaboration has become the standard reference work for a wide range of users from train staff and infrastructure managers to railway enthusiasts and modellers.

TRACKmaps October 2016

Introduction to this Edition

This book was last updated in 2006 and represents a tremendous amount of work in catching up the intervening years. The track diagrams in this book now concentrate on the Anglia and London North Eastern Routes of Network Rail together with a number of private railways and industrial concerns. They are, in general, up to date as at October 2016. Major additions include works such as Bacon Factory Chord, Cambridge and Peterborough station remodelling, Doncaster North Chord, Hitchin Grade Separation and the Canal Tunnels at St. Pancras. There have also been significant removals include the lifting of redundant lines in former coal mining areas and further lifting of track in former marshalling yards. Some works already commenced or planned but not yet finished are shown such as the Sheffield Tram-Train Project and Crossrail. The steady closure of signal boxes and re-control to major signalling centres continues apace and a number of freight sites, previously private, have now taken back under Network Rail's direct control through the Project Mountfield initiative.

This 4th edition has a number of other changes to its predecessor. The Index has been extended to include as many individual locations as possible, now totalling over 4,000. The ELR index has been retained and an LOR index added.

There has been some re-configuration of maps, especially in the Lincolnshire and Yorkshire areas, to reduce duplication of locations. As per other books in the series, the consolidation of leisure and miniature lines continues, as these now number around five hundred country-wide and are well served by other publications. Those heritage lines that do remain have, wherever possible, been moved closer to a relevant Network Rail location.

Acknowledgements

The Editor is indebted to Network Rail and its staff for access to many internal documents and there are many other contributors to this publication; some significant providing layouts, site checking or proofing details and some in a small way giving personal observations, answering individual questions or giving access to engineering drawings and construction diagrams. The Editor is particularly grateful for the assistance of Alex Betteney, Ian Hughes, Iain Scotchman, Ian Delgado, Neal Cummings, Alan Sheppard, Peter Green, Barnaby Clark, Denzil Peacock and Kevin Adlam in producing this edition, together with contributions by Myles Munsey, Michael Oakley from his Railway Data series (see the Bibliography), Mick Donovan, Andrew Brade, Jonathan Butson, Tony Cullingworth, P. Devonport, John Lacy, Kate Oldroyd, Mervyn Rogers, Peter Smith, Claire Tracey, Tony Watson and Darryl White. Acknowledgement is also due to Phil Deaves whose website on railway codes has been an effective reference in sorting out ELR queries, to Peter Scott, the editor of Minor Railways, to the Branch Line Society and to representatives of various heritage lines who have provided information. Many of the references used are provided in the Bibliography which appears at the end of this Book.

Martyn Brailsford

1st Edition 1988 (reprinted 1994)
2nd Edition 1998 (reprinted 2005)
3rd Edition 2006
4th Edition 2016

Published by TRACKmaps
PO Box 5259, Beckington, Frome, BA11 9DD. Website: www.trackmaps.co.uk

Edited by Martyn Brailsford

Cartography by David Padgett
Typesetting by John Szwenk

Printed by Brightsea Print Group, Clyst Honiton EX5 2UL
Cover design by Jan McFarlane at ArtWebCo, Swindon SN2 8YY

Publisher's Note

Every effort has been made by the Editor to ensure the accuracy of the information in the book is as correct as possible at the time of going to press. Notwithstanding, the Publishers welcome corrections, updates or suggestions for application to future editions. Contributions are preferred through the Contact Us page on the website or by post to the address above.

KEY

———————	Running Line	*86.34* _(Not italic if Station mileage)	Distance in Miles and chains from specified zero 1 Mile = 1760 yards / 1.6km 80 chains = 1 Mile 1 chain = 22 yards / 20.11m
———————	Siding	*57.600*	Distance in Kilometres
———————	Electrified overhead (25kV AC unless stated)	| 93	Whole mileposts, shown on the appropriate side of the line
———————	Electrified 3rd rail (750V DC)	| 32	Whole kilometre posts
———————	Electrified 4th rail (LUL) (630V DC)	*81.30]*	End of mileage run
———————	Electrified, overhead & Conductor rail	*113.76* ―――― **COM** *105.70*	Lineside mileage change
··················	Proposed or under construction.	DOW	ELR-Engineer's Line Reference (Prefix and suffix numbers indicate sub-divisions and their boundaries)
———●———	Line obstructed	[LN752]	Line of Route Code
——○- - -	Line 'in situ' but out of use, partly dismantled, buried, or overgrown	**3**	Platform with number (May be supplemented by sub-divisions. e.g. (a), (b), (c), 'N' or North etc)
——:——	Change of Signalling mandate	⑦	Indicates number of carriages per platform (approx 20m lengths)
LNW ‖ LNE	Network Rail Territory boundary	⠿	Proposed platform
Barnsley | York ROC (BY) | (S)	Signal Box / centre area limits (Within an area, plates on automatic signals may reflect actual line description)	▭	Former Royal Mail platform
✕ ❖	Diamond Crossing / Switch Diamond	▭	Platform out of use
—)- - -(—	Tunnel	⊔	Other feature (labelled)
⌣	Bridge under Rail or Viaduct	▨	Loading bank / dock
—Y—	Selected Motorway / Trunk Road bridges over rail	*Worksop* *(WP)* ⊠	ASC, IECC, SB, SC, SCC or ROC with code (underlined text relates)
—+—	Network Rail operated level crossing	▨	Control Panel
—¦—	User-worked crossing with Telephone	◼	Gate Box
←——→	Track signalled in both directions (a double arrow indicates normal direction of travel)	▫ ⊙	Ground Frame GF / Ground Switch Panel GSP or Shunting Frame SF. Ⓢ Indicates 'Shut in' facility
—⋈—	Private siding boundary, or gate	✳	Radio electronic token block / Token exchange point
⌐——⟍	Sand Drag / Trap Point	¶	Proposed closure
—◯—▫	Turntable / Ramp	○	Water tower
—‡—	Gantry Rails (Freightliner Terminal)	∧	Summit, height in feet
—×—×—×—	Fence	*(Easington)* •	Indicates a former Jn, Station or Signal Box
⋏⋏⋏⋏⋏⋏⋏	Wall / Bank / Cliff		
▬▬▬ ▲	Hot Axle Box Detector (HABD), Wheel Impact Load Detector (WILD) or Wheelchex Device		

Guide references are given to pre-nationalisation, pre-grouping and sometimes pioneer railways e.g. LNE: GC

Traditional Line Descriptions may be quoted, e.g. **EAST SUFFOLK LINE**

GENERAL ABBREVIATIONS

Abbr	Description	Abbr	Description	Abbr	Description
A	Acid Application	ft	Feet	REC	Reception
BP	Associated British Ports	GC	Gantry Crane	RETB	Radio Electronic Token Block
C	Alternating Current	GDS	Goods	REV	Reversing or Reversible line
RR	Arrival	GL	Goods Loop	ROC	Rail Operating Centre
SC	Area Signalling Centre	GS	Goods Shed	RR	Run-Round
dy	Boundary	H	Headshunt	S	South
CH	Branch	HABD	Hot Axle Box Detector	S & T	Signal & Telegraph
R	British Rail	HH	Hopper House	SB	Signal Box or Southbound
ET	Controlled Emission Toilet Discharge	HL	High Level	SC	Signalling Centre
L	Crossing Loop on Single Line	HST	High Speed Train	SCC	Signalling Control Centre
OM	Change of Mileage	IECC	Intergrated Electronic Control Centre	Sdg(s)	Siding(s)
R	Cripple Siding	Jn	Junction	SD	Sand Drag
W	Carriage Washer	Jt	Joint	SIMBIDS	Simplified Bi-Directional Signalling
&W	Carriage & Wagon	km	kilometres	SN	Shunt Neck
■	Connections Disconnected	LC	Level Crossing (locally operated)	SP	Switch Panel
A	Down Avoiding	LHS	Locomotive Holding Siding	SS	Shunt Spur
C	Direct Current	LL	Low Level	TA	Tamper siding
E	Down Electric	loe	limit of electrification	TB	Turnback Siding
ED	Diesel Electric Depot	LP	Loop	TEP	Token Exchange Point
EP	Departure	LPG	Liquified petroleum gas	TL	Traffic Lights
F	Down Fast	LS	Locomotive Shed	TMD	Traction Maintenance Depot
G	Down Goods	LW	Locomotive Washer	T&RSMD	Traction & Rolling Stock Maintenance Depot
GL	Down Goods Loop	M	Middle	U&D	Up & Down
L	Down Loop	M ch	Miles and Chains	UA	Up Avoiding
M	Down Main	M&EE	Mechanical & Electrical Engineer	UE	Up Electric
MD	Diesel Maintenance Depot	MGR	'Merry-go-round'	UF	Up Fast
MUD	Diesel Multiple Unit Depot	MN	Main	UFC	Underframe Cleaning
N	Down	MOD	Ministry of Defence	UFN	Until Further Notice
PL	Down Passenger Loop	MU	Maintenance Unit	UG	Up Goods
R	Down Relief	N	North	UGL	Up Goods Loop
RS	Down Refuge Siding	NB	Northbound	UH	Unloading Hopper
S	Down Slow	Ng	Narrow Gauge	UL	Up Loop
SB	Down Surburban	NIRU	Not in regular use	UM	Up Main
T	Down Through	NR	Network Rail	UPL	Up Passenger Loop
E	East	NT	No Telephone (on LC)	UR	Up Relief
B	Eastbound	OHC	Overhead Crane	URS	Up Refuge Siding
GF	Emergency Ground Frame	OHLE	Overhead Line Equipment	US	Up Slow
MD	Electric Maintenance Depot	OOU	Out of Use	USB	Up Suburban
MUD	Electric Multiple Unit Depot	ONS	Overhead Neutral Section	UT	Up Through
ngrs	Engineers' Sidings	OTM	On-track Maintenance	V or Vdct	Viaduct
ol	End of Line	P	Points padlocked	W	West or Wash Point
RTMS	European Rail Traffic Management System	PAD	Prefabricated Assembly Depot	WB	Westbound or Weighbridge
SP	Emergency Signalling Panel	PL	Passenger Loop	WD	War Department or Wheelchex Device
TCS	European Train Control System	PSB	Power Signal Box	WILD	Wheel Impact Load Detector
A	Flushing Apron	PW	Permanent Way	WL	Wheel Lathe
P	Fuelling Point or Footpath	Qy	Query concerning distances etc, unresolved	yds	yards

SUPPLEMENTARY ABBREVIATIONS FOR THIS BOOK

A	Network Rail Anglia Route	LNE	Network Rail London North East Route
CTRL	Channel Tunnel Rail Link	LNW	former London and North Western Railway
DLR	Docklands Light Railway	LNW	Network Rail London North West Route
EC	former Eastern Counties Railway	LSW	former London and South Western Railway
ECML	East Coast Main Line	LT&S	former London, Tilbury and Southend Railway
EM	Network Rail East Midlands Route	LUL	London Underground Limited
GC	former Great Central Railway	M&C	former Maryport & Carlisle Railway
GE	former Great Eastern Railway	Mid or M	former Midland Railway
GN	former Great Northern Railway	N&SWJn	former North and South Western Junction Railway
GW	former Great Western Railway	NE	former North Eastern Railway
HS1	HS1 Limited	NL	former North London Railway
H&B	former Hull and Barnsley Railway	NLL	North London Line
L&B	former London and Blackwall Railway	SC	Network Rail Scottish Route
L&Y	former Lancashire & Yorkshire Railway	SR	former Southern Railway
LD&EC	former Lancashire, Derbyshire & East Coast Railway	SX	Network Rail Sussex Route
		TFL	Transport for London
LMS	former London Midland and Scottish Railway	WX	Network Rail Wessex Route
LNE	former London and North Eastern Railway	W	Network Rail Western Route

LEVEL CROSSING ABBREVIATIONS

Abbreviation	Description	Abbreviation	Description
(ABCL) *	Automatic Barrier Crossing, Locally monitored	(MWL) *	Crossing with Miniature Warning Lights
(AHBC) *	Automatic Half-Barrier Crossing	(OC) or (OPEN)	Open Crossing (non-automatic), without barriers or gates
(AOCL) *	Automatic Open Crossing, Locally monitored	(RC)	Remotely Controlled crossing with barriers
(AOCL+B)	AOCL with Barriers	(R/G) *	UWC with Red and Green warning lights operated by approaching trains
(AOCR)	Automatic Open Crossing, Remotely monitored		
(BW)	Bridle Way (generally shown if telephone provided)	(TMO)	Traincrew Operated crossing
(CCTV)	Full barrier crossing with Closed Circuit Television monitored by Signaller	(TMOB)	Traincrew Operated Barrier
(FP)	Footpath crossing (generally shown if telephone provided)	(TMOG)	Traincrew Operated Gates
(MCB)	Manually controlled Crossing with Barriers	(UWC)	User-Worked accommodation or occupation crossing, with telephone
(MCB-OD)	MCB with Obstruction Detection	(UW~)	User-Worked crossing where ~ is substituted with 'B' Barriers, 'G' Gates, 'K' Kissing gates or 'W' Wickets
(MCG)	Manually controlled Crossing with Gates		
(MGH)	Manned Gates, Hand worked	(WL)	Barrow or Foot Crossing with White Light indicators
(MGW)	Manned Gates with Wickets		
(MSL) *	Crossing with Miniature Stop Lights		

* (-X) shown after these abbreviations (e.g. AHBC-X) indicates that the crossing works automatically for movements in the wrong direction.

In some cases, the code of the controlling signal box may be shown, e.g. Thonock Lane Farm (UWC) (GC).

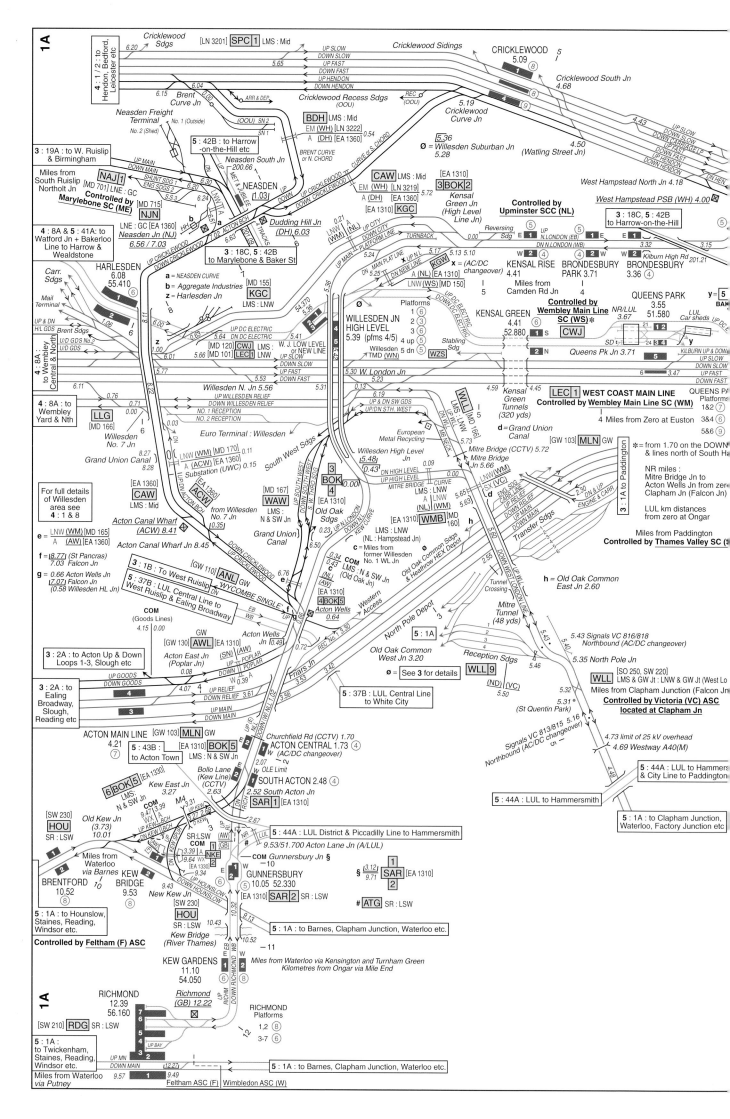

NORTH LONDON LINE ● TOTTENHAM & HAMPSTEAD LINE

[EA 1310] BOK 2 LMS : LNW (NL : Hampstead Jn)

Hampstead Heath Tunnel (1166 yds)

1.63-1.56 Supported Cutting

Controlled by Upminster SCC (NL)

LNE & LMS Jt : GE & Mid Jt
Mortimer St Highgate Rd Vdct 0.23-26

Covered Way (185yds)

[EA 1370] GOJ [EA 1370]
2 JRT TAH 1

LNE & LMS Jt : GE & Mid Jt

UPPER HOLLOWAY 3.00 ⑥

LEY ROAD ROGNAL 2.44

HAMPSTEAD HEATH 1.53 ④ Miles from Camden Road Jn

Gospel Oak Jn 1.10

GOSPEL OAK 1.01

Junction Rd Jn

Upper Holloway (UH) 2.76

Cripple Sdg GSP

Belsize Slow Lines Tunnel (1 mile, 107 yds)

Belsize Fast Lines Tunnel (1 mile, 11 yds)

Lismore Circus Umbrella Tunnel 2.22 2.17 2.29

[LN 3201] SPC 1 LMS : Mid

* = Hampstead Tunnel (1.74-76 (3.72-76)

Tottenham North Curve (T.N.C) Tunnel No. 1 (160 yds)

Kentish Town Jn

KENTISH TOWN 3.40 (Moorgate) 1.42 (St Pancras)

[LN 3213] MCL LMS : Mid

Miles from St Pancras via Kentish Town

Gospel Oak - Barking Electrification
Lines due for electrification 2018

SPC 1 MCL Controlled by West Hampstead PSB (WH)

KENTISH TOWN WEST 0.34

[EA 1310] BOK 2 LMS : LNW (NL : Hampstead Jn)

Camden Road Tunnels

Controlled by Upminster SCC (NL)

[LN 101] ECM 1 LNE : GN 14A : to Finsbury Park

[LN 3201] SPC 1 LMS : Mid

BOK 1 [EA 1320]

[MD 701] MCJ LNE : GC CHILTERN LINE
3 : 18C : to Harrow-on-the-Hill

SOUTH HAMPSTEAD 2.33

[MD 120] CWJ LMS : LNW

Sth Hampstead Tunnels

PRIMROSE HILL 5.49

Camden Jn 1.59

Primrose Hill Jn 5.57

Primrose Hill Tunnels (1182 yds)

3 : 18C : to Marylebone

Camden Jn

Miles from Euston

Camden Viaduct

CAMDEN ROAD 5.01

Camden Rd Central Jn [EA 1320] BOK 1

Camden Rd E. Jn

Dock Jn North 0.76/2.73

Copenhagen

5 : 49A

CALEDONIAN ROAD AND BARNSBURY 3.74 Platforms

2CRC1 LMS : NL

From Camden Road West Jn ALL directions are DOWN & Line Designations change

[MD 145] [EA 1320] (Hampstead Rd Jn)

Miles from former Broad Street Station

4 : 1 : to London St Pancras

4 : 1 : to Farringdon & Blackfriars

4 : 1 : to London St Pancras

4 : 1 : to Farringdon & Blackfriars

14A : to Kings Cross

[CN 3214] CBI

[LN 115]

Ω = Primrose Hill to Caledonian Road & Barnsbury North London Viaducts and Arches

M = Maintenance Sdg to HS1

a = Camden Rd Incline Jn 0m 44ch/0.706(e)
b = York Way N Jn 1.382(LSP)/0m 13ch
c = Belle Isle Jn 0m 57ch(KX)/0m 53ch *
d = Cedar Jn 0.522(e)/0.305(LSP)
e = York Way S Jn 0.000/1.409(LSP)
f = ECML Bridge Covered Portal 1.425(LSP)

g = A|HS1 (NL) (AF) 0m 37ch *
h = A|HS1 (NL) (AF) 0m 24ch
i = LNE|EM (K)|(TWH) 0m 37ch *
j = LNE|HS1 (K)|(AF) 0m 24ch

k = HS1/NLL CONNECTION
l = ST PANCRAS ECML CONNECTION

* Mileage from Canal Tunnel Junction

[01] LEC 1 LMS : LNW (London & Birmingham)
WEST COAST MAIN LINE

Gospel Oak - Barking Electrification
Lines due for electrification 2018

[EA 1370] TAH 1 LNE & LMS Jt (Tottenham & Hampstead Jt)

UPPER HOLLOWAY 3.00

14B : to Alexandra Palace

Harringay Jn

HARRINGAY 3.32

Hornsey Train Servicing Centre

LNE [LN 165] HPW

Harringay Park Jn

10B : to Enfield Town & Cheshunt

[EA 1160] BGK LNE : GE

SEVEN SISTERS 5.48

TOTTENHAM HALE 6.00

10B : to Cheshunt

Lea Valley Viaduct 6.56-62

BLACKHORSE ROAD 7.21

10B : to Chingford

Seven Sisters Jn 5.40/0.00

HARRINGAY GREEN LANES 4.61

CROUCH HILL 3.65

Crown Hill Tunnel (90 yards)

14A : to King's Cross

[LN 101] ECM 1 LNE : GN

S. Tott West Jn

S. Tott East Jn

SOUTH TOTTENHAM 5.69
S. Tottenham Jn (S) 5.71

1 TAH 2 [EA 1370]

$ = SSL [EA 1300] LNE:GE
UP & DN SEVEN SISTERS CHORD

South Tottenham Station Junction (S)

Tottenham South Jn 5.41

Coppermill (North) Jn

WALTHAMSTOW QUEENS ROAD 8.11

[EA 1370] TAH 2 LMS : Mid (Tottenham & Forest Gate Jn Rly)

1 TSE 2 [EA 1290]
(Tottenham West Jn)
★ COM

S. Tottenham Liverpool St (S) (L)
6.22 | 5.54

Clapton Jn

Temple Mills & Stratford

10B

Controlled by Upminster SCC (NL)

14A : to Finsbury Park

Canonbury Tunnel Canonbury W. Jn

[LN 110] CFP LNE : GN

(Dalston Western Jn) [EA 1320] LMS : NL

1 BOK DWW 1

1 DWW 2 [EA 1320]

Navarino Rd Jn

Platforms

Controlled by Upminster SCC (NL)

HACKNEY DOWNS 2.78

HOMERTON 2.01

HACKNEY WICK 2.68 River Lea

DALSTON KINGSLAND 2.06

CALEDONIAN ROAD AND BARNSBURY 3.74 Platforms

HIGHBURY & ISLINGTON 3.36 Platforms

CANONBURY 2.73 Platforms

Zero Datum for ELL

A 2.17 COM TFL 0.11

Upminster SCC

[EA 1180] GRE BR

HACKNEY CENTRAL 1.32

Victoria Park (Victoria Park Jn) 2.48 (0.00)

LMS : NL / LNE : GE

§ = Reading Lane Jn 2.55

4 Miles from former Broad St Station
(but reverses at Dalston Western Jn to Navarino Rd Jn)

DALSTON JUNCTION 0.20

ELL [EA 1325] ELL LMS : NL

Controlled by East London Line SCC (EL)

HAGGERSTON 0.52

5 : 46B : to New Cross/ New Cross Gate

LONDON FIELDS 2.35

Miles from Liverpool Street

CAMBRIDGE HEATH 1.61

2A : to Liverpool St.

[EA 1160] BGK LNE : GE

Controlled by Liverpool Street IECC (L)

2B to Stratford

(1.74 Regent's Canal)

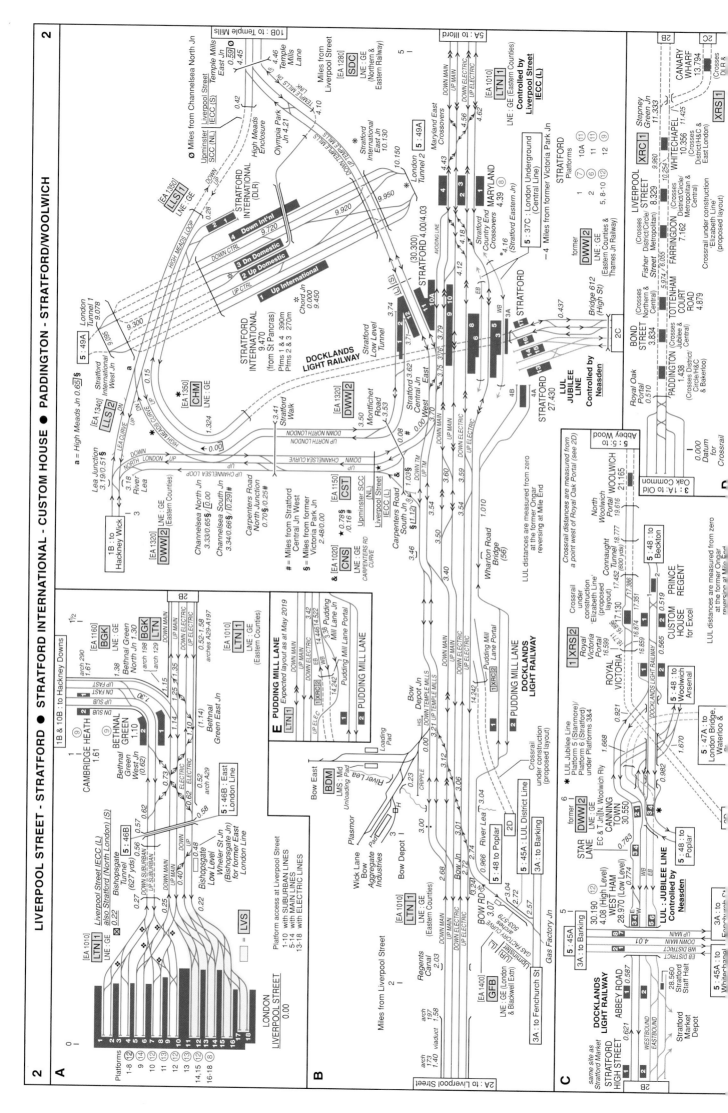

LIVERPOOL STREET - STRATFORD ● STRATFORD INTERNATIONAL - CUSTOM HOUSE ● PADDINGTON - STRATFORD/WOOLWICH

LONDON, TILBURY & SOUTHEND LINE : FENCHURCH STREET - SHOEBURYNESS • SOUTHEND PIER

Panel A

BARKING

LUL distances are measured from zero at the former Ongar reversing at Mile End
Km posts on north side of line

Ω = 7.42 is the mean of LTS platforms also signal box (LUL only)

a = DOWN T & H / DOWN TILBURY
b = UP TILBURY / UP T & H
c = Barking East Jn
d = Barking Line GF 13.53

BARKING Platforms
1 ⑨
4 ⑭
5 ⑬
7 ⑫
8 ⑬

Barking Sidings
(District & Hammersmith & City Lines stabling)

23.080 UPNEY (LUL)
24.550 BARKING

BTE
TLL LMS : Mid (LT&S) [EA 1390]

Gospel Oak - Barking Electrification
Lines due for electrification — 2018

5A : to Ilford
5A : to Stratford

WOODGRANGE PARK 12.05
11.79 Woodgrange Park Jn
11.47 Forest Gate Jn
FGW TAH 3 [EA 1370]
LMS : Mid (LT&S)

EAST HAM EMU DEPOT (EM)
c2c - National Express
1 FSS 2 LMS : Mid (LT&S) [EA 1380]

Panel — left (Fenchurch Street area)

Pig's Bay QinetiQ
Distances in kms very approximate

LONDON FENCHURCH STREET 0.00
FSS 1 LNE : GE (London & Blackwall) [EA 1380]
arch 1 0.33 0.20
TMO High Street 0.00
TMO 0.9

TOWER GATEWAY
5 : to Bank
5 : 48 : to Poplar

SHADWELL
Royal Mint St Jn
LIMEHOUSE
viaduct (1.04)
Regents Canal Jn
Christian St Jn 0.61
5 : 45A : to Whitechapel
Ø Whitechapel & Bow Joint (Met. District & Mid (LT&S))

BOW ROAD 3.07
GFB [EA 1400]
Gas Factory Jn
FACTORY CURVE
2B : to Bow Jn & Stratford
z = BOW CHURCH

BROMLEY-BY-BOW (LUL) 31.580
DEVONS RD
DLR to Stratford
5 : 48 : to Poplar
GFB FSS 1 LMS : Mid (LT&S)

WEST HAM (LUL) 30.190
R. Lea & Bow Creek
5 : 47B Jubilee Line (LUL)
2C : to Canning Town (DLR)

PLAISTOW (LUL) 29.390
DIST AND H/SMITH & CITY LINES
UPTON PARK (LUL) 28.150
EAST HAM (LUL) 26.740

WANSTEAD PARK ⑦ 11.15
LEYTON MIDLAND RD ⑧ 9.22
LEYTONSTONE HIGH ROAD ⑧ 10.00
WALTHAMSTOW QUEENS ROAD 8.11
5 : 38A : LUL Central Line
5 : 38A : to Ilford

Sth Tottenham
1B : to South Tottenham

Miles from London St. Pancras via Upper Holloway

Panel B

LT&S Lines controlled by Upminster IECC (UR)

UPNEY (LUL) 23.080 2 1
BECONTREE (LUL) 21.210
DAGENHAM HEATHWAY (LUL) 19.840
DAGENHAM EAST (LUL) 18.500
ELM PARK (LUL) 16.170
HORNCHURCH (LUL) 14.660
UPMINSTER BRIDGE 13.410

UPMINSTER 12.190
3.30 from Romford
5B : to Romford
LUL SB (FM)
Depot
see 5 : 45B
Upminster IECC (UR/NL)
Upminster East Jn
FSS 2 [EA 1380] UPG LMS : Mid (LT&S) [EA 1410]

Platforms
1A ⑫
2,3 ⑦
6 ⑫

OCKENDON 3.05
OCKENDON SINGLE LINE
West Horndon 19.15
Stifford Viaduct
CHAFFORD HUNDRED 5.38
(For Lakeside Shopping Centre)
M25 16.73
Whipps Farm

LMS : Mid (LT&S)

Dagenham East Crossovers
EASTBOUND WESTBOUND
DN MAIN UP MAIN
DISTRICT LINE

FSS 2 [EA 1380] LMS : Mid (LT&S)

Panel C

LT&S Lines controlled by Upminster IECC (UR)

Pitsea Jn 26.52
UP SDG DN SDG
26.60 32.43

BENFLEET for Canvey Island 29.11 ⑫
LEIGH-ON-SEA 32.43 ⑫
CHALKWELL 33.69 ⑫
WESTCLIFF 34.66 ⑫
SOUTHEND CENTRAL 35.55
Platforms
1 ⑫
2 ⑫
3 ⑭
4 ⑫

SOUTHEND EAST 36.49
THORPE BAY 37.73
London End Jn 38.74
Carriage Sidings (SN)
SHU c2c National Express
SHOEBURYNESS 39.40

Controlled by Upminster IECC (UR)
All crossovers are bi-directionally signalled

Kelsey No 1 (UWC) 30.11
Kersey No 7 (UWC) 30.65
Salvation Army (UWC) 31.14

FSS 3 [EA 1380] LMS : Mid (LT&S)

Salvation Army (UWC) 30.65
Kersey No 2
Sea wall

Panel — Pitsea / Basildon (upper right)

Miles from Fenchurch Street

PITSEA 26.42
Pitsea Jn 26.52 32.43
Pitsea Hall (208) 32.37
Vange Wharf (CCTV) 31.43 32.24 Pitsea Hall (208)
DN TILBURY
4A : to Tilbury & Pitsea
4B : to Grays and Tilbury : 4B

BASILDON 24.26 ⑫
LAINDON 22.69 ⑫
WEST HORNDON 19.15 ⑫

All Lines controlled by Upminster IECC (UR)

DOWN MAIN
UP MAIN

Panel — Barking / Tilbury (centre right)

Miles from Fenchurch Street

DOWN MAIN UP MAIN
DOWN T & H UP T & H
DOWN TILBURY GDS
UP TILBURY MN

Barking, Tilbury line Jn East
Barking, Tilbury Line Jn West (up)
BWT BKG UP DN T & H LINES
13.42 13.18 13.12 13.10

TAH 4 3
24.550 BARKING (St Pancras) 13.62
7.42 Ω (BS/Signals only)

River Roding 7.08
Balloon Rd
Storage
Inlet Line
6.50 6.40 6.35

Panel D — SOUTHEND PIER RAILWAY
(Southend-on-Sea Borough Council)

NORTH STATION
3ft gauge (920mm)
automatic points
colour-light signals
Length c. 1m 9ch
SOUTH STATION (Pierhead)
Work shop spur

October 2016

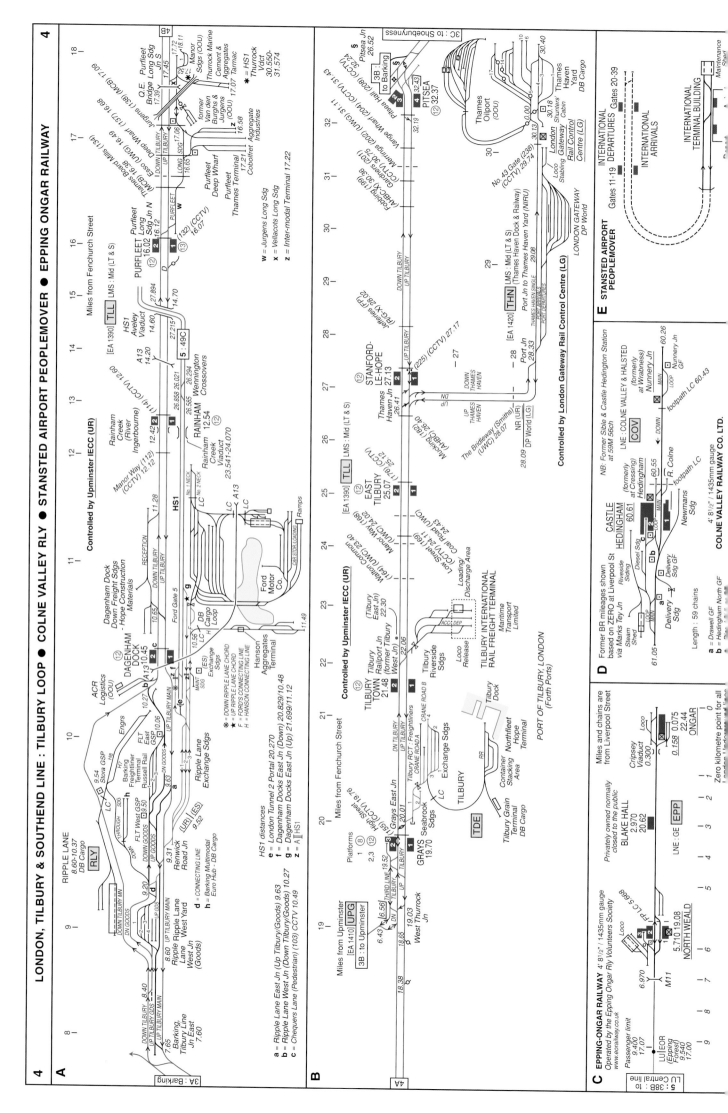

LONDON, TILBURY & SOUTHEND LINE : TILBURY LOOP ● COLNE VALLEY RLY ● STANSTED AIRPORT PEOPLEMOVER ● EPPING ONGAR RAILWAY

5

A

Gospel Oak - Barking Electrification
Lines due for electrification 2018

[EA 1370] TAH 2

3A : to Wanstead Park

Forest Gate Stn Jn 5.37
FOREST GATE 5.21
Forest Gate Jn 5.63/0.00

MANOR PARK 6.19

Miles from Liverpool Street

DOWN MAIN / UP MAIN
DOWN ELECTRIC / UP ELECTRIC
DOWN BCH / UP BCH
DOWN PASS AVOIDING / UP PASS AVOIDING

FGW [EA 1030]
Woodgrange Park Jn [0.31] 11.79
WOODGRANGE PARK (8) 12.03
3A : to Barking

2B : to Stratford

ILFORD EMU Depot (IL)
Abellio Greater Anglia, Bombardier
Crossrail
Plessey Rds
ICS Layout shown is post Crossrail alterations to Ilford Depot subject to confirmation

Carriage Inspection Shed
Country End
Ley Street Yard Sidings
Carriage Washer Roads
Bombardier Paint Shop
Bombardier Shop 'A'
No.1 Carriage Line / No.2 Carriage Line
Wheel Lathe
Traverser
London End

ILFORD 7.28
Ilford Depot London End Jn 7.45
Ilford Depot Country End Jn 8.30
Aldersbrook Up / Carriage Holding Sidings

CHADWELL HEATH 9.79
10.08 / 10.13
T/B Sdg
GOODMAYES 9.23
Goodmayes Sdg (OOU)
SEVEN KINGS 8.45
8.54 / 8.63 / 8.73

LTN 1 [EA 1010] [EA 1011]
LTN 1 LNE : GE (Eastern Counties)
Controlled by Liverpool Street IECC (L)

B

11 Miles from Liverpool Street

Arches 1-17 ROMFORD
Romford London End Jn 12.26
ROMFORD 12.30
Romford ROC 12.06
Romford Engineers' Depot
Romford Jn 12.39 / 0.13
0.00 (12.39)
12.00

GIDEA PARK 13.41
Gidea Park Station Jn
Gidea Park Carriage Sidings
Gidea Park Country End Jn
Layout at Gidea Park subject to confirmation
13.30 / 13.55 / 14.03 / 14.15 / 14.23

HAROLD WOOD 14.76
BRENTWOOD 18.16
M25
Ingrave Summit 19.20
16.47 / 17.35 HABD

SHENFIELD 20.16 (Southend Line)
Shenfield Stabling Sidings
Sth Country End Jn 20.22 / 20.50
London End Jn 19.45
Platforms 1-5 / 6
Southend Loop
DOWN SOUTHEND / UP SOUTHEND
UP PASS LOOP
UP PLATFORM LOOP or UP SOUTHEND
[EA 1050] SSV LNE : GE
10A : to Southend
21.00 / 21

EMERSON PARK 1.64
UPMINSTER 3.30
UPMINSTER BRANCH
ROU [EA 1040]
LMS : Mid (LT & SI)

i = Inlet Road
o = Outlet Road

LTN 1 LNE : GE (Eastern Counties)
[EA 1010] [EA 1011]
Controlled by Liverpool Street IECC (L)
All crossovers on the Main Line are bi-directionally signalled

C

Miles from Liverpool Street

INGATESTONE 23.50
23.00
Ingatestone (FP) 23.00
Church Lane 24.60
Church Lane Crossovers 24.75 / 25.41
Margaretting (FP) 25.39
Ingatestone (2)

CHELMSFORD 29.60
Chelmsford Viaducts 29.40 / 29.53 / 29.64
River Can Viaduct 29.26-36
River Chelmer Viaduct 30.25
Arbour Lane Crossover 30.20 / 30.30
Mill Siding
Brick House Crossovers 33.24
Boreham Viaduct 32.69-72
Incline
Lower Yard - Foster Yeoman Stone Term.

HATFIELD PEVEREL 35.74
River Ter Viaduct 35.22

WITHAM 38.47
38.26 / 38.34 / 38.55
24.22 / 24.15 / 38.55
24.15 COM
YARD RD
HABD 5D
WHITE NOTLEY 21.10
CRESSING 20.00
BRAINTREE FREEPORT 18.54
BRAINTREE 17.71
Fairheads NO.39 (UWC) 20.77
19.75
Cousins (34) 19.18
BRAINTREE BRANCH
BRA [EA 1070]
LNE : GE (Maldon, Witham and Braintree)
WITHAM (38.47) 24.22 / 24.15
New House Farm (UWC)(43) 21.85 / 21.11
Cut Throat Lane (R/G) 24.05
Miles from Bishop's Stortford

Controlled by Liverpool Street IECC (L)

KELVEDON 42.21 / 42.02
Church Street (AJBCX) 41.57

MARKS TEY 46.49
Marks Tey Jn 46.56 (mileage reverses but increases to Sudbury)
Church House Farm (UWC) 47.50
Church No.2 (FP) 47.43 / 47.25
Church No.1 (FP) 46.06 / 46.30
East Anglian Railway Museum
Chappel S. / Chappel N.
Sand Terminal / Tarmac
WB
Hopper Loading Rails

D

STOUR VALLEY LINE
BURES 53.45
Mount Bures (ABCL) 52.61
Chappel Viaduct (River Colne)
CHAPPEL AND WAKES COLNE 50.18
Workshop / Museum GF 50.26
= Goods Shed 50.30
DN & UP SUDBURY
Pitmore Viaduct (River Stour) 55.36
55.46-47
Lamarsh School (UWC) 54.17
SUDBURY (Suffolk) 58.32
Ladbridge (34) 57.42
Cornard (UWC) 57.52
Ladbridge (ABCL) 58.25
SUD [EA 1080] LNE : GE (Colchester, Stour Valley via Marks Tey Jn)
Controlled by Liverpool Street IECC (L)

E

Controlled by Colchester (CO)
MARKS TEY 46.49
LTN 1 [EA 1011]
Crufts Hill (35) 49.41
Lexden Viaduct (River Colne) 49.63
Crutch No.2 (FP) 47.43
Crutch No.1 (FP) 47.25
6A : to Colchester
LNE : GE (Eastern Counties) (CO)
Controlled by Liverpool Street IECC (L)
[EA 1011]

October 2016

5

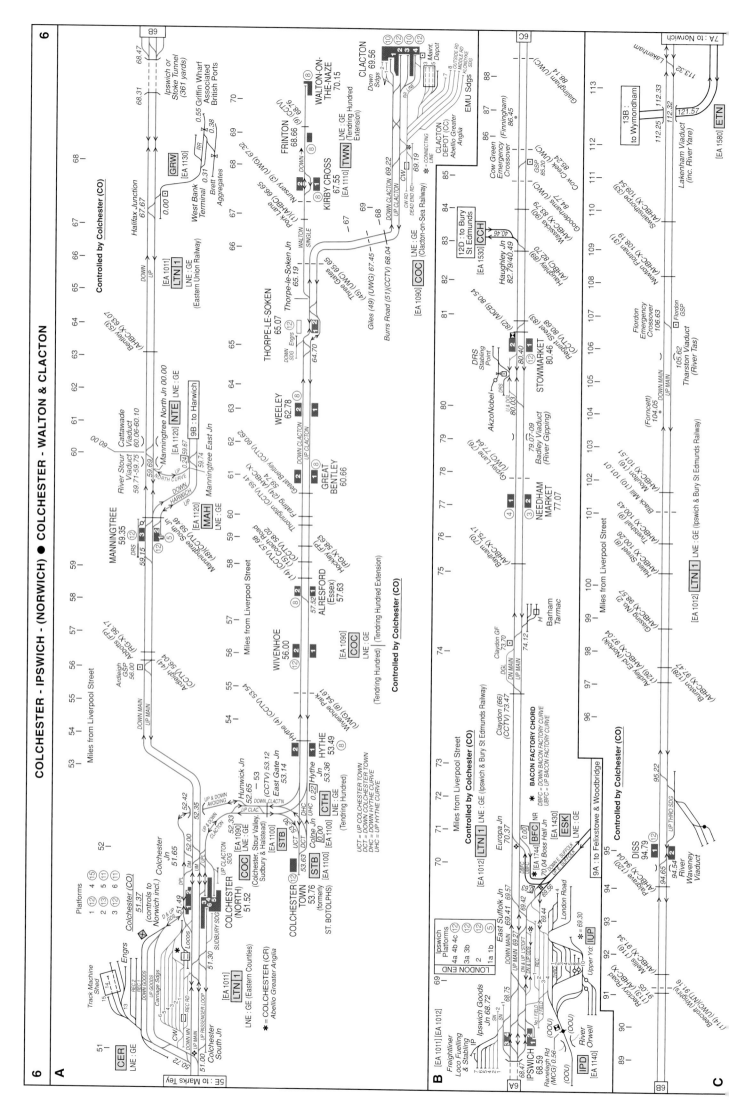

A — NORWICH (Thorpe)

8 : to Lowestoft, Yarmouth & Cromer

[EA 1480] WHC 1 LNE : GE (East Norfolk)

DN CROMER BRANCH
UP CROMER BRANCH

Bungalow Lane (1A) (R.G.'X') 2.18
Giffords (R.G.'X') 1.32
Whitlingham Lane (UWG) (4) 1.63

DOWN MAIN
UP MAIN

(TB) [BL] Brundall

Whitlingham Jn 1.69

[EA 1470] NOL LNE : GE

Thorpe (CO) Bridge 1.47·50

Miles from Norwich Thorpe

(River Yare)

One Mile Bridge 1·00·04

NORWICH (Thorpe) 0.00

Platforms
1 & 2
3 & 4
5
6

Miles from Liverpool Street via Cambridge 124.09
via Ipswich 114.77

Jubilee Carriage Sidings (J)

Area/Line designations eg 'C' : 'D' etc

Carriage Sidings 'S'

Central

Controlled by Colchester (CO)

2 LTN LTN 2 NOL
[EA 1013]

Thorpe Jn 0.29
LOCO NECK 'N'
Former Fuel Sdg
Bridge 357 123.60

Riverside Freight Depot

Sugarstone Stockpile

THORPE YARD 'Y' THG

HEADSHUNT 'H'

Royal Dock

B — THE WELLS AND WALSINGHAM RAILWAY 10¼" gauge Former BR distances from Wymondham are bracketed

WALSINGHAM 3.74 (c 28.62)
3.75
Mid-Norfolk (13B) →

Barnards Cutting (1 in 29)

WIGHTON (SETON'S HALT) 2.29
WIGHTON HALT 1.75

WARHAM 1.11
FWW 2 LNE : GE

THE MIDDEN HALT 0.23

The Tunnel (B1105)

WELLS ON SEA 0.02 (32.50)
0.00

Loco Shed
Ash pit
Workshop
Loco

2 LTN LTN 2 NOL
[EA 1013]

a = Through Sdgs GF

Wensum Jn 0.60
0.28

Crown Point Control Tower (CP) 0.58

CROWN POINT DEPOT (NC)
Abellio Greater Anglia

Underframe Cleaning Shed

Lavatory Flushing

Wensum Depot Engrs

NCW BR
[EA 1470] NOL LNE : GE

THROATHOLE (WENSUM CURVE)

DOWN LOWESTOFT
UP LOWESTOFT
RECEPTION 1
RECEPTION 2

0.38

BY-PASS LINE
DEAD END
CW
SS

0.75

123.43

C — CARLTON COLVILLE - EAST ANGLIAN TRANSPORT MUSEUM
(3 miles SW of Lowestoft)

CHAPEL ROAD
Chapel Road Trolleybus Stop

Exhibition Buildings

Commercial Vehicle Depot

Tram Depot

EAST SUFFOLK LIGHT RAILWAY 2' 0" gauge 10 chains

Electric Tramway, 4' 8½" (18 chains)
Trolleybus
550 volts, DC

Trolleybus wire for stabling

Trolleybus Depot

Woodside Tram Stops

WOODSIDE

Hedley Grove

D

Swing Bridge Jn 123.38
123.37

Trowse Swing Bridge (TB) 123.37
(Controls Cromer Branch)

Trowse Swing (TB)
Swing Bridge Jn 123.38

Trowse (Swing Bridge) Jn

Trowse Swing Bridge (River Wensum)

TROWSE DN & UP LP
UP MAIN
DOWN MAIN

Discharge Pit
Tarmac

Miles from Liverpool Street
123.00 : via Cambridge
113.68I : via Ipswich

UP THETFORD
DN THETFORD

UP MAIN
DOWN MAIN

Trowse (Lower) Jn

TROWSE 123.11

Victoria Sidings (OOU)

[EA 1013] LTN 2
[EA 1012] LTN 1 LNE : GE

123

6C : to Diss & Ipswich   13B : to Wymondham & Ely

[EA 1580] ETN LNE : GE (Norwich & Brandon Railway)

HOVETON & WROXHAM 8.61
2

WROXHAM 8.63

8 : to Norwich
8.69

WHC 1 LNE : GE
8 : to Cromer

Belaugh Green 7.64 [9.72]

COLTISHALL 6.04

DOWN UP

Hautbois Loop 4.17

BUXTON 3.23
River Bure (Buxton River Bridge)

Brampton Loop 2.41

BRAMPTON HALT 2.30

3.63

BURE VALLEY RAILWAY (1991) LTD - 15" gauge 'THE BROADLAND LINE'

Miles from Aylsham (Bure Valley Railway)

Spratts Green 1·12 [16.44]

Aylsham Tunnel (182 yards)

AYLSHAM 0.00
SB (Control Centre)
0.28·37
Workshop Shed
Running Shed

1
2·3

Former GE/LNE/BR trackbed (ELR: WMC), with mileages measured from Norwich in [brackets]. Some of the former mileposts remain on the same side as the Bure Valley ones.

Radio controlled signalling

E — WHITWELL AND REEPHAM RAILWAY 4' 8½" / 1435mm gauge

0.23
0.00

Proposed extension into original platform

Loco (ex-Goods Shed)
Pit
0.04

NSM LMS & LNE Jt : M & GN Jt

Original Whitwell and Reepham station platforms are at 40m 07ch (0.06) from South Lynn Junction via Melton Constable.

F — BRESSINGHAM STEAM MUSEUM TRUST & GARDENS
(2½ miles West of Diss)

Gor's Curve
Roydon Bridge
Diamond Curve
Roydon Bank
Roydon Curve
Wortham Straight
Nursery Curves
Nursery Railway 2' 0" gauge 2½ miles
Museum

Loco Shed
DEP ARR
Dual gauge
Loco Shed
LS

Lake

Bressingham Drain

Waveney Valley Railway 15" gauge 113 chains

Garden Railway 10¼" gauge 61 chains

Loco Shed

4' 8½" Gauge Line 40 chains

Causeway Bridge

Rhodes Curve

LING FARM HALT

© Copyright TRACKmaps. No reproduction without permission

October 2016

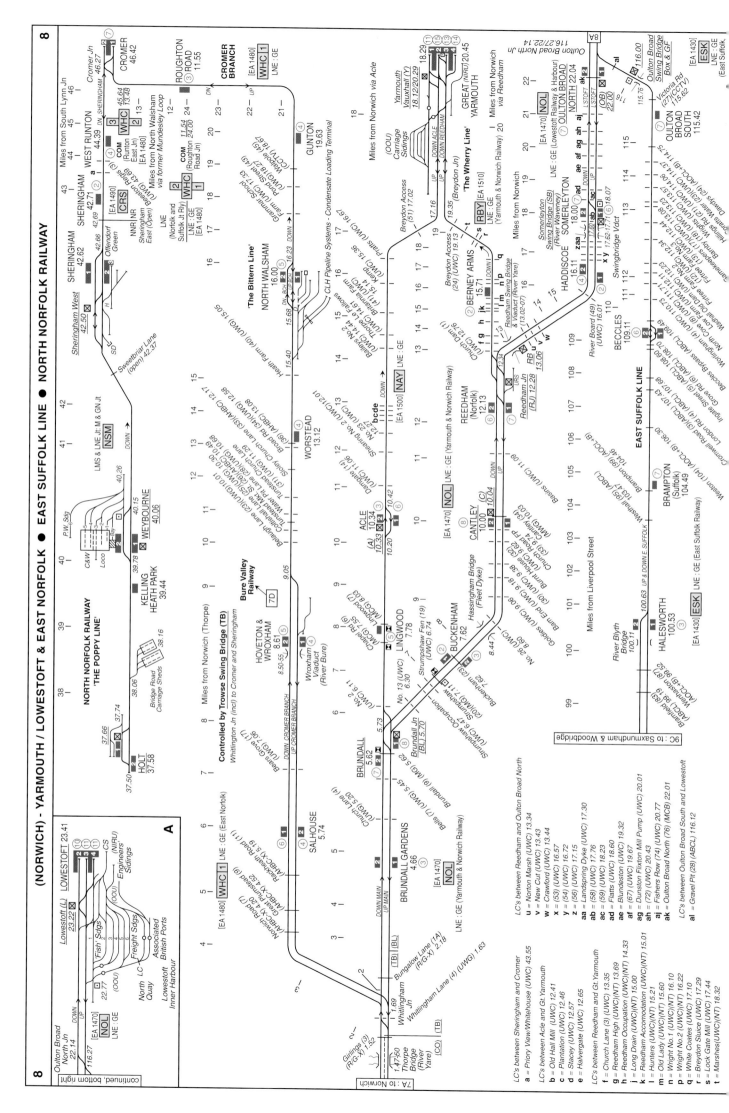

(NORWICH) - YARMOUTH / LOWESTOFT / EAST NORFOLK ● EAST SUFFOLK LINE ● NORTH NORFOLK RAILWAY

Controlled by Saxmundham (ES)

SAXMUNDHAM (ES) 91.11
[EA 1430] ESK LNE : GE (East Suffolk Railway)

Saxmundham Jn & GF 91.41
Bratts Black House (UWC) 92.19
Snowdons (UWC) 93.68
Knodishall (3) (TMO) 92.49
West House (5) (TMO) 93.32
Saxmundham Rd (8) (TMO) 94.02
LEISTON 95.20
Leiston Station (TMO) 95.15
Sizewell (TMO) 95.79
LEISTON Direct Rail Services for Sizewell Power Station EDF Energy & Magnox
Crane
NR boundary
UP & DOWN SIZEWELL
Leiston Station (12)
Leiston Road (TMO) 94.79
SIZ LNE : GE (East Suffolk Railway) [EA 1520]

Brick Kiln (59) (UWC) 90.30
Chantry Rd (61) (RC) 91.16 / Albion St. (62) (MCB) 91.20
ESK LNE : GE (East Suffolk Railway) [EA 1430]

Beversham (50) (ABCL) 87.15
Snape (54) (UWC) 88.22
Red House Farm (49) (UWC) 85.45
Blaxhall (47) (AOCL+B) 86.31
Blackstock (44) (UWC) 85.29

WICKHAM MARKET 84.43

FELIXSTOWE (Town) 84.30
FEL LNE : GE [EA 1440]
FED [EA 1460]
FELIXSTOWE BEACH LINE
FELIXSTOWE BEACH (CCTV) (CO) 84.69
Felixstowe Creek Sidings
Stora Enso Pad
Site of Felixstowe Dock Jn 85.34
(85.22)
85.29
NR Boundaries
LC
South Freightliner Terminal
Landguard & Sealand Terminals

FELIXSTOWE TOWN BRANCH
Felixstowe Beach Jn 83.57
Controlled by Colchester (CO)
PORT OF FELIXSTOWE (Felixstowe Dock and Railway Coy) Hutchison Ports (UK)
Level crossings

TRIMLEY 82.64/0.00
TFN [EA 1450] LNE : GE
Keepers Lane (26) (UWC) 82.33
Thorpe Lane (27) (AHBC) 82.01
Melton Sewage (UWC) 79.54
No. 5 Gates (AHBC) 81.81
No. 3 Gates 83.41
No. 6 Gates (28) (UWC) 82.30

EAST SUFFOLK LINE
a = Kingston Farm (UWC) 78.55
b = Jetty Avenue (UWC) 78.66
c = Maltings (UWC) 79.42
d = Melton Sewage (UWC) 79.54

NORTH QUAY BRANCH
Blofield Hall LC
Gun Lane (UWC) 82.16
Morston Hall (21) (AHBC) 80.64
Levington (15) (AHBC) 80.00
Fagbury FP LC
Central Freightliner Terminal Trinity Walton Dooley Terminals
ARRIVAL
1.55
1.18
North Freightliner Terminal
Traverser
2.27

MELTON 80.31
Hawkins (20) (AOCL+B) 80.28
Sun Wharf (22) (UWC) 80.05
Dock Lane (27) (AOCL+B) 79.04
Ellingers (31) (UWC) 78.62
Ferry Lane (19) (AOCL+B) 79.07
Lime Kiln (21) (AOCL+B) 79.29

WOODBRIDGE 79.00
Broom Hill Viaduct 78.13 a b
River Fynn Viaduct 77.15
Routes (8) (R/G) 77.36
78.04 (Orwell)

FEL LNE : GE (Felixstowe Railway & Dock Company)
Controlled by Colchester (CO)
[EA 1440] FEL

Ufford (36) (ABCL) 81.60
Ufford (UWC) 82.16
Bealings (14) (ABGL) 75.79
75.12
FELIXSTOWE
DOWN / UP

DERBY ROAD 74.67
74.30

FELIXSTOWE
DOWN EAST SUFFOLK
UP EAST SUFFOLK
Westerfield Jn 72.23

WESTERFIELD 72.20
E. Suffolk Jn 72.08
BFC 70.63
DOWN E. Suffolk Boss Hall Jn
UP E. Suffolk 70.04
East Suffolk Jn 69.56
69.41
Europa Jn 70.37
6B : to Stowmarket
LTN1 [EA 1012] [EA 1744]

★ BACON FACTORY CHORD
DBFC = DOWN BACON FACTORY CURVE
UBFC = UP BACON FACTORY CURVE
DBFC 0.00 / UBFC 0.00

[EA 1430] ESK LNE : GE
UP EAST SUFFOLK
DOWN EAST SUFFOLK

6B : to Ipswich

Miles from Liverpool Street
70 71 72 73 74 75 76 77 78 79 80 81 82 83 84 85 86 87 88 89 90 91 92

Controlled by Saxmundham (ES)
[EA 1430] ESK LNE : GE (East Suffolk Railway)

8 : to Lowestoft
East Green (63) (UWC) 93.06
North Green (65) (UWC) 92.27
Middleton (70) (ABCL) 94.52
Willow Marsh (71) (AHBC) 95.31
Hubbards (UWC) 98.12
Frielands (75) (UWC) 97.23
Barhams (76) (UWC) 96.09
DARSHAM 95.35

Darsham (72) (AHBC) 94.62
93 94 95 96 97 98 99

HARWICH BRANCH
Miles from Liverpool Street

Manningtree East Jn (0.24) 59.74
MISTLEY 61.14
DN LOOP
footplain (R/G) 61.01
Up Sdg GF 61.19
MAH LNE : GE (Eastern Union & Harwich Railway) [EA 1120]
MAYFLOWER LINE

Bradfield (R/G) 62.37
62.62
Jaques Hall (UWC) 63.31
WRABNESS 65.06
Wrabness Emergency Crossovers 64.72
64.00
Colchester Parkeston
Coppéras (11) (UWC) 66.49
Sea wall
67.49
HPQ
Parkeston Yard DB Cargo
Parkeston Goods Jn 68.02 / 68.12
Car Terminal DB Cargo Ramps
Carriage Sidings
New Yard
Freight Sidings
UP UP SIDINGS
DN ROCK SIDING
CARLESS CURVE
Yeoman Aggregates
Harwich Refinery - Carless Solvents
Shed
FRONT / MIDDLE / BACK
TP SIDING

HARWICH INTERNATIONAL (Port of Parkeston Quay)
CRIPPLES
Parkeston West (11A) (MCB) 68.67
Parkeston East (11B) (CCTV) 68.79
Parkeston (P) 68.62
CONTAINER TERMINAL Stena Sealink
STORAGE SDG
THIRD SDG / NIRU
HARWICH SINGLE
69.25 DN UP
BANK SDG 69.45
Alexandra Road (12) (CCTV) 70.37
HARWICH TOWN 70.61
DOVERCOURT 70.19
(OOU)

Miles from Liverpool Street
60 61 62 63 64 65 66 67 68 69 70

October 2016

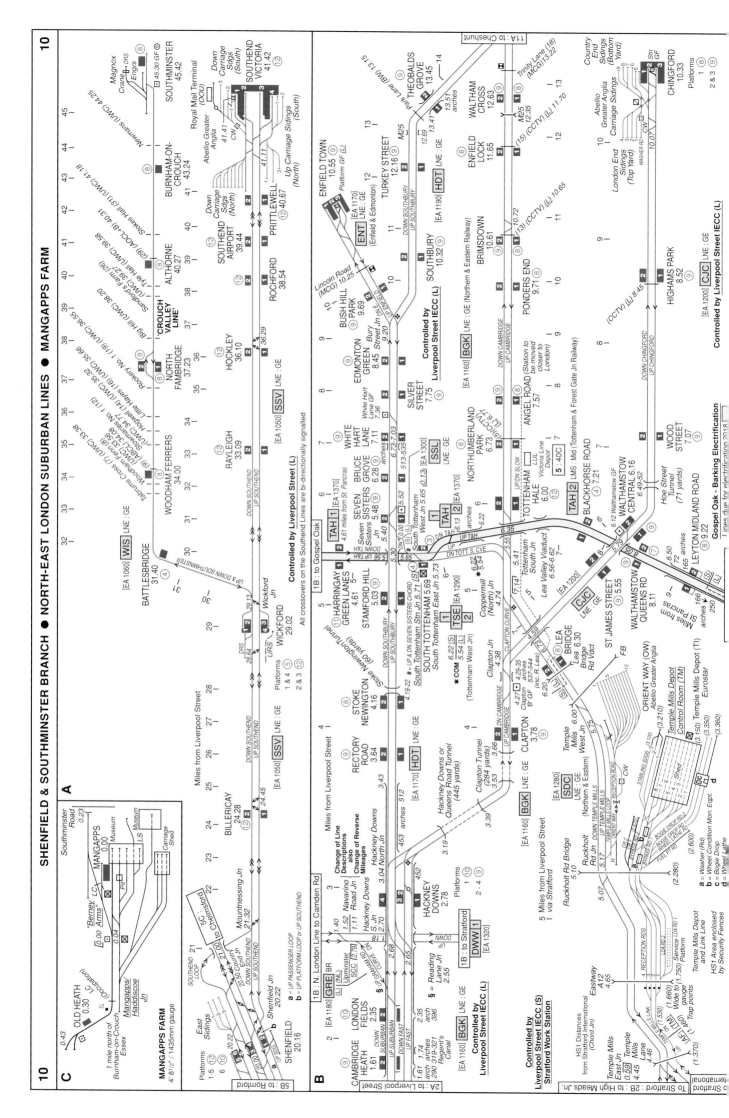

CHESHUNT - HERTFORD EAST / STANSTED - CAMBRIDGE - (ELY) • CAMBRIDGE - NEWMARKET

A

Controlled by Liverpool Street IECC (L)

[EA 1190] HDT
10B : to Southbury
Cheshunt Jn 13.71 14.28l
CHESHUNT 14.01
Trinity Lane (18) (MCG)13.22
Windmill Lane (20) (TL) 14.07
Cadmore Lane (21) (UWC) 14.32
Wharf Road (29) (UWG) 15.65
Sipe Lane (28) (AHBC-X) 16.05
BROXBOURNE 17.17
Platforms 1 & 2 ⑫ 3 ⑧ 2 & 3 ⑫ 1 & 4 ⑧
17.04 17.24 GF A
Cranbourne (2) (R&G-X) 19.42
RYE HOUSE 18.71
Rye House Tarmac
Broxbourne Jn 18.38
Creasey's (Rye Meads) (1) (UWG) 19.09
Long Bridge Vdct (River Stort)
ST MARGARETS 20.25
Roydon Lock (3) (UWG) 20.10
Stanstead (FP) 21.43
Mill (20) (CCTV) 21.36
Eastwicks (FP) 21.22
ROYDON 20.09
Wilbes (FP) 21.02
Briggens Mill (20) (UWG) 22.09
Hartford (9) (UWG) 22.07
WARE 22.16
Widbury Hill (CCTV) 22.36
Ware (13) (CCTV) 22.21
Viaduct Maintenance (18) (UWG) 23.13
DOWN HERT / UP HERT
HERTFORD EAST 24.19
[EA 1210] HEB LNE : GE (Northern & Eastern Railway)
Mead Lane (R&G-X) 23.57
Spellbrook (30) (CCTV) 28.17
Fowlers (UWG) 28.73
SAWBRIDGEWORTH 26.57
Roger's (UWG) 25.20
Roberts (22) (CCTV) (L) 26.53
HARLOW MILL 24.36
Harlow Mill 24.20
DOWN CAMB / UP CAMB / RECEPTION 23.75
Harlow Mill Yard
Aggregate Industries
HARLOW TOWN 22.59
Harlow Town 22.40
Patmore Mill (FP) 22.50
[EA 1160] BGK LNE : GE (Northern & Eastern Railway)
Controlled by Liverpool Street IECC (L)
10B : to Waltham Cross
DN CAMB / UP CAMB

B

Controlled by Liverpool Street IECC (L)

Carriage Sidings
Tamper
BISHOPS STORTFORD 30.27 ⑫
[EA 1160] [EA 1161] BGK
Cannons Mill Lane (FP) (R&G-X) 31.31
STANSTED MOUNTFITCHET 33.28
Air Ministry Sidg 33.54
Stansted South Jn 33.54
Stansted North Jn 0.00/34.25
Stansted East Jn & M11 34.26
CAMBRIDGE CHORD [EA 1220]
Tye Green Jn Airport Tunnel (1 mile, 184 yds)
STANSTED AIRPORT 36.67 Platforms 1 (18), 2 (10), 3 (14) (P1 buffer stop at 37.04)
[EA 1161] BGK LNE : GE Northern & Eastern Railways) [Eastern Counties]
Coopers Lane Jn 36.24
ELSENHAM 35.45
Fullers End Footpath (UWG) 35.15
Ugley Lane (52) (UWG) 37.13
NEWPORT (Essex) 39.72
Hogs Croft (55) (UWG) 38.52
Elephant (56) (FP) 40.13
Newport (58) (CCTV) 41.31
Trees (61) (UWG) 41.55
AUDLEY END 41.55
Audley End Tunnel (456 yards)
Littlebury Tunnel (407 yards)
Littlebury (65) (R&G) 43.46
Ickleton Road (69) (UWG) 46.35
M11 Spur 46.35
Duxford : Huntsman / Hexcel
Aerolite Resin Loading
Urea Discharge Pit
WB / LC / (NIRU) 48.00
WHITTLESFORD PARKWAY 49.01
Fairheads (R&G) 45.06
GREAT CHESTERFORD 45.56
M11 Spur (AHBC-X) 45.75
Hinxton (UWG) (AHBC) 47.11 / 47.62
Duxford (75) (AHBC) 47.71
Controlled by Cambridge (CA)
11C
12A : to Ely
DGL

C

Miles from Liverpool Street via Clapton

Whittlesford Crossover 49.46 / 49.53
Dernford (8a) (UWG) 49.75
Sawston (82) (UWG) 50.46
Sawston (82) (CCTV) 50.46
Dernford (8a) (R/G) 50.53
SHELFORD 52.36
Shelford (87) (CCTV) 51.36
Granhams (89) (UWG) 51.96
Shepreth Branch Jn 53.06
Shepreth Branch Jn Dukes (91) (UWG) 53.06 / 53.10
Weavers (UWG) 52.54
Pemberton (92) (UWG) 54.04
[LN 125] [EA 1230] SBR
24C : to Royston
UP ROYSTON DN ROY 55 HABD 53.10
CAMBRIDGE 55.52
Cambridge South Jn 55.28 / 55.35
DN SLOW / DN MAIN / UP MAIN 54.47
[LN 125] [EA 1161] BGK
a = PLATFORM LINE
Platforms 1 ⑫ 2 ⑩ 3 ⑧ 4 ⑪ 5 ⑥ 6 ⑦ 7 ⑬ 8 ⑬
Loco Holding Sidings
Engine (Mill Rd) Spur
Cambridge North (Mill Rd Jn)
Coldham Lane (an) 56.28/0.00
Coldham Lane Jn 56.51/0.23
Chesterton Jn 57.54 / 57.56
River Cam 57.48
CAMBRIDGE NORTH 57.75 ⑫
(Under Construction)
[EA 1530] CCH
Chesterton Jn (96) (CCTV) 57.54
Barnwell Jn
RECEPTION / ARRIVAL / DEPARTURE
Chesterton Jn Yard
CAMBRIDGE DEPOT (CA) Arriva TrainCare
★ = Fuel ✱ = Wash
Cherry Hinton High Street (5) (CCTV) 2.17
Cherry Hinton Bypass (6) (CCTV) 2.53
Teversham (8) (AHBC) 3.44
Coxes Farm (10) (UWC) 3.69
Laundry Lane (1) (ACCL+B) 0.29
NEWMARKET SINGLE
Barnwell Jn
Fulbourn (14) (AHBC) 4.36
•1.62 (Brookfields SB)
WATERBEACH 61.01
GSP 60.78
Milton Fen (99) (AHBC) 59.10
Six Mile Bottom (11) (AHBC) 62.70
Westley Road (93) (R/G) 7.78
Bottisham Road (94) (R/G) 8.14
Moyces (94) (AHBC) 9.06
DULLINGHAM 10.54
Burgess Drove (107) (RG-X) 61.20
Bannolds (108) (AHBC) 61.48
Dimmocks Cote (119) (UWG) 65.46
Nairns (117) (UWG) 66.25
Dimmocks Cote (X) (AHBC-X) 66.25
Wood Ditton (99) (AHBC) 13.17
NEWMARKET 13.67
West River Vdct 14.31
12D : to Bury St Edmunds
12A : to Ely
[EA 1161] BGK LNE : GE (Eastern Counties)
Controlled by Cambridge (CA)
11B

© Copyright TRACKmaps. No reproduction without permission

October 2016

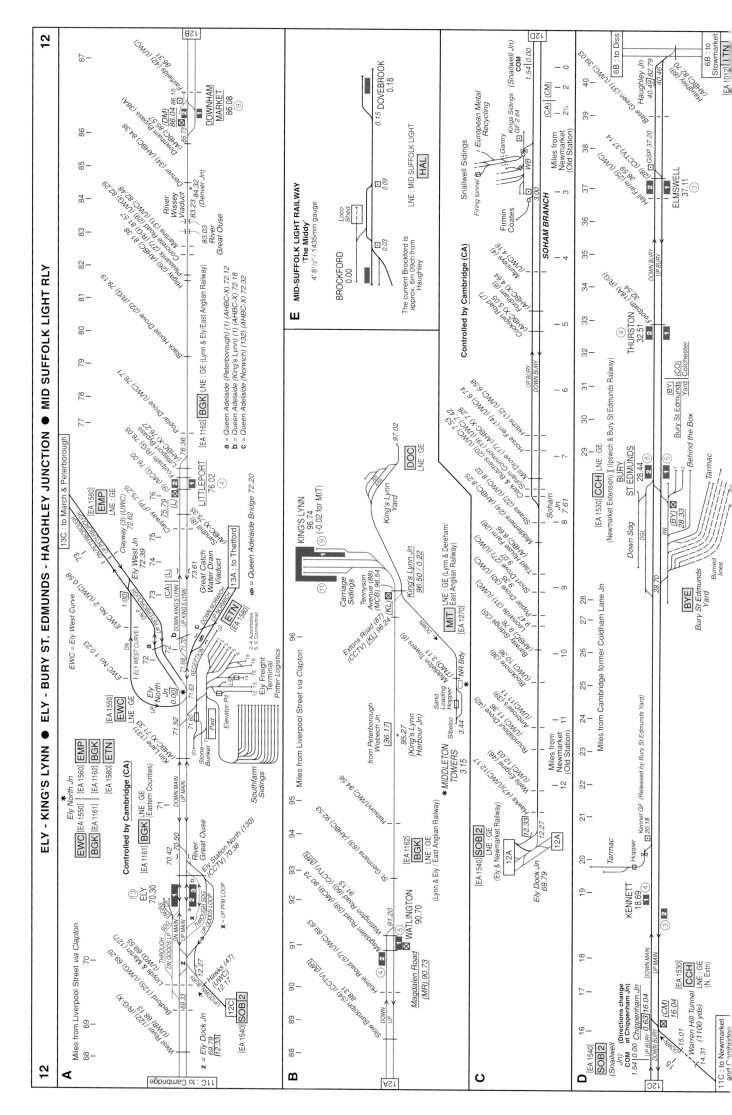

A

13B

Croxton (45) (AHBC-X) 96.44
Goodrham's No 42 (UWC) 93.28
97.63 (Roudham Jn)
Goodrham's No 41 (UWC) 94.70

THETFORD 93.50
Dock

Controlled by Cambridge (EN)

Two Mile Bottom (32) (AHBC-X) 91.16
Crown Commissioners (33) (RG-X) 91.35

Santon (29) (AHBC-X) 88.72

Miles from Liverpool Street via Clapton & Cambridge

Forestry (27) (UWC) 87.17

BRANDON 86.32
DB Cargo
DGL
87.16 (MCB-OD)
URS 86.52
ETN [EA 1580] LNE : GE (Norwich & Brandon)
LNE : GE (Eastern Counties)

Paris (28) (UWC) 85.68
Parrots (23) (UWC) 85.50
Little Ouse 85.26

LAKENHEATH 82.39

Hockwold (47) (UWC) 98.50
Shadwell (47) (UWC) 98.67
Hockham Road (50) (UWC) 99.03

Hollow (UWC) 82.44
Hlams en (UWC) 83.04
New Bridge (UWC) 80.30

MID NORFOLK RAILWAY

SHIPPEA HILL 77.17
(MCB-OD) 77.23
Cambridge (CA) Cambridge (EN)

Pools (2) (AHBC-X) 79.16
Chivers (1) (AHBC-X) 78.54
SH 78.54

DN NORWICH
UP NORWICH
Mile End (141) (AHBC-X) 73.63

COUNTY SCHOOL 17.36
Wells & Walsingham Railway (7B)

Palmers No 142 (UWC) 73.43

12A : to Peterborough
12A : to King's Lynn

(Padnal) 73.18
Palmers (UWC) 72.32
72.18
72.20 72.32
Ely Queen Adelaide
Jn Bridge
71.67

Cambridge (Peterborough) (1) (AHBC-X) 72.12
Queen Adelaide a = (Peterborough) (1) (AHBC-X) 72.12
b = Queen Adelaide (King's Lynn) (1) (AHBC-X) 72.18
c = Queen Adelaide (Norwich) (132) (AHBC-X) 72.32

12A

B

7A : to Norwich
Lakenham Vsct [EA 1012]
LTN 1
6C : to Diss & Ipswich

122
112.32
121.01-03
112.57

Harford Bridges (R. Yare) 121.29
Eaton (43) (AHBC-X) 120.29

c Rosemary Lane (93) (UWC) 120.60

Keswick (91) (AHBC-X) 120.02
URS Hethersett

UP THETFORD
DOWN THETFORD

(EN) (CO)

Miles from Liverpool Street via Clapton & Cambridge

Intwood (90) (AHBC-X) 119.48

[EA 1580] ETN LNE : GE (Norwich & Brandon)

Bowick Road (87) (AHBC-X) 114.34
Spinks Lane (1) (RG-X) 115.14

WYMONDHAM ABBEY 0.62
Church Lane (2) (TMO) 0.60
GF2 0.44
GF1 0.59
Wymondham South Jn 113.69/0.03

0.08
NR
113.60
Down Sdgs
Park Lane (UWC) 113.34

WYMONDHAM 113.72
Up Sdg

Suton (82) (AHBC-X) 112.30

KIMBERLEY PARK 3.56
Kimberley Park (10) (TMO) 3.59
HARDINGHAM 5.41
Privately owned normally closed to the public

Baldwins (82) (UWC) 110.33
Sporvences (2) (UWC) 109.66

SPOONER ROW 111.27

Rose Lane (UWC) 109.33

NOE LNE : GE

THUXTON 6.73
Garvestone (Town Lane) (UWC) 7.39
Thuxton (Town Lane) (13) (UWC) 6.71

YAXHAM 9.39
Yaxham (AHBC-X) 9.41

ATTLEBOROUGH 108.19

Sporle (2) (UWC) 108.02
Snow's Lane (UWC) 107.52
Powell Farm (56) (UWC) 106.75
Hatham (UWC) 106.15

Hardingham No 1 (61) (AHBC-X) 105.09
Hardingham No 2 (62) (UWC) 105.30

Miles from Liverpool Street via Clapton & Cambridge

ECCLES ROAD 104.36

Popham Road (55) (MCB-OD) 104.31

Grain Loading
Bottom discharge

Exchange Sidings

DEREHAM 11.32
Neatherd Road 11.29

Swanton Road (32) (UWC) 11.72
Richard Johnston Ltd. grain terminal (NJRU)

Hearn No 59 (SW) 104.10

a = Norwich Road 11.38 (OOU)
b = Dereham Central 11.25 (OOU)
1 = 11.19
2 = 11.24

DOWN MAIN
UP MAIN

Hoe Ham (54) (MCB-OD) 102.75
Dog Derry Farm (UWC) 102.15
Scarning (UWC) 101.44

HARLING ROAD 101.35

Controlled by Cambridge (EN)

Hoe (Hall Rd) (35) (MCB-X) 13.61
Wendling (Hoe Rd) (98) (TMO) 15.77

(OOU)

Roudham Hall (UWC) 100.17

NORTH ELMHAM 15.75
North Elmham (TMO) 15.7

Wartling (Hoe Rd) (96) (UWC) 15.6

13A

C

12A : to Ely

Manea Cambridge (M) (CA)

Second Drove (13) (AHBC-X) 73.35
Third Drove (16) (AHBC-X) 75.38
North Fen (11) (AHBC-X) 75.24
Beald Drove (10) (UWC) 74.25
Coltie Drove (9) (AHBC-X) 74.59
Cheatisham (9) (AHBC-X) 73.76

New Bedford River Viaduct 78.15-77.77
Welney Road (21) (AHBC-X) 78.50

Miles from Liverpool Street via Clapton & Ely

Wisbech

Old Bedford River Viaduct 78.57-78.41

(M) 80.11
MANEA 80.18
(23) (MCB) 80.13
(M) 80.26 (M) 80.34

Welham Lane (3) (UWC) 79.50

y = Bates (UWC) (M) 80.26
z = Watsomes (UWC) (M) 80.34

Stonea (S) 82.03

[EA 1560] EMP LNE : GE (Eastern Counties)

Redmoor (ACCL) 82.26
Wisbech Bypass (ACCU) 82.26

Waldersea (15) (AHBC-X) 90.06

URS

(EN)

Coldam (11) (UWC) 83.21

Badgeney Road (44) (AHBC-X) 84.69
Still Drove (43) (MS) 84.31
Horsemoor (1) (AHBC-X) 85.07

(OOU)
WIG [EA 1570] "WISBECH SINGLE"
LNE : EC (Wisbech, St Ives & Cambridge Jn Railway)
LINE CLOSED

(MS) (M)

(MS)

March South Jn 85.35
MUP March Up Yard
MUP [85.34]

March Down Yard GBRf

MARCH 85.76

March East Jn 85.68 (46) (MCB) 85.69
March South Jn (MS) 85.34
March East Jn (ME) 85.68

MUP

Bridge 2314 (Twenty Foot River)
87.29
Elm Road (2) (UWC) 86.60

WIG [EA 1570]
Wisbech Sdg
86.18

ø = Portable Train Weigher
∗ = Control Tower

RECEPTION
A2 A1
A4 A3

MWL

Factory Sdgs

a = March West Jn 86.16
z = March East Jn 85.78
x = March Whitemoor Jn [0.13] 86.18

EAST
WEST
x
0.00
CVE

March West Jn 86.16

Norwood Road (47) (AHBC) 86.30

DOWN MAIN
UP MAIN

Whitemoor Drive (54) (AHBC-X) 87.31
Whitemoor (ME) 87.31

Middle Drove (59) (RG-X) 87.75
Kisby (6) (UWC) 88.24

Three Horse Shoes (THS) 91.05

RECEPTION
B1
B2
B3
MAINTENANCE
WAGON FUELLING
C1
C2
C3
D1
D2
D3
B5
B6
B7
B8
LOCO RELEASE
New Ballast Stockpile
Used Ballast Stockpile
MIDDLE ROAD
BALLAST 1
BALLAST 2
SPOIL
SPOIL 2
LOCO RELEASE
'Phase 2 Area'

Whitemoor Local Distribution Centre

Approx 60ch from March Whitemoor Junction

WHITTLESEA 94.60
WD 93.53
Down Sdg
94.54 (W)

Three Shoe Drive (69) (AHBC-X) 91.15
Three Shoe Drive (69) (AHBC-X) 90.76
Station Road No 2 (AHBC) 90.03

Eastrea (73) (AHBC-X) 93.28

Burnt House Drive (71) (UWC) 92.58

Baily's (71) (UWC) 93.01

Miles from Liverpool Street via Clapton & Ely

EMP LNE : GE (Eastern Counties)
[EA 1560]

Kings Dyke 96.75

Harts Drove (81) (RG) 95.02
Ramsey Road (82) (AHBC) 95.31

Black Bush (83) (AHBC-X) 95.51
(90) (MCB) 94.68

Funtham's Lane (CCTV) 97.16
(88) (MCB) 96.73
HABD

(88) (UWC) 98.40
LNE : A (P) (K)

16A : to Peterborough

© Copyright TRACKmaps. No reproduction without permission

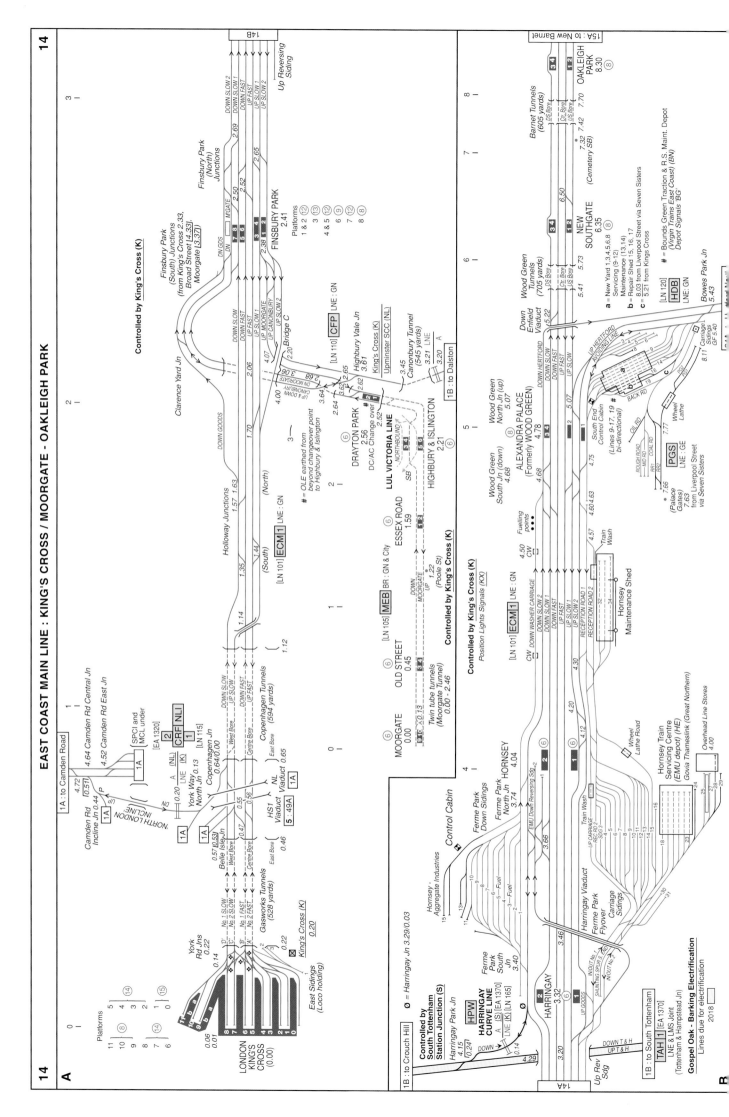

EAST COAST MAIN LINE : KING'S CROSS / MOORGATE - OAKLEIGH PARK

EAST COAST MAIN LINE : NEW BARNET - HITCHIN - (PETERBOROUGH)

15

A

Down Sdgs (OOU)
NEW BARNET 9.12
North Crossover
South Crossovers GF 9.03
South Up Sdg
Vdct. 8.64 9.00 8.74 9.18 9.03

Hadley Wood North Tunnels (232 yards)
Hadley Wood South Tunnels (384 yards)
HADLEY WOOD 10.46 10.27 10.39 10.60 10.70

Potters Bar Tunnels (1214 yards)
DN TUNNEL UP TUNNEL
12.00 11.25 11.43
POTTERS BAR 12.57 12.36 12.53 13.00

DOWN SLOW DOWN FAST UP FAST UP SLOW

BROOKMANS PARK 14.37

WELHAM GREEN 15.50
Marshmoor 16.06

HATFIELD 17.54 17.67 18.00

Reversing Siding
19.60 20.00
WELWYN GARDEN CITY 20.25
Position Light Signals (WGC)
20.45 20.35 20.11
BK PL THRO SDG H
UP HERTFORD SDG
Up Sidings

EMU Sidings
Govia Thameslink (Great Northern)
Digswell 21.18
Welwyn (or Digswell) Viaduct 21.38-61 513 yards
SD CW

[LN 101] [ECM|1] LINE : GN

Miles from King's Cross

Controlled by King's Cross (K)
Position Lights Signals (KX)

14B : to Oakleigh Park & King's Cross
15B

B

WELWYN NORTH 22.00
Welwyn Tunnel (1046 yards)
Welwyn South Tunnel (446 yards)
21.37-60 Welwyn (or Digswell) Viaduct 513 yards
DN MAIN UP MAIN
23.11 23.32 23.44 23.12
Woolmer Green Junction 23.68
GSP
Robbery Lane Viaduct 23.58
KNEBWORTH 25.03

Langley Junctions 26.59 (28.15) Down
HABD's 26.62
26.23 26.59
Langley South Jn 27.25
Up 28.01 26.45

STEVENAGE 27.45 27.30 27.02 27.67
(Stevenage Old Station) 28.38
A1(M) 29.22
DOWN SLOW DOWN FAST UP FAST UP SLOW

Tarmac
Stone
HITCHIN 31.74 31.79 31.49 31.18 31.27 31.17
30.60 HABD's
Hitchin South Jns
Hitchin 'A' 31.50

Cambridge Jn 32.11 33.32
Hitchin North Jn 32.53
33.09 33.42 Cadwell 35.56 (Three Counties)
DOWN CAMBRIDGE FLYOVER
DN CAM UP CAM
YARD LINE
Up Yard
Down Yard Engineers'
Plant Maintenance Depot

Hitchin 'B' 32.43
NRU
24C : to Royston & Cambridge
LNE : GN (Royston & Hitchin) [LN 125] [SBR]
[LN 126] [DCF] NR

ARLESEY 37.03
Jiggs Lane (BW) 38.61

[LN 101] [ECM|1] LNE : GN

Miles from King's Cross

Controlled by King's Cross (K)

24B : to Hertford North
[LN 120] [HDB] LNE : GN
Controlled by King's Cross (WL) [WL]

15A 15C

C

Abbots Ripton (stn)
Leys Summit 62.00
Abbots Ripton 63.42 HABD
64.25
Woodwalton Jn 65.43
Connington South Jn 67.30 67.03 67.20 67.38
Connington Sidings (OOU)
ARR/DEP
Connington North (89) (CCTV) 68.28
HABD 69.28 69.12
Holme (87) (CCTV) 68.93
Holme Lode (88) (CCTV) 70.02
Stilton Fen Emergency Crossovers
Stilton Fen 70.78
GSP
(Yaxley & Farcet) 72.49
DOWN SLOW DOWN FAST UP SLOW (LOOP) UP MAIN UP FAST

Plasmor
BIGGLESWADE 41.13 40.42 40.65 41.02
East Road (35) (RG) 33.54
Holme Green (37) (RG) 40.06
Broadway (Little Stukeley) (86) 62.60

SANDY 44.10 43.59 43.68 44.63 45.15
Sandy South Jn
Sandy North Jn
Down Sdgs (OOU) URS
DOWN SLOW DOWN FAST UP FAST UP SLOW

No. 42 Lyndsell (RG) 42.10
42.10 HABD's
No. 42 Lyndsell (RG) 42.10

Tempsford 46.31 (50) (CCTV)
Everton (50) (CCTV) 46.55
47.40 (Tempsford)
ST NEOTS 51.58 51.47 51.23
St Neots South Jn 52.26
St Neots North Jn
DRS URS
HABD's 54.07
No. 66 (RG) 54.70 No. 71 (RG) 55.63 (FP)
Offord (FP) 54.70 (CCTV) (72) 55.76
56.00 (Offord & Buckden)

Great Ouse Vdct (143)
HUNTINGDON 58.70 58.35
58.15-58.18 H'don South Jn
H'don North Jn
59.20
Down Sdgs North
DOWN SLOW DOWN FAST UP MAIN

[LN 101] [ECM|1] LNE : GN

Miles from King's Cross

Controlled by King's Cross (K)
[24B] King's Cross (K) Peterborough (P)

Miles from King's Cross
Controlled by Peterborough (P)

15B

D

Connington South Jn
CTP

Fletton Jn 75.02
75.05 75.11 74.76 74.71
Flyover 75.02 Fletton 'C' GF
LOOP (OOU)
NVR/NR 0.00 0.02
FLETTON BRANCH
Nene Valley Railway
(Longueville Junction) 45.53
1.47
River Nene
75.65 75.68
DOWN SLOW DOWN FAST UP SLOW UP FAST
Orton Mere 76

[FOM] LNE : GN

42D : to Orton Mere
16A : to Peterborough
42D : to Peterborough Nene Valley
13C : to March

Miles from King's Cross

© Copyright TRACKmaps. No reproduction without permission

October 2016

15 15C

EAST COAST MAIN LINE : PETERBOROUGH - GRANTHAM - NEWARK

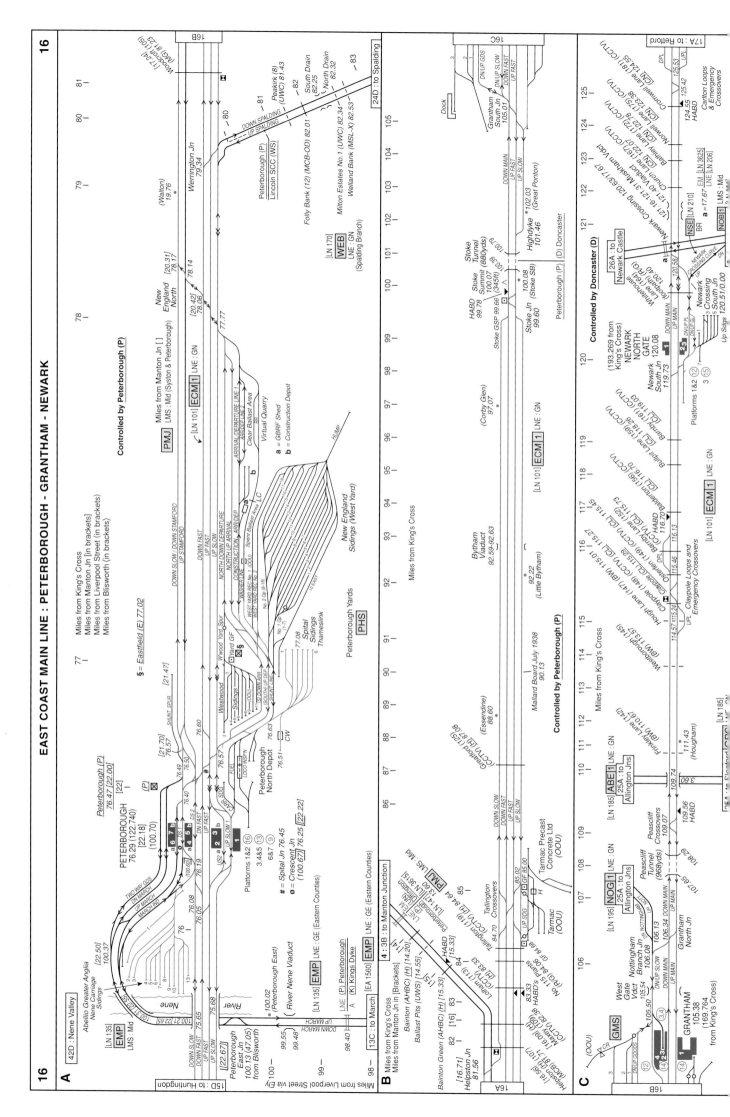

EAST COAST MAIN LINE : (NEWARK) - RETFORD - DONCASTER

October 2016

A — Miles from King's Cross

Controlled by Doncaster (D)

ECM1 [LN 101] LNE : GN

Pipers Wood Summit 149.40
Bawtry Viaduct
Bawtry Emergency Crossovers
Ranskill Loops and Emergency Crossovers
Barnby Moor & Sutton
Retford North
Retford Western Jn
Askham Tunnel (57 yards)
Markham Summit
Tuxford Emergency Crossovers
Carlton
Carlton Loops

16C : to Newark

B — Miles from Huntingdon South Jn via March

Beckingham [Doncaster (B) (D)]

ECM1 [LN 101] LNE : GN

Haxey & Epworth 106.24
Finningley 112.04 [SPD]4 LNE : GN & GE Jt
Beech Hill (AHBC-X)

29C : to High Marnham
29C : to Shirebrook
26C : to Lincoln

Arksey Loop
ECM1 LNE : GN [LN 101]

18A : to York

DONCASTER WORKS "The Plant"
River Don

WABTEC RAIL LTD

WABTEC RAIL LTD SHOPS
A - Heavy Vehicle
B - Light Vehicle
C - Wheel Machine
D - Wheel
E - Erecting
F - Smith/Dampers/Wheelset Paint
G - Components
H - Electrical Testing

J - Shotblast
K - Paint (x2)
L - Wagon
M - Class 321 Renatus Project
N - Wet Blast Cleaning
Pits on Rds 4,5 & 12 in Heavy & Light Vehicle Shops

Unipart Rail Old West Carriage Shop
Asbestos Shop
Wheel Line
Hexthorpe Dead End

32A : to Hexthorpe Jn and Mexborough

DONCASTER 155.77 (251.060) from King's Cross

Platforms (Accommodation varies according to routes, etc)
0
1
2
3
4
5
6,7
8

Marshgate Sidings
Marshgate Jn
Don Jn
Bentley Jn

35A : to Wakefield
17D
32B : to Scunthorpe

C — Miles from Brancliffe East Jn

32A : to Hexthorpe Jn & Mexborough
PED5 [LN 826] LNE : GC
Hexthorpe Sidings
DB Cargo
Up West Sdgs

Miles from Penistone via Barnsley GC & Wath
h = SJB [LN 832]
Bridge Jn - St. James's Jn (Goods) HEXTHORPE GOODS SINGLE

30B : to Gainsborough Central
RETFORD HL (GN)138.49 LL (GC) 64.32
Thrumpton (TN) 64.47

WHR [LN 748]
MAC3 [LN 736] LNE : GC

Roberts Road Electro-Motive Diesels

S. Yorkshire Jns
St. James's Jn (Pass)
Bridge Jn
Balby Jn
St. James's Jn (Goods) 22.38
Balby Bridge Tunnel (95 yards)
Doncaster IEP Depot - Hitachi

Concrete Sleeper Factory - Trackwork MOLL
Wood Yard

Belmont Up Yard
Belmont Down Yard
Decoy North Jn 117.46
Decoy South Jn
Decoy Up Yard
Decoy Down Yard
DDY
DUV
SPD5 [LN 150]

Doncaster Railport Freightliner
Intermodal Roads
West LC
East LC
New Ballast Stockpile
Used Ballast Stockpile

Potteric Carr Jn
DB Cargo
UDS [LN 150] LNE & LMS : S. Yorkshire Jt. Cttee. (GC, GN, L&Y, Mid, NE)
BKS [LN 758]

§ = Track materials re-cycling area
f = USED BALLAST SIDING
g = LOCO RELEASE

'SOUTH YORKSHIRE JOINT LINE'

St. Catherine's Jn 15.17 [Z1.60]
c = from Brancliffe E. Jn
d = from Manchester V. via Wakefield
Former Doncaster R.M. Terminal
BAY 154 PLATF'M
YDS [LN 762] BR ST. CATH'S CURVE

M18 15.16
Low Ellers Curve Jn
Flyover West Jn
Flyover East Jn
Decoy North Jn
a = Flyover East Jn - Decoy North Jn
b = Decoy North Jn
FWR1 FWR2 [LN 235]
LCR [LN 160]
Loversall Carr Jn
Rossington GSP
Rossington Emergency Crossover 151.28
Bessacarr Carr Jn
Bessacarr Halt 115.48
Carr Lane (383) 115.72
Auckley (MCB-OD) 112.73
Hayfields (UWC) 114.06
SPD4 [LN 170] LNE : GN & GE JT.

Miles from Huntingdon South Jn via March

34A : to Brancliffe East Jn

17A
17B

D 157

ECM1 LNE : GN [LN 101]
Arksey 157.76

17C

[LN 758] BKS LNE & LMS Jt : S. Yorks. Jt. Cttee. (GC, GN, L&Y, Mid, NE)

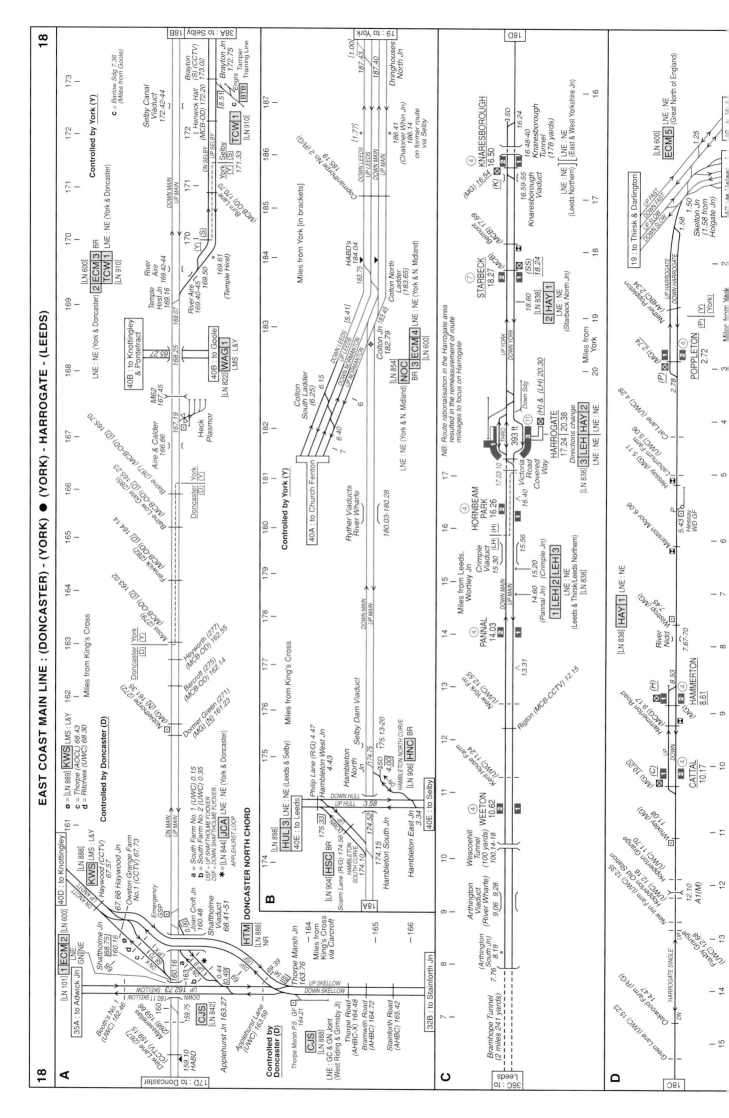

EAST COAST MAIN LINE : YORK

A

NORTH BAY RAILWAY: SCARBOROUGH
59ch length / 20" gauge

SCALBY MILLS
PEASHOLM
BEACH (not open to passengers)
Lake
Loco Turning Loop
Loco Shed
Ballast Sdg
FB
LC (FP)
N

B

DERWENT VALLEY LIGHT RAILWAY
Derwent Valley Light Railway Society
4' 8½" / 1435mm gauge
(3½ miles east of York)

MURTON PARK
A64
HOLGATE DEPOT
Traverser 1
Traverser 3
T/T APPROACH

C NATIONAL RAILWAY MUSEUM, YORK (Great Hall)
4' 8½" / 1435mm gauge

ex York North Engine Shed
Great Hall
The Works
Warehouse
See Main Plan

18D : to Harrogate
20A : to Thirsk

[LN 838] HAY 1
LNE : NE (York & Harrogate)

Skelton Bridge (River Ouse)
3.12–3.16
Skelton Bridge Jn
3.23
3.11

[LN 600] ECM5
LNE : NE (Gt. North of England) (York & Newcastle)

★ = Skelton Jn
1.58 from Holgate Jn
1.50 from York Stn

DOWN HARROGATE
UP HARROGATE
DOWN SLOW
DOWN FAST
UP SLOW
UP FAST

(formerly Severus Junction)
York Yard North 0.79
Landing Lane Bridge 1.05

No. 1 UP ARRIVAL
No. 2 UP ARRIVAL
HEADSHUNT

Klondyke Yard
UP YARD
Group 'A' 1-8 Long term storage
Group 'B' 9-12
No. 1 INDEPENDENT
No. 2 INDEPENDENT
No. 3 INDEPENDENT

PW Yard
TRANSFER LINE
WAREHOUSE LINE

York LMD Siemens
Trainwash
(Clifton SB) 0.32
0.54
Engineers' Leeman Rd Yard
CET/Refuelling Apron
Stabling Sdgs

ECM5 [LN 600] [LN 864]

7¼" gauge
National Railway Museum (Sth. Hall) (ex Goods Shed)
See 19C
National Railway Museum
(ex Engine Shed)
LOCO LINE
DOWN FAST
UP FAST

Wagon Repair Sdgs
Parcels Sdgs
Service Centre: Engrs
NRM DK 0.25
York (IECC) (Y, L S, CF) 188.38

York ROC

York Yard South 0.21
Holgate Reception Sdgs
[LN 618] [LN 724] HOS
LNE : NE (York Main Goods Lines)

Dringhouses North Jn (1.00 from York)
Holgate Jn 188.07 [0.00]
188.01
Bridge 47
[LN 600] [LN 854] ECM4
LNE : NE (York & N. Midland Rly) (also York & Doncaster)
to former Chaloner Whin Jn

18B : to Doncaster & Church Fenton

187.43
187.40
187

Scarborough Bridge (River Ouse)
Scarborough Bridge Jn
Waterworks Jn
MAINTENANCE
0.22
0.19
0.16
0.09
0.06
0.20

DN SCARBOROUGH
UP SCARBOROUGH
DOWN
UP

(Y) (S) Strensall
[LN 880] YMS LNE : NE (York & Scarborough)
Boothan Stay (6) (UWC) 1.51
Boothan (5) (A/BC-X) (S) 1.51
(Burton Lane Jn) 1.04

39D : to Scarborough

Strensall Walnuts (51) (UWC) 7.19
Strensall (49) (UWC) 7.03
Riverside Farm (49) (MOB) 6.48
Strensall No. 2 (38) (ICCTV) (S) 6.11
Strensall No. 1 (33) (ICCTV) (S) 6.00
Oakbusts (29) (UWC) 5.26
Manor Farm (29) (UWC) 5.03
Barkers (24) (ICCTV) 4.59
Haxby Station (23) (ICCTV) (S) 4.18
Farmstead Rise (16) (UWC) 3.45
Haxby Road (14) (ICCTV) 3.27
Farmstead Rise (16) (UWC) 3.27
Haxby Road (1) (UWC) 3.19
New Earswick (11) (UWC) 3.00
Hall Farm (9) (UWC) 2.54
Kettleshing Farm (9) (UWC) 1.70

York (IECC)
YORK
§ 188.40 [0.00]
COM
[LN 600] [LN 854] ECM5
4 ECM5

Platforms 1 2 3 4 5 6 7 8 9 10 11

188.19
188.28
188.13

YORK Platforms		Signal Post codes:
1	⑨	(BD) Barnetby - Doncaster
2	⑧	(BG) Barnetby - Gainsborough
3	D12,U13	(BL) Barnetby - Lincoln
4	⑧	(CB) Cleethorpes - Barnetby
5	⑳	(MB) Marsh Jn - Brocklesby
6	⑬	
7	⑫	(B) Former Brodklesby SB
8	⑦	(P) Former Pasture Street
9	D19,U20	(ST) Former Stallingborough SB
10	⑯	(S) Former Sheffield PSB
11	⑯	

York Rail Operating Centre (ROC)

Miles from Kings Cross
188
187

YORK:
(46ft)
(303.376 from Kings Cross)
Origin and Zero mileage for:
York & North Midland to Altofts Jn
York & Newcastle
York & Harrogate
York & Scarborough

§ = 188.11½ from King's Cross via the old route through Selby

October 2016

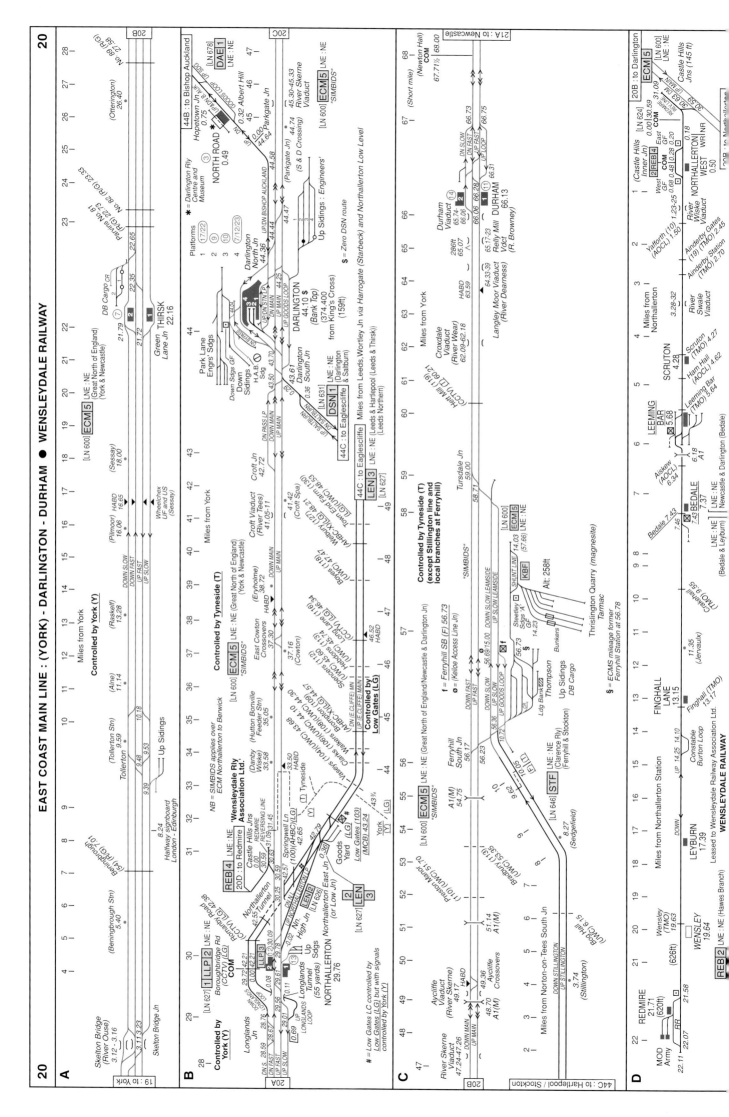

EAST COAST MAIN LINE : (YORK) - DARLINGTON - DURHAM ● WENSLEYDALE RAILWAY

EAST COAST MAIN LINE : CHESTER-LE-STREET - TYNE YARD ● LOW FELL - STOCKSFIELD

A   **B**   **C**

Miles from York

69 — 70 — 71 — 72 — 73 — 74 — 75

Controlled by Tyneside (T)

20C : to Durham

Plansworth Viaduct

69.54-60

HABD 70.20

Chester Moor or Dene Viaduct 70.77-71.07

CHESTER-LE-STREET 71.72

⑤

2   1

Chester-le-Street Viaduct 72.19-20

73.32

Ouston Crossovers

DOWN MAIN / UP MAIN

Birtley Jn 75.26

21B

[LN 600] ECM 5 LNE : NE (York & Newcastle) "SIMBIDS"

Miles from Newcastle (C), via Elswick

14 — 13 — 12 — 11 — 10 — 9 — 8 — 7 — 6

STOCKSFIELD 13.11

⑥   1   2   ⑤

Mickley (R/G) 11.40

(PE) 10.49

PRUDHOE 10.47

⑤ 1   2 ④ (MCB) 10.49 / 10.45

[LN 682] NEC 2 LNE : NE (Newcastle & Carlisle)

UP MAIN / DOWN MAIN

9.10 (6.36) (West Wylam Jn)

(W) WYLAM 8.35

1 ⑤   ④ 2 (MCB)

Clara Vale (AHBC-X) 7.40

Golf Course Bridleway (UWG) 7.08

Boat House (UWC) 6.34

21B

43E : to Carlisle

C

Miles from Newcastle (C), via Elswick

6 — 5 — 4 — 3 — 2

BLAYDON 4.03 34ft (B) 5.22

Addison (AHBC) 5.03

⑤   1   ⌧

Chain Bridge (RC) 5.19

LINE : NE (Newcastle & Carlisle)

(B) Blaydon (T) Tyneside

River Derwent Viaduct 4.07

Swalwell Jn 3.78

2 COM 3.78 / 5.28

NEC 2 (Newcastle & Carlisle) 4 / NEC 1 (Gateshead, Norwood & Blaydon) [LN 682]

Skiff Inn (UWC) 4.18

Miles from Newcastle (C), High Level Bridge Jn, (Blaydon Jn), (Gateshead, Norwood & Blaydon) [LN 682]

METROCENTRE 3.33 ⑤

1

DUNSTON 2.17

1   2 ④

1.71 Norwood Jn

[LN 682] NEC 1 LINE : NE (Gateshead, Norwood & Blaydon)

UP CARLISLE / DOWN CARLISLE

1.42

1.26

[LN 684] NLF LNE : NE (Dunston Extn)

LOW FELL SINGLE

LOW FELL ROYAL MAIL TYNESIDE 0.50 (NIRU)

ROYAL MAIL LOW FELL

21C

22A : to Newcastle

1.06

1.01

78.07

Bensham Tunnel (125 yards)

79 — 78 — 77 — 76

Miles from York

DOWN MAIN / UP MAIN

[LN 600] ECM 5 LNE : NE (York & Newcastle) "SIMBIDS"

Low Fell Jn

Low Fell Sdg

0.13

0.00

77.40

77.37 DN / 0.00 DN

P

GOODS / SLOW / UP

Lamesley Crossover 76.66

TYNE NORTH ARR/DEP

76.57

TYNE YARD DB Cargo [TEY]

DEPOT LINE

Maintenance Depot

DB Cargo

Down Departure Sdgs

'V' LINE

Tyne North Cabin GF

Engineer's Sdgs

Up Staging Sidings

Tyne South Cabin GF

Middle Cabin GF

CW

WW

ARR

FP

Exchange Sdgs

Hump Top

Reclamation

former Down Primary Sdgs

Virtual Quarry

15 16 18 19 20 21 23 24 26 28 30

SHUNTNECK

M1

former Tyne Yard South Box 75.62

TYNE SOUTH ARR/DEP

TRANSFER/DEPOT LINE

UP / SLOW / DOWN / DOWN MAIN / UP MAIN

Birtley Jn 75.26

21A

[LN 600] ECM 5 LNE : NE (York & Newcastle) "SIMBIDS"

Controlled by Tyneside (T)

October 2016

EAST COAST MAIN LINE : NEWCASTLE - MORPETH - WIDDRINGTON

A

Heaton North Jn   2.70
Flushing Apron
2.55
2.58
Pile Sdg GF
Heaton GSP   2.35
former Electrification Depot

Heaton Traction and Rolling Stock Maintenance Depot (HT)
(Enlarged scale)
Arriva Rail North

DOWN GOODS LOOP NORTH
WASHER LINE BY-PASS
Maintenance Servicing Depot
No.4 SERVICE
Former Carriage Washing Shed

Chillingham Rd   2.18
DOWN GOODS LOOP SOUTH
DOWN MAIN
UP MAIN
UP GOODS LOOP
CW
HCS
FUEL
GAUGE DEPARTURE (1-5)
DMU
RECEPTION LINES (1-4)
SPARE VEHICLE SDG B
SPARE VEHICLE SDG A
STABLING 1-8
PRIMARY DEPARTURE (1-7)

WALKERGATE
CHILLINGHAM ROAD
TYNE & WEAR METRO
SIDINGS LINE
DEP LINE 2
(CT)
49 : to Tynemouth

All lines controlled by Tyneside (T)

[LN 600] ECM 7   LNE : NE
"SIMBIDS" (Newcastle & Berwick)

DOWN MAIN
UP MAIN
UP/DN SLOW
DEPOT LINE NECK
DEPOT / ARRIVAL
Heaton South Jn   1.65
Red Barns 0.65-0.70
Argyle Tunnel (98 yards)
1.79
1.51 (Heaton)
1.25 (Riverside Jn)
1.18
1.04
Ouseburn Viaduct
Heaton Carriage Sdgs Control Tower
46A : to Sunderland

Miles from Leeds, Wortley Jn via Harrogate (Starbeck), Northallerton L.L. and Sunderland
100

MANORS
Dean St Crossover 0.40
0.58   0.56 Metro Tunnel
0.46
0.28   0.36
Pilgrim St Crossover
Viaduct
[LN 627]
LEN 3   LNE : NE (Newcastle & Berwick)

High Level Bridge 1337ft long 112' high
GATESHEAD 100.40 Tyneside Central Freight Depot (OOU)
SHUNT SPUR
St James' Bridge Jn 100.23
Park Lane Jn 100.65
DOWN SUNDERLAND
UP SUNDERLAND
T.E.C.LINE
OAKWELL
GATE SDG
101.45
101.33
High Level Bridge Central Jn 101.39
High Level Bridge Jn 0.00
GREENFIELDS EAST
Greenfields Jn
W.CURVE 0.00 | 101.33
0.16
0.21
0.00 | 101.15 (High Street Jn)
[LN 676] 2 PLG 1   LNE : NE

NEWCASTLE
120 ft
(432.323 from King's Cross)
80.16 0.00
[LN 600] 6 ECM 7 [LN 600]
LNE : NE (Newcastle & Carlisle)

Platforms
1 ⑧
2 ⑱
3 ⑮
4 ⑬
5,6 ③/5/10
7-8 ⑥/2/10
9-12 ⑤

[LN 622]
NEN   LNE : NE (Newcastle & Carlisle)

FORTH BANKS / PARADISE BRANCH
Castle Sdgs GF
0.51
0.57   Forth Banks Engineers Sdgs GF
0.73
Engrs Sdg (OOU) OTM
arches 1-29
0.25 0.22

5 ECM 6 [LN 600] LNE : NE
Newcastle West Jn   80.05 80.04
"SIMBIDS"
Elswick
80   0.11
Newcastle South Jn   79.75
Viaduct 79.70
Newcastle East Jn (Castle Jn)   101.59   0.14   0.11

King Edward Bridge
King Edward Bridge North Jn   79.57
King Edward Bridge East Jn   0.00   0.30
King Ed. Br. S. Jn   0.62
79.66
79.53   79.49
79.29   79.26
Askew Road Tunnel (53 yards)
Viaduct 79.42
UP FAST
DOWN FAST
UP SLOW
DOWN SLOW
GATESHEAD WEST
GATESHEAD

ECM 5   LNE : NE
[LN 600]
21B : to Durham / Carlisle
[LN 682] NEC 1   LNE : NE (G.N.&B.)

Tyneside (IECC) 0.32
SE CVE 0.00
Ø = [LN 620] KEB
* = [LN 674] HLK   LNE : NE (G.N.&B.)
(G.N.&B.) = Gateshead, Norwood & Blaydon
0.27 Metro tunnel
[LN 674] HLK
[LN 676] HLK   LNE : NE (G.N.&B.)
49

DOWN FAST
UP FAST
DOWN SLOW
UP SLOW
DN MAIN
UP MAIN
0.64
0.48

B

Miles from Newcastle

23A : to Alnmouth
Felton Lane (M) 25.16
Widdrington Sdgs 24.60 24.63
RR Exchange Sdgs
Loading Pad
Widdrington Grange (CCTV) (M) 23.23 23.24
WIDDRINGTON 23.20
Widdrington Opencast Disposal Point Closed ④

Ulgham Lane (CCTV) (M) 22.52
Butterwell Jn 0.00 (N)   20.63
Ulgham Lane (CCTV) (M) 20.17
NR Bdy
NORTH BRANCH [LN 700]
DOWN
GF 'A'
GF 'B'
GF 'C'
WB
BUNKER LINE
BWO
Butterwell Disposal Point UKCSMR Ltd
SOUTH BRANCH 5.38
Signal B6 (NR)
23C : to Ashington [0.71]
[LN 600] ECM 7   LNE : NE (Newcastle & Berwick)
"SIMBIDS" Butterwell (B)

Longhirst (CCTV) (M) 20.17
PEGSWOOD 18.44
UP MAIN
DOWN MAIN
[LN 694] EJM BR

Morpeth North Jn 17.30
Bothal (River Wansbeck) 17.48-57
120.46 | 17.48-57
120.32
DOWN FAST
DOWN SLOW
UP MAIN
DOWN
NE CURVE
Miles from Manors Jn via Percy Main
20.07
20.04
20.32
MORPETH 16.50
Morpeth North (CCTV) (M) 16.79
16.79 UP MAIN
16.63
16.56
REV SDG
a
b
c
BLYTH & TYNE
DOWN
[LN 696] HJM
[LN 694] HJM
LNE : NE (Blyth & Tyne)
Park House Farm (UWC) 19.38
Hepscott Jn 19.44
23C : to Bedlington

a = Coopies Lane 20.40 (AHBC)
b = Barmoor through siding (No. 2)
c = Electrification Depot

Morpeth (M)
Tyneside (T) Morpeth
Plessey (River Blyth) 12.17-23
11.51
Plessey Crossovers
Stannington (CCTV) (M) 13.4
Clifton (M) 14.56
[LN 694] EJM   LNE : NE (Blyth & Tyne)
23C : to Bedlington

CRAMLINGTON 9.74 ⑤
Dam Dykes (CCTV) 8.46 8.45
HABD's
[LN 600] ECM 7   LNE : NE "SIMBIDS"
Dudley Bridleway 7.13
Killingworth Bridleway 6.28
UP MAIN
DOWN MAIN
Killingworth (CCTV) 5.76
Great Lime Road 5.50-53
4.41

Benton Crossovers 4.10
Benton (North) (M) 0.00 0.48
METRO
0.05
0.64
[LN 694] BNE   LNE : NE
49 : to Tynemouth
49 : to Gosforth
B & T

Controlled by Morpeth (M)

Miles from Newcastle
Mileages in [brackets] are Light Railway Order mileages

A

22B : to Morpeth

Lucker (CCTV) (TW) 49.17

Newham (CCTV) (A) 47.09

CHATHILL 46.01
Chathill Crossovers 45.67

[A] Tweedmouth (TW)
47.08 HABD
Alnmouth (A)

Stamford (CCTV) (A) 39.34
Falloden (CCTV) (A) 40.39
No. 162 (UWC) 43.65
Christon Bank (CCTV) (A) 42.46
No. 161 (UWC) 43.00

Little Mill (CCTV) (TW) 40.38
Little Mill Crossovers Alt 217ft 39.30
HABD 40.38

Miles from Newcastle

Aln Valley Railway
River Aln 35.40-35.50 34.76
Up Sdg Engrs'

ALNMOUTH 34.69
[A] (R) (2) (for ALNWICK)

Warkworth (CCTV) (A) 33.71
Wooden Gate Crossovers 33.65 34.25
Wooden Gate (CCTV) (A) 31.67

ACKLINGTON 28.43

River Coquet 29.72-30.01

Chevington North Crossovers 26.55 26.37
Clyvington (CCTV) (M) 25.49
DOWN CHEVINGTON LOOP 26.34
UP CHEV LP 25.58
HABD 25.48 25.55

Controlled by Morpeth (M)

Controlled by Alnmouth (A)

B

1:11C : to Edinburgh

Miles from Edinburgh (Waverley)

ENG | SCOT 54
[LN 600] [7][ECM][8] COM
LINE | SC [SC 147]
(544.741)

Tweedmouth (King's Cross 544.751) (TW) 54.06 HABD

(Marshall Meadows) 56.35 68.01

Miles from Newcastle

Royal Border Bridge (River Tweed)
Down North Sdgs
DOWN MAIN 67.36
UGL 67.38
DGL 67.08 67.11

BERWICK UPON TWEED [11]
§ 67.00 117ft
(540.189 from King's Cross)

Vact 66.72 66.30 66.41
66.33 66.74

Tweedmouth (TW) 65.78
Tweedmouth Sdgs DB Cargo
RECEPTIONS 1 / 2 / 3

Spittal (R/G) 65.42 65.01

Scremerston (CCTV) (TW) 63.46

Goswick (CCTV) (TW) 60.67
No. 193 (R/G) (TW) 60.66 HABD

Beal (CCTV) (TW) 58ft
Fenham Hill FP 52.37
59.32 Beal Crossovers

Fenham Low Moor (CCTV) (TW) 55.31

Smeafield (CCTV) (TW) 54.79

Craig Mill (CCTV) (TW) 52.48
Crag Mill Loops
52.41 52.43

former Slater Quarry

Belford Burn FP 51.74
Easington FP 51.15 51.72

Belford (CCTV) (TW)
Belford Crossovers 51.39
51.54 51.55

DN MAIN / UP MAIN / DN PL / UP PL
DRS Engrs'
GR

[LN 600] [ECM][7] LINE : NE (Newcastle & Berwick)
"SIMBIDS"

NB = SIMBIDS applies over ECM Northallerton to Berwick

LINE : NE (Newcastle & Berwick) [LINE : NB (Edinburgh & Berwick)]

§ = 57.35 from Edinburgh (W)

22B : to Newcastle

Controlled by Tweedmouth (TW)

C

22B : to Butterwell Jn

Miles in (brackets) are Light Railway
Order mileages (from Butterwell GF "A")

Potland Burn Disposal Point UKCSMR Ltd (OOU)
New Moor (AOCL) (NR) 4.17(1.33)
(NR) 4.18(1.31)
Loading Pad
5.38
Sig. B6 (NR)
(EG) Edinburgh (TW)

'Light Railway' [2.19 - 0.71]

Lynemouth : Alcan (Rio Tinto) Smelter Mothballed

Hirst Lane (MCG) 3.21

Lynemouth 6.41
Lynemouth 6.19

Empty Wagon Reception Sdgs
20' Container
Coke Siding
Alumina Siding
Pad Ingot loading area
Uncoaler WB
Lynemouth Power Stn EPH
(AOCL)

STRANGE LINE DOWN / UP (OOU)

Alcan Branch Jn 5.33
Controlled by Lynemouth

Hepscott Jn
19.44
DOWN LYNEMOUTH 4.14
UP LYNEMOUTH 3.05 (NR)

NR -4 Alcan

[LN 694] [EJM] 22B : to Morpeth [BWO]

[LN 702] [BWC] LINE : NE

ASHINGTON 2.77 NR/UK Coal 2.43
3 / 2

Miles from Manors Jn via Percy Main

Hepscott (A/HBC) 19.27
Park House Farm (UWC) 19.38

North Seaton (MH) 1.58
Green Lane (A/HBC) 0.47
Marcheys House Jn (MCB) 1.76
North Seaton (MCB) 0.36

Cambois (A/HBC) 1.35 [BWC]
School Corner (UWC) 0.47

Bedlington N. (N) 0.31
Bedlington Jn 0.32
Coatsworth Farm No. 2 (UWC) 16.26 16.08
Choppington (A/HBC) 17.06

Freemans (MCB) 1.31

Bedlington North (BN) 15.71

Marcheys Jn (MCB) 0.00 DOWN UP CAM
Winning Crossing Jn 0.32 [LN 702]
Winning (WG) 0.36

[WSB] [LN 706]
West Sleekburn Jn 15.65
a = West Sleekburn (UWC) 0.16
a

Bebside (A/HBC) 14.67
Plessey Road (CCTV) 13.16

BEDLINGTON
Bedlington South (MCB) 15.60
Bedlington Furnaceway Sdgs DB Cargo
Bedlington (BS) 15.12

Newsham North Jn 12.74
Newsham (MCB) 12.45
Newsham (N) 11.30
Hartley (A/HBC) 11.12 11.30
Red House Farm (UWC)

Morpeth (M) on Bedlington N. 15.71

[LN 706] [WSB] LINE : NE (Blyth & Tyne) (Cambois Branch)

Cambois (TMO) 2.10

Port of Blyth (TMO) 2.55
Battleship Wharf GF 2.51
Battleship Wharf
NORTH 3.22 BLYTH LOOP

NORTH BLYTH
Alcan : Import Berth Closed

Loading Bunkers

DOWN BLYTH & TYNE UP BLYTH & TYNE
'BLYTH & TYNE SINGLE'
UP 'BLYTH & TYNE' 7.41
Holywell (A/HBC) 7.41
Earsdon 2.53 7.08

[LN 694] [BNE] [EJM]
LINE : NE (Blyth & Tyne)
COM

Seghill North (A/HBC) 9.06
Mares Close (UWC) 9.75
9.36
(Seaton Delaval)

Benton (North) Jn 0.00/4.24
Benton Crossovers 4.10

Tyneside (T) 0.48
Newsham (N)
METRO 0.64
0.05

[ECM] [7]

22B : to Morpeth

22B : to Newcastle

D — ALN VALLEY RAILWAY 4' 8½" / 1435mm gauge

ALNWICK LIONHEART

[ACK] LINE : NE

23A

Railway on greenfield site, but have aspirations to run onto former Alnwick to Alnmouth trackbed, towards Alnmouth.

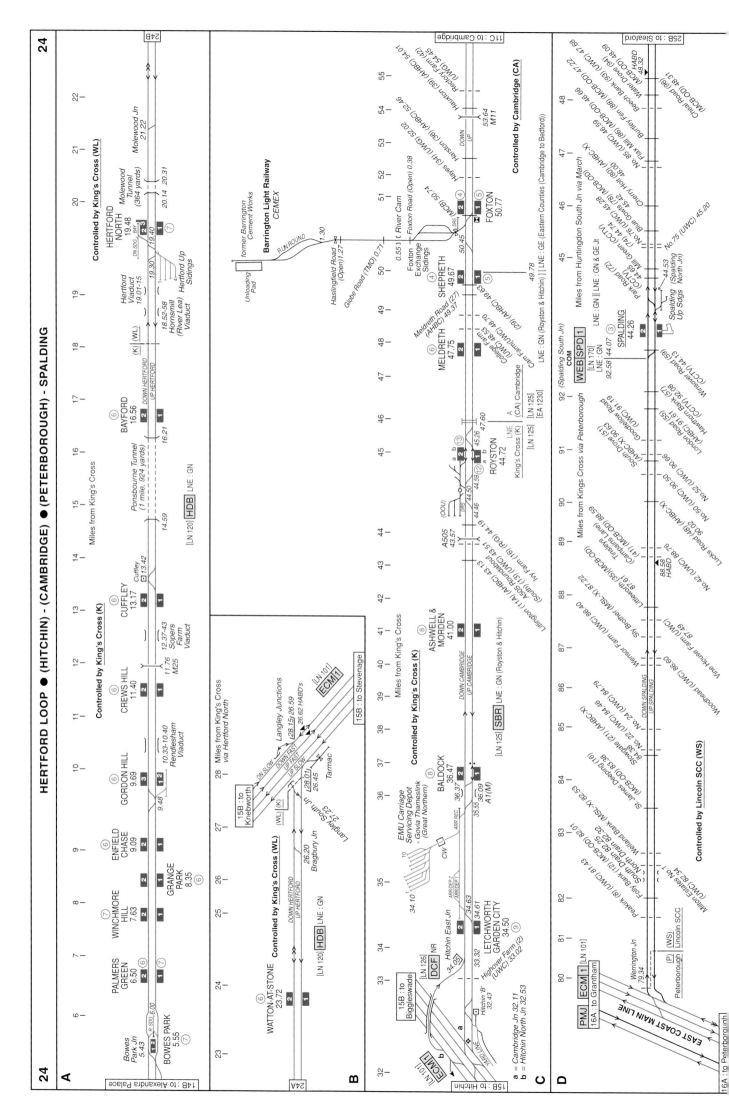

BOTTESFORD - SLEAFORD - BOSTON ● (SPALDING) - SLEAFORD - (LINCOLN)

October 2016

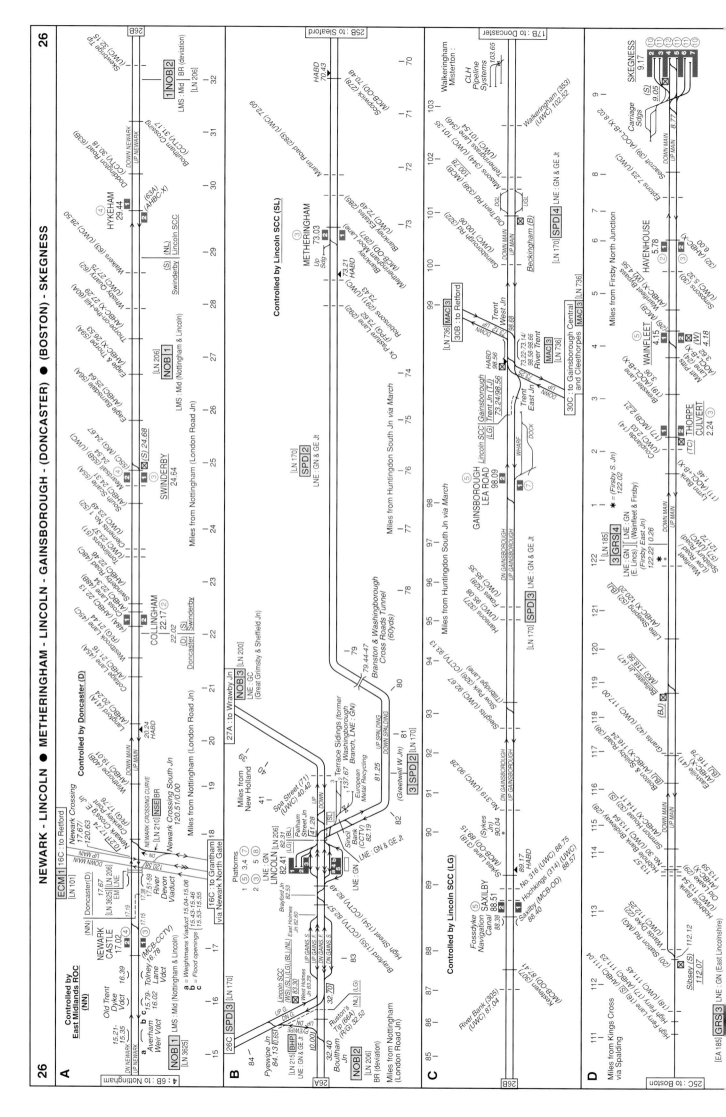

NEWARK - LINCOLN ● METHERINGHAM - LINCOLN - GAINSBOROUGH - (DONCASTER) ● (BOSTON) - SKEGNESS

A

27B

UP BARNETBY
DOWN BARNETBY

Holton-le-Moor (20) (MCB) 21.11
[LN 200] NOB 3 LNE : GC (Great Grimsby & Sheffield Jn)

Claxby Gatehouse (21) (AHBC-X) (H) 22.07

Claxby & Usselby (29) (AHBC-X) (H) 23.69

Walesby (30) (AHBC-X) (H) 24.46

Hamiltons (31) (UWC) 25.58

Market Rasen (R/G) 26.52
Footpath (R/G) 26.52
Maypole Viaducts
26.32-26.37

No. 35 (UWC) 27.19
MARKET RASEN 26.54

Lissingley (41) (AHBC-X) (H)
Busslingthorpe 40) (W) 29.90

UP MAIN
DOWN MAIN

Snelland (49) (AHBC-X) (W) 32.20
Thornally (49) (AHBC-X) (H) 32.15

Reasby Manor (53) (AHBC-X) (L) 33.60
Stainton (55) (AHBC-X) (L) 34.51
Scothern (5?) (UWC) 35.55
Langworth (58) (MCB) 35.96

34.28 Langworth Viaduct

Engineers'

Wickenby (45) (MG) 30.53

International Petroleum

Welton (L) 35.74

Reepham (63) (CCTV) 36.61
Stonefield Farm (69) (UWC) 37.04
Cherry Willingham (67) 38.18
No. 68 (UWC) 38.18

Lincoln (BL) (L)

26B : to Lincoln

B

HOMBERSTON NORTH SEA LANE
1.19
LCs
LCs
LCs
Floodgates

Carriage Shed
Sector Plate
LC
LC
Loco Shed
Sector Plate
LC
Griffin Hall Museum
Floodgates
LC
2 3
1
LAKESIDE CENTRAL 0.56

Floodgates LC
LC
DISCOVERY 0.25
LC
LC's
CLEETHORPES KINGSWAY 0.00

15" gauge
CLEETHORPES COAST LIGHT RAILWAY

Miles from New Holland

C

LINCOLNSHIRE WOLDS RAILWAY
4' 8½" / 1435mm gauge

NORTH THORESBY 147.72
147.74
LUDBOROUGH
146.27
146.25 miles from King's Cross
Fulstow Road
147.62
Locomotive Shed
146.02

ELR LNE : GN (East Lincolnshire)

Miles from New Holland

Smithfield (15) (AHBC-X) (H) 19.34
Folkly Lane (13) (UWC) 18.03
North Kelsey (13) (AHBC-X) (H) 18.25

Howsham (8) (AHBC-X) (H) 16.17

UP BARNETBY
DOWN BARNETBY

[LN 200] NOB 3 LNE : GC (Great Grimsby & Sheffield Jn)

27A

4 : 44B : to Manchester

Controlled by York ROC (CB)   MAC 3

33C : to Scunthorpe
DOW [LN 752]
Controlled by York ROC (BD)

33.31
33.24
(33.34)

Wrawby Jn 12.55 (94.12) (33.34)
94.12
93.30
94.06
12.67
12.55
(BL) Controlled by York ROC (BL) 12.55
(H)

30C : to Gainsborough Central   MAC 3
[LN 736]
Controlled by York ROC (BG)

30C : to Cleethorpes MAC 3

E

Platforms (Maximum, not partial)
1 (16)   5 (16)
2 (17)   6 (17)
3   (7)   7 (5/6)
4   (5)   8 (19)

Sheffield North End
Granville Street
DN
DN QM
SDG
B/UM

28 : to Meadowhall & Darnall

SHEFFIELD 158.40 178 ft
158.52
158.54
158.52 Sh.N.Jn
1a 1b
2a 2b 3b
3a
4a 5b 4b
5a
6b 8b
6a 7a 8a
2c
158.32
TRAM 50
Turner St. Footbridge
Sheffield Station/ Sheffield
Hallam University
LNE : GC BEW [LN 815]
28 : to Woodhouse Jn

THROUGH LINE
DOWN STATION SDG
UP STATION SDG No 1
UP STATION SDG No 2

SHEFFIELD FUEL POINT
Fuel Point
SHEFFIELD TISDLOCK
Shrewsbury Road
158.24
Sheffield 158.27
Sheffield 158.51
158.19 Granville Road
'CW'
'C'
'A'

Shrewsbury Road Carriage Sidings Arriva Rail North

DOWN HEELEY LOOP
DOWN MAIN
UP MAIN

UP BEIGHTON
DB = DOWN BEIGHTON

Miles from Langwith Jn via Clowne (former Westthorpe Colliery Line, LNE : GC)
WEC WRR = WESTTHORPE RUN ROUND
WSL = WESTTHORPE SHUNT LOOP

Beighton Jn (48.06)
155.48
155.46
WRR
155.43
2:17 Beighton Jn
11.60
154.27 (Killamarsh)
Westthorpe Run Round

York ROC (S)
47.60

DOWN BARROW HILL
UP BARROW HILL

152.47 HABD

28 : to Rotherham

156
155
154
153
152

East Bank Tunnel (80 yards)
Queens Road 157.44
157.15 London Road
Heeley 156.62
UP HEELEY LP
156.16
156.01 158.05

TJC 1 LMS : Mid (Chesterfield & Sheffield)
[LN 804]

Miles from St Pancras via Leicester & Toton

Both routes controlled by York ROC (S)

Miles from St Pancras via Leicester & Toton

CHR LMS : Mid (North Midland)
[LN 806]

Renishaw Siding Mill (UWC) 151.07

DWS [LN 808]
DWS

DORE AND TOTLEY
(0.000) Dore West Jn
0.27 HABD
(5) (0.60) 154.72
#
154.04
154.00 154.16
DOWN
SOUTH CURVE (91 yds)
154.20
153.71
153.61
Dore South Jn
Dore Station Jn
154.54 154.62
154.54

LNW
LNE : (S) York ROC

MAS LMS : Mid (Dore & Chinley)
[NW 9001]

UP MAIN MANCHESTER
DOWN MAIN MANCHESTER CRS

Totley Tunnel East (TE)
154.62 (TE)
Totley Tunnel (3 miles, 950 yards)
155.20

[LN 807]
MAS LMS : Mid (Dore & Chinley)

Bradway Tunnel (1 mile, 266 yards)
152.49
152.40 474ft

DRONFIELD 151.44
(5)
2
1

Barrow Hill Roundhouse Railway Centre (Staveley)
28A
BHM
Barrow (Barrow Hill) North Jn
149.62
Barrow Hill 149.34 NVR bdy
BW HILL 149.31 GDS
RECEPTION 2
RECEPTION 3
RECEPTION 4
CR's
150.00
149.46
Barrow (Barrow Hill) South Jn
148.76
Up Sidings

East Midlands ROC (CS)
149.39
York ROC (S)

Whiting Moor Road Viaduct 148.45
149.69-149.75
Unstone Viaduct (River Drone)
(Sheepbridge)
146.69 HABD

151
150
149
148

(CB) East Midlands ROC
York ROC (S)
DOWN BARROW HILL
UP BARROW HILL
147.60

CHR LMS : Mid (North Midland)
[LN 806]

146.59
146.36
146.70 DOWN MAIN
146.65
146.61
146.64 Tapton Jn
146.28
146.34
146.20 CHESTERFIELD

9 SPC TJC 1
[LN 3201] [LN 804] LMS : Mid (North Mid)

Chesterfield North Jn
146.36

(DC)
(CS)
(TC) (CB)
Down Sdgs 146.60
1 & 2 (8)
3 (12)

Controlled by East Midlands ROC

145.21 Chesterfield South Jn
144.68 Horns Bridge
EM LNE
DOWN MAIN
UP MAIN
EREWASH
EREWASH
DN
UP

UBH = UP BARROW HILL
DBH = DOWN BARROW HILL

147
146
145

4 : 5 : to Trent Jn & Derby

A

BARROW HILL ROUNDHOUSE RAILWAY CENTRE (Staveley)
4' 8½" / 1435mm gauge

Deltic Preservation Society Depot

Connecting Line

VAN ROADS 1
COMMERCIAL ROADS 2
Roundhouse contains 24 rds all with pits
Loading/Unloading Area

STORAGE RDS
COAL ROAD
ASH PIT RD
FRONT RD
RUNNING LINE
a = PREPARATION PIT RD
GARDEN RD

150 ROUNDHOUSE 150.04

Springwell Branch

Occupation Crossing 149.60 150.00

Staveley Engine Shed 149.56

Whittington Road

Storage Sdgs

NR Bdy 149.34

(Mileage reversal point for running line)

ROUNDHOUSE HALT 149.79

27E

BHM 149.63 (South Yorks & River Don)

M1 159.43

(Treeton North Jn) 159.19

Treeton Jn 158.65

Woodhouse Mill Jn

−159

−158

UP BARROW HILL

DN GDS LINE

Treeton

UP CANKLOW GOODS LOOP 160.11

DOWN BARROW HILL

SHUNT NECK

Canklow 160

159.58

(Catcliffe Jn) 159.15 TNC

SHE DEP (DN)
SHE ARR (UP)
159.22

Catcliffe Viaduct

BTJ

Masborough Sorting Sidings South Jn 160.57

River Rother Viaduct 47.02-47.06

47

47.24

UP GDS LINE

Woodhouse Viaduct 47.16-21

Treeton Jn 157.37

−157

Woodhouse Jn 46.52

LN 736 MAC3
LNE : GC (Sheffield & Lincolnshire Jn. Rly)

46.56

LN 816 BEW LNE : GC

CHR 156
LMS : Mid (Nth. Midland)

Beighton Jn 48.07

Beighton Stn Jn 47.42

BX MCO

48

York ROC

155.56-48
155.43

Westthorpe Run Round 11.60

v = WESTTHORPE RUN ROUND
w = WESTTHORPE SHUNT LOOP

30A : to Worksop

Rotherham Steel Terminal DB Cargo

LN 809 BTJ LNE : Sheffield District

Miles from St Pancras via Leicester, Toton & Treeton

Shepcote Lane New Sdgs
Tinsley : Avesta SPACE (Stainless Plate And Coil Expansion) OUTOKUMPU

161 Miles from St Pancras via Leicester, Toton and Barrow Hill

CHR LMS : Mid (North Midland) [LN 806]

159.76

EAST DEPARTURE

Sheffield International Rail Freight Terminal DB Cargo

EAST ARRIVAL
EAST DEPARTURE

160.52

Tinsley Park Jn 160.68

Tinsley Park

Avesta SMACC (Stainless Melting and Continuous Casting) OUTOKUMPU

46

45

Miles from Manchester (London Road) via Woodhead

UP WORKSOP
DOWN WORKSOP
UP BRANCH
DOWN BRANCH

WOODHOUSE 46.18

WH

Woodhouse Jn 46.52

2
1

−6 Miles from Woodburn Jn

LN 830 WME LNE : GC (South Yorks & River Don)

Controlled by York ROC (S)

−5

ROTHERHAM CENTRAL 4.60

Rotherham Central (proposed)
Rotherham Central Jn 4.45

LN 818 HCD BR

−4 Rotherham Main (UWC) 4.01

161.45
161.56

Tinsley : Avesta (TMO) 161.04/ARR/ARR

Tinsley Avesta

Controlled by Woodburn Jn (W)

WEST DEPARTURE
WEST ARR

SEL BR

161.24 Shepcote Lane W. Jn
LN 810 LN 809

Proposed electrification as part of the Tram-Train Project (750V DC overhead)

Ickles Viaduct 161.28
161.40

−3 2.79 Tinsley East Jn
2.61 Tinsley North Jn

2.38 M1
2.22 Tinsley South Jn
SW CURVE
SX CURVE

161.20
161.63

161.20 Shepcote Lane Jn
LN 812 BLJ BR

1.36 Broughton Lane Jn
LN 830 WME LNE : GC

Controlled by Woodburn Jn (W)

0.56 (Attercliffe)

DN
UP

44

43

DARNALL 43.23

42.40

0.00

Miles from Manchester (London Road) via Woodhead

M1 (Tinsley Vdct) 162.16

M1 (Tinsley Vdct)

50 TRAM

MEADOWHALL INTERCHANGE 161.70

MEADOWHALL INTERCHANGE 161.52

Wincobank South/Tinsley Jn

BRIGHTSIDE 161.27

x = BRIGHTSIDE RECEPTION No.1
y = BRIGHTSIDE RECEPTION No.2

Brightside Loop

Valley Centertainment

Arena/Don Valley Stadium

Attercliffe Sidings Cemex

ATTERCLIFFE ROAD 159.34

EMR 159.65

Attercliffe Viaduct 159.73

158.76 Nunnery Main Line Jn 158.77

BR LMS : LNW Nunnery Jn 159.33/.41.68

Woodburn Jn (W) 159.16

York ROC (S) 158.60

158.67

Miles from St Pancras via Leicester, Toton & Sheffield

STOCKSBRIDGE

UP WORKSOP
DOWN WORKSOP

42.29

42.22 Tram over see 50

1 NUJ2 W Woodburn Jn 42.40

29B : to Stocksbridge

LN 804 TJC 3 LMS : Mid (North Midland)

Miles from St Pancras via Leicester, Toton & Barrow Hill

32A : to Swinton & Mexborough via Aldwarke Jn

−164 Parkgate (proposed)
Parkgate Jn 5.59
LN 815

Millmoor C F Booth

LMS : Mid (Sheffield & Rotherham)

WBH

York ROC (S)
Woodburn Jn (W) 3.57

UP TINSLEY
DOWN TINSLEY

0.62
0.20
0.00

162.18
161.77
161.91

Holmes Jn (or CHORD) Brinsworth St 0.36
Holmes Curve

Rotherham (Station Jn) 162.24

ROTHERHAM MASBOROUGH 162.00
163.74

COM 161.77

LN 804 TJC
z = MASBOROUGH DOWN GOODS LOOP

Masborough (Stn. Stn. Jn)

UP MAIN
DOWN MAIN

3
2

York ROC (S)
183.43
163.22

DN B HILL
UP B HILL

UP BARNSLEY
DN BARNSLEY

162.00-02
161.70

Wincobank Vdct

Chapeltown Viaduct 165.63

166.28

Tankersley Tunnel (1498 yds) 165.68

166.00

CHAPELTOWN 165.68

LN 868 SHB LMS : Mid / BR (Stairfoot)

Buttercliffe Lane (UWC) 164.12

Ecclesfield Emergency Operating Panel 164.09

34B : to Barnsley

Controlled by Barnsley (BY)

−165

Miles from St Pancras via Leicester, Toton & Sheffield

164

Grimesthorpe Jn
Mill Race Jn 160.18
160.34

LN 804 TJC
LMS : Mid

Brightside Stn. Jn 161.12

LMS : Mid (Sheffield & Rotherham)

Wincobank Jn 161.70

162

161

160

159.65
159.27
159.01
159.17

Victoria Vdct 159.17
* = Spans 13-15 also known as Wicker Arches

* Victoria Vdct arches 1-42
DOWN
41.08 41.39 41.48

VICTORIA 41.22

LMS : Mid (Sheffield & Rotherham)

LMS : Mid (Sheffield, Ashton-under-Lyne and Manchester Railway)

Miles from Manchester (London Road) via Woodhead

WADSLEY BRIDGE 38.36

LN 750 MAC3 LNE : GC

38.40
38.77

Penistone Road Viaduct (A61) (5 Arches)

Herries Road Bridge

Broad Street Tunnel (109 yards) (Tram over)

→ N

SHIREBROOK - WHITWELL / HIGH MARNHAM & BRANCHES ● STOCKSBRIDGE STEELWORKS

A

28 : to Sheffield

Miles from Manchester
(London Road) via Woodhead

34   35   36   37

STOCKSBRIDGE LINE   UP

[LN 750] MAC 3

LNE : GC
(Sheffield, Ashton-under-Lyne
and Manchester Railway)

DOWN

NR bdy 0.00 |33.20

33.35 (Deepcar)
0.07   *(Deepcar)* Deepcar Exchange Sdgs

NR bdy   Deepcar (Viaduct (River Don)
0.46

0.21   Ellen Cliff Loop 0.65

Stocksbridge Light Railway SKL
1.17
1.30

1.56

Stocksbridge
Tata Steel

2.26

1.78

B

30A : to Shireoaks & Worksop

— 152

WHITWELL
150.56 ④

LMS : Mid [LN 768] PSE
(Mansfield & Worksop)

— 151

DOWN MANSFIELD
UP MANSFIELD   LINE

Whitwell Tunnel (544 yards)
150.28
150.03

(EC) ⊠

Elmton & Creswell Jn
149.37

② CRESWELL
149.26 ④

— 149

HOOD

Miles from St Pancras
via Corby & Newstead

— 148

Norwood (MG) 147.71

[LN 768] PSE LMS : Mid

LANGWITH
② WHALEY-THORNS
147.14

*Shirebrook
South Jn 10.19*

— 147

— 146

146.44 (SJ)
Shirebrook
East Jn 145.62
0.45 145.11
0.54 145.10
DOWN MAIN
UP MAIN   (SJ) UP BROUGH

SHIREBROOK
④ 145.06

— 145

WH Davis
Wagon
Works

(Langwith Jn)
Shirebrook
0.54
c = LNE : GC (LD & EC)

9.72

*Warsop
Up Yard (OOU)*
10.59 Warsop Jn
[0.00]
Shirebrook Jn
[0.45] (SJ) 145.14
145.04

[LN 784] HIM 1 BR

[LN 772] SWP
LNE : GC (LD & EC)

ROBIN

(Sheepwash Viaduct
144.63

Shirebrook Jn (SJ)
East Midlands ROC (KS)

— 144

*Littlewood Vdct
143.43-47*)

144.20
UM
EM
LNE
143.00 |
[LN 768] PSE LMS : Mid
[LN 3273] PBS 3 LMS : Mid (Mansfield & Worksop)

— 143

DN

**Controlled by
East Midlands ROC**

4 : 5 : to Mansfield & Trent Junction

Miles from former Chesterfield Market Pl.

— 11   12   13   14   15   16   17   18   19   20   21   22   23   24

*Welbeck Colliery
CLOSED*   *Welbeck West 3.15*

⊡ DN 3.54
⊡ UP *Welbeck East 2.65*

NR Boundary 2.63 (River Meden)
2.38)
0.05 *WELBECK*

[LN 802] WKC LNE

(Warsop)
12.18
UP MAIN
DOWN MAIN

0.38 UP WELBECK
UP WEL
0.00

LOCO SPUR

Welbeck
Colliery Jn
13.17

[LN 784] HIM 1
LNE : GC (LD & EC)

*Thoresby Colliery
CLOSED* [LN 788] TYC

(Clipstone
West Jn)
15.15

(Clipstone
East Jn)
15.40

**Clipstone (C)
15.20**

(Edwinstowe)
16.47
UP MAIN
DOWN MAIN

Bunker 1.22
WB   1.18

DOWN

17.21 17.16
17.21 Thoresby
Colliery Jn (T) ⊠

[LN 784] HIM 1
LNE : GC

17.52

OLLERTON
18.16

Controlled by Thoresby Colliery (T)

*Broughton Brake Tunnel
(350 yards)*

[LN 786] BEC BR

UP BEVERCOTES
BRANCH DOWN

NR Boundary
4.22

3

(OOU)
beyond
1.00

Miles from Chesterfield Market Pl.

1.65

1.49 — 2

— 1

DOWN 0.33 Bevercotes
No.1 GF

0.30   ⊡ *(Boughton)*
20.55

20.15
20.14 No.2 GF
20.12 Boughton Jn
20.13 No.1 GF

UP MAIN
DOWN MAIN

*Tuxford
No.1 GF* ⊡ 23.57
23.75 *Tuxford
No.2 GF* ⊡ 23.75
(Tuxford)

*Limbs No.1
(UWC) 22.29*

C

Controlled by Thoresby Colliery (T)

Miles from Chesterfield Market Pl.

25   26   27

*High
Marnham*
27.60

27.45 V to
former
Power
Station
27.48

[LN 786] 17A : to Retford
LNE : GN
24.78
DN 131.23 UP

17A : to Newark

29A

[LN 784] HIM 2
LNE : GC/BR
(LD & EC)

[LN 784] 1 HIM 2

*Tuxford West
Junction Sidings
Rail Innovation and
Development Centre*

24.58

⊡ 24.54
*Tuxford
West Jn*
GF

29C

29

October 2016

© Copyright **TRACK**maps. No reproduction without permission

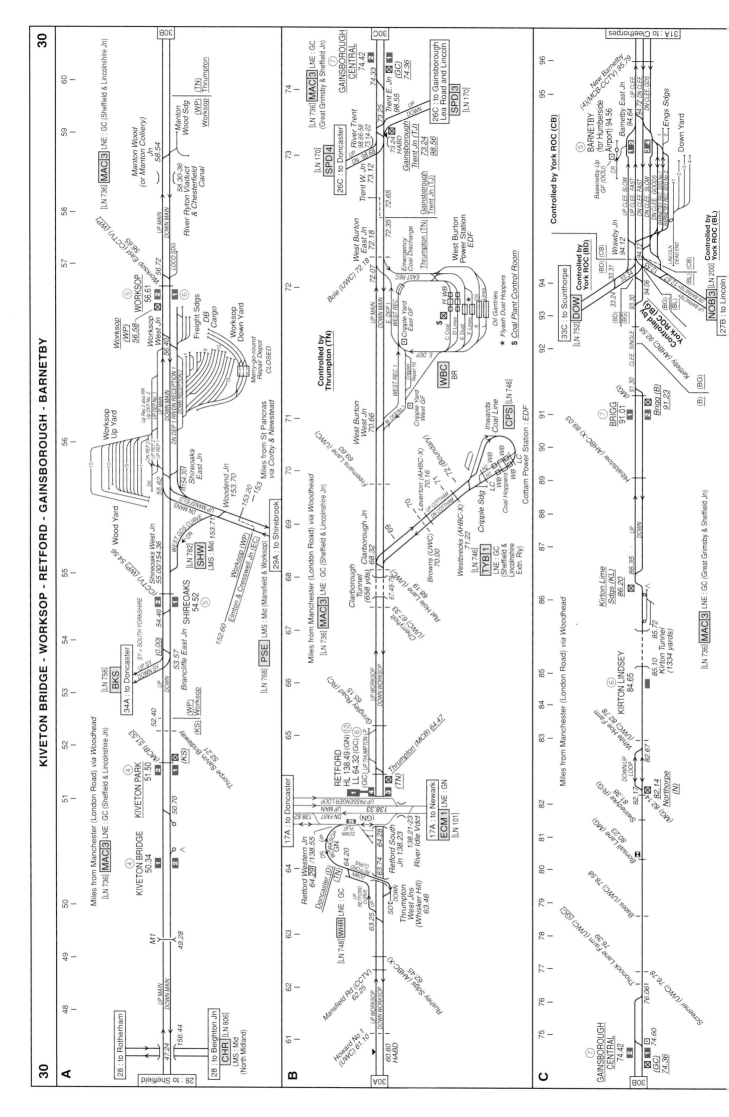

A

Cleethorpes Traincare Facility
Siemens
Fuelling Apron 112.11
CW 112.40
CLEETHORPES 112.40 or 10 non - DMU
CLEETHORPES SINGLE

NEW CLEE 110.78
Fish Dock Road (41) (MCB-OD) 110.31
First Dock Road (41) (MCB-OD)

GRIMSBY DOCKS 110.11
MAC 3 | LNE : GC
GRIMSBY LP 110.48
Pasture Street (38) 109.26
Garden Street (37) (MCB-OD) 109.03
GRIMSBY TOWN 109.20
Wellowgate (36) (MCB-OD) 109.14
Littlefield Lane Crossing (34)
Frieghtgate (35) (MCB-OD) 108.73
(Great Grimsby & Sheffield Jn)

GRIMSBY DOCKS 109.59 110.02

Marsh North Jn 108.05
(Marsh East Jn) 108.08
MWN [LN 740]
31C
Marsh West Jn 107.69

GREAT COATES 107.19
Great Coates (30) (MCB-OD) 107.11

HEALING 105.75
Great Coates (30) 106.69

STALLINGBOROUGH 104.75
Church Lane (UWC) 104.20
Stallingborough (MCB-OD)

Little London (22) (MCB-OD) 103.55
Roxton Siding (21)

Harborough Jn 101.13
UP & DN HARBOROUGH CHORD
HABROUGH 101.13
Old Jn (12) (UWC) 100.38
Habrough Jn 100.53
Rye Hill Farm (UWC) 1.12
Ulceby (South) Jn 100.31

BROCKLESBY 99.32
Ulceby (MCB-OD) 100.32
BRI 1 [LN 742]
Croxton 97.40
Wheelchex
Gawood's 98.90 (UWC)
Pushpole (8) (UWC) 98.64
Ulceby Chase Farm (7)
Brocklesby West Jn 99.20
Brocklesby East Jn 99.39
(Great Grimsby & Sheffield Jn)

UP CLEETHORPES
DOWN CLEETHORPES
UP CLEETHORPES GOODS
DOWN CLEETHORPES GOODS
MAC 3 [LN 736] | LNE : GC
(Great Grimsby & Sheffield Jn)

31B

30C : to Barnetby

Miles from Manchester (London Road) via Woodhead
Controlled by York ROC (CB, B, MB, ST, P)

B

River Humber

Oil Terminal
Petroleum Sdgs. No. 4 East
Robinson Rd LC (TMO)
East Dock Road LC (Open)
(Queens Road Jn)
LNE : GC
Grimsby District Light
1 PYE 2 COM
Queens Road Jn
1 PYE [LN 740]
Chris Smaller GF 0.75
Kiln Lane (AOCL) 0.51
Freight Terminal Sdg
Global Shipping
31C

Immingham East Storage
Immingham East Sdgs 107.02
700 Series Sdgs
Simon Storage Sdgs
Ridleys Sdg
600 Series Sdgs
(Methane Gas)
Pad
106.31
106.43
106.50 0.00
DN GRIMSBY
BRI 2
APR
DEP 106.21
NR
Gresley Way LC (Open)
IAWS LC (Open)
§ = Immingham Token Exchange Point
(former Immingham East Jn SB) 0.08
S = Immingham Token Exchange Point
§

IMMINGHAM TMD
DB Cargo
Controlled by York ROC (MB)

Simon Storage East (Texaco)
No. 2 Kings Rd
Alexandra Rd North LCs (Open)
SHED SD
No. 2 & 3 Quays
Transit Quays
No. 1 Quay
MIDDLE RD
SHED SIDE MIDDLE ROAD
107.32
Engineers Sdg (ESSO Bay)

Eastern Jetty
Western Jetty

Simon Storage West
Dock Tank Farm
CAGE
Western Storage
LC (UWB)
Henderson Quay (No.8)
Seawheel Sdgs
Mineral Quay
IMMINGHAM DOCK
Associated British Ports (NCBO)
ABP EXXTOR Container Term
STORA ENSO
Mineral Quay Sdgs
§ = Simon Storage LC (UWB)
★ = Simon Storage West (TMO)

ENGINE LINE
D = Diesel Shed
Immingham C&W
DB Cargo
Depot Walkway (UWC) 106.10
SAND HOPPER SDG
FUELLING SHED
STORES
COAL ROAD
106
DEAD END MAINTENANCE ROADS
No. 1 DEPARTURE
No. 2 DEPARTURE
STAGES ROAD
LOAD BK.
Service Rds
Pad

DFDS Seaways Nordic Steel Terminal
Discharge Bunker CPL
NCB Terminal
Rotary Tippler Servicing Shed
UP GRIMSBY
DOWN GRIMSBY
105.07
LC
Dock Boundary
105
(MB)
[R]

C

* COM — 4.79 108.73
* also change of Directions
Toxide UK GF
Woad Lane (AHBC) 3.36
4.06
4.19
4.33
Pyewipe Road (P) (MG) 4.19
ABP
2 PYE 3 [LN 740]
PYE 3 [LN 740]
Great Coates
No. 1 108.34 (GC)
31A
'GRIMSBY LIGHT SINGLE'
UP GRIMSBY
DOWN
1 2 3
Marsh Lane (AHBC) 1.25
Grimsby District Light West Marsh Sidings
LNE : GC
PYE 2 [LN 740]
MWRS = MARSH WEST RECEPTION SDG
31B

River Humber
Humber Terminals
Royal Dock
Freshney Cargo Sers
Moody Lane (AOCL) 108.69
108.74
UNION DK BRANCH
ABP [LN 738]
Alexandra Dock
Freshney 109.17
West Side Rd
Union Dock
◇ = Car Loading Pad
109.79
GRIMSBY DOCKS Associated British Ports (NCBO)

B (lower)

Miles from Manchester (London Road) via Woodhead and Retford

BARTON-ON-HUMBER 110.18
Pasture Road (114) (ABCL) 109.63
Killingholme DB Cargo
2.70
Humber Sea Terminal
Admiralty Sdgs DB Cargo
Barrow Road (21) (MG) 106.57
Oxmarsh (20) (MG) 106.38
NEW HOLLAND 106.52
New Holland Bulk Services
BAR [LN 744]
LNE : GC
(Great Grimsby & Sheffield Jn)
BARROW HAVEN 108.05
Barrow Road (21) (MG) 106.57
(106) (Open) 108.07
Barrow Haven Viaduct 108.08

Chapel Farm (UWC) 105.16
GOXHILL 104.55 [G]
Goxhill (15) (MG) 104.51
Butterswood (13) (MG) 106.38
Thornton Abbey (12) (ABCL-X) [G]
THORNTON ABBEY 103.04
Bystable Lane (10) (MGH-Key) 102.10 [G]
Meadow Croft Fm
Garola Ho. (7) (UWC)
Barton Road (12) (ABCL-X) [G]

Humber International Terminal APB
APB Cabin
Regent Oil (TMO) 1.04
Immingham Lindsey Refinery Total & Petrofina
IMMINGHAM Lindsey Refinery
Humber Road Jn
Immingham Bulk Terminal British Steel
Ore Loading Bunker
Overhead Conveyor
Western Entrance (CCTV) 104.55
104.67
104.72 (TMO)
104.74 (OC)
104.74 CONTAINER LOAD AREA
104.79
Immingham North LC (OC)
Humber Rd LC
Immingham West Jn 105.06
0.00 105.10 Humber Rd LC
COM
KIL 1 [LN 742]
2 KIL 1 [LN 742]
NR Bdy 0.06
NR Bdy
0.02 0.06 0.48

Departure Sidings
Arrival Sdgs North
Control Tower
IMMINGHAM Humber Road Sdgs
Immingham Reception Sidings 104.30
Humber Coal Rly. & Dock
Phillips 66
Storage Gantry
Loading Sidings
Loading Sidings Gantry
Controlled by (IR)
UP IM 103.19
DN IM
104.05
103.45
103.54
Ambiance (15) (UWC) 104.38
KIL 2 [LN 742]
LNE : GC (Barton & Immingham Light)
BRI 2 [LN 742] [LN 740]
LNE : GC
NCB Terminal

Killingholme Tar (20) 2.70
Shell Mex (20) 2.44
Yorkshire Tar (20) 2.39
New mn (19) 2.34
(Open) 2.19

Ulceby North Jn 100.44
Ulceby Gate
ULCEBY 100.31
(1-3 North Sidings, 4-9 South Sidings)
Ulceby South Jn 100.36
BAR [LN 744] [LN 742]
BRI [LN 742]
0.45
Controlled York ROC (MB)
UP BARTON
DOWN BARTON
w = Danny's (UWC) 100.49
x = Wartons (UWC) 101.14
y = Robinson (8) (UWC) 101.36
UP IM
DN IM
31A
101.40
101.39
(MB) 101-
[LN 744] [LN 742]
100.73

Miles from Manchester (London Road) via Woodhead and Retford
Controlled York ROC (MB)
31

October 2016

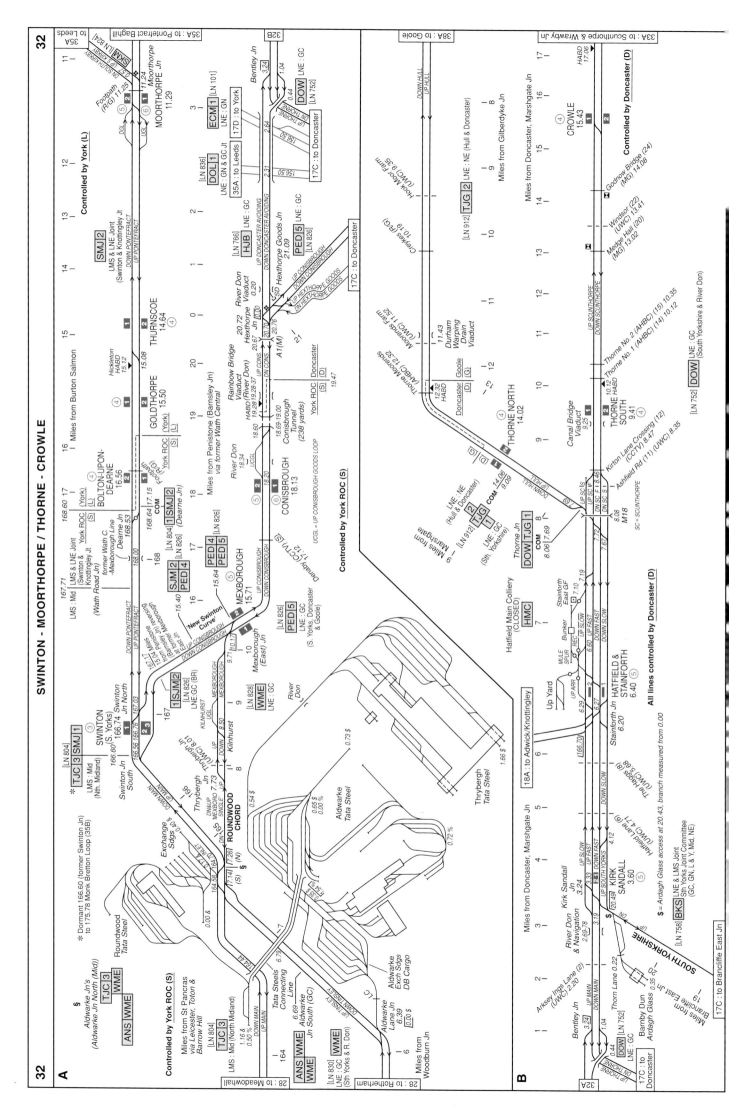

ALTHORPE - SCUNTHORPE - WRAWBY JUNCTION

A

Doncstr Scunthorpe (D) (S)

Miles from Doncaster, Marshgate Jn

Keadby Canal Bridge 18.18

32B: to Doncaster

Keadby Canal (28) (MCB) 18.3 [E]

Keadby River Bridge (River Trent) 19.70 (former Bascule Bridge)

M181

ALTHORPE 19.21 19.34 ⑤

[LN 752] DOW

LNE : GC (S. Yorks & R. Don)

Gunhouse Jn 20.32

GUNHOUSE L.P. 20.62

Frodingham Viaduct 21.28

20.56

LNE : GC (Trent, Anchsolme & Grimsby)

UP MAIN / DOWN MAIN

Scunthorpe

Frodingham Jn 23.13

Freight Sidings DB Cargo

No.1 REC / No.2 REC

[LN 754] SAN SCUNTHORPE FOREIGN ORE BRANCH

Santon Ore Mining (UWC) 25.11 (32A)

Foreign Ore Branch Jn 25.34

(S) York ROC (BD)

Controlled by Scunthorpe (S)

Santon Foreign Ore Branch 0.25 / 0.00

33C

33B

Frodingham Depot Volker Rail

NOP / SCD / COM

a = (Dawes Lane Jn)
b = Trent Jn 0.00/23.51
c = Dawes Lane (AOCL) 0.32

British Steel Coal Handling Plant

Hopper & Control Panel

A ARRIVAL / RECEPTION SDGS / STANDAGE DOCK / DEPARTURE ROAD

Nth Lincoln Jn 24.25

Cripple Sdgs

Eccles Sdgs

Anchor Exchange Sdgs

North Lincoln Sdgs

Dawes Lane Coke Ovens (Closed)

Redbourne Semi-Finished Steel Stockyard

1-3 Inwards
4 Loco release
& Loop Sdgs
5-16 Outwards

Muck Bank

Mills Exchange Sidings

Medium Section Mill

Former Bloom & Billet Mills

SCUNTHORPE FOREIGN ORE BRANCH

Foreign Ore Terminal 0.74

Ore Tippler Plant

TIPPLER LINE 1.16

ORE BEDS

SSH Scunthorpe (S) 23.27

TRANSFER 23.40 / TRANSFER 23.65 DN SCUNTHORPE GOODS / TRENT RECEPTION LINE 24.10

High Yd 1-3 / 4

TRENT SDGS: DB Cargo Low Yd 9

IR = Iron Road
TS = Tube Side
MR = Middle Road

Rail Sidings

Plate Mill (Mothballed)

Winn's Sdgs

Scunthorpe

RDL

NG = New Gantry
OP = Old Portal

Rail Service Centre

CEW Dock

HRB = Heavy Repair Bay

AFRPS Loco Shed

'Appleby'

Appleby Coke Ovens

Quench Car Track

Coke Oven Weighbridge

APPLEBY FRODINGHAM WORKS British Steel (Greybull Capital)

North Lincoln Road

HIGH LINE

Platelayers Stock Ground

Scrap Recovery & Iron Ponds

Northants Bridge

Bridge 44

Stores Road

66 Road

Blast Furnaces

QVWR

Bottom Loop

Coal Running Road

SMSRR

Torpedo Repair Bay

Gate 15

Gate 7

15 Loop

14 Loop

Rod Mill

New Loop

Slab Bay

Welfare Loop

Soaker Side

Stripper Bank

West Bank

Mill Shop Running Road

= 5 Bay Loop

Mould Shop (Closed)

CC BOS Scrap Bay

CC = Continuous Casting
BOS = Basic Oxygen Steel Plant

SM = Scrap Main
SL = Scrap Loop
DER = Dead End Road

APPLEBY-FRODINGHAM Railway Preservation Society Excursion Platform 'Frodingham'

HRB - Heavy Repair Bay

SMSRR = South Melting Shop Running Road
QVWR = Queen Victoria West Road

B

Miles from Frodingham West Jn

ROXBY GULLET Biffa Waste Management

Loading / Unloading area

Bagmore Farm 3.60

[LN 756] NOP

Normanby Park GF 2.11

33A

(British Steel Line) LC

Dragonby Sdgs DB Cargo

FLIXBOROUGH WHARF LTD

Faber Prest Distribution Ltd Steel Terminal

Crane

River Trent

LC

C

Miles from Doncaster, Marshgate Jn
Controlled by York ROC (BD)

33A

Scunthorpe (S) York ROC (BD)

Appleby (33) (MCB-OD) 26.60

Keadwood Lane (UWC) 27.40 (36)

Worlaby (UWC) 28.10 (36)

Kings College (UWC) 30.75

Moor Lane (45) (UWC) 31.42

Elsham (MCB-OD) 31.58 / 31.33

M180

UP SCUNTHORPE / DOWN SCUNTHORPE

[LN 752] DOW / LNE : GC (Trent, Anchsolme & Grimsby)

30C : to Immingham and Cleethorpes

33

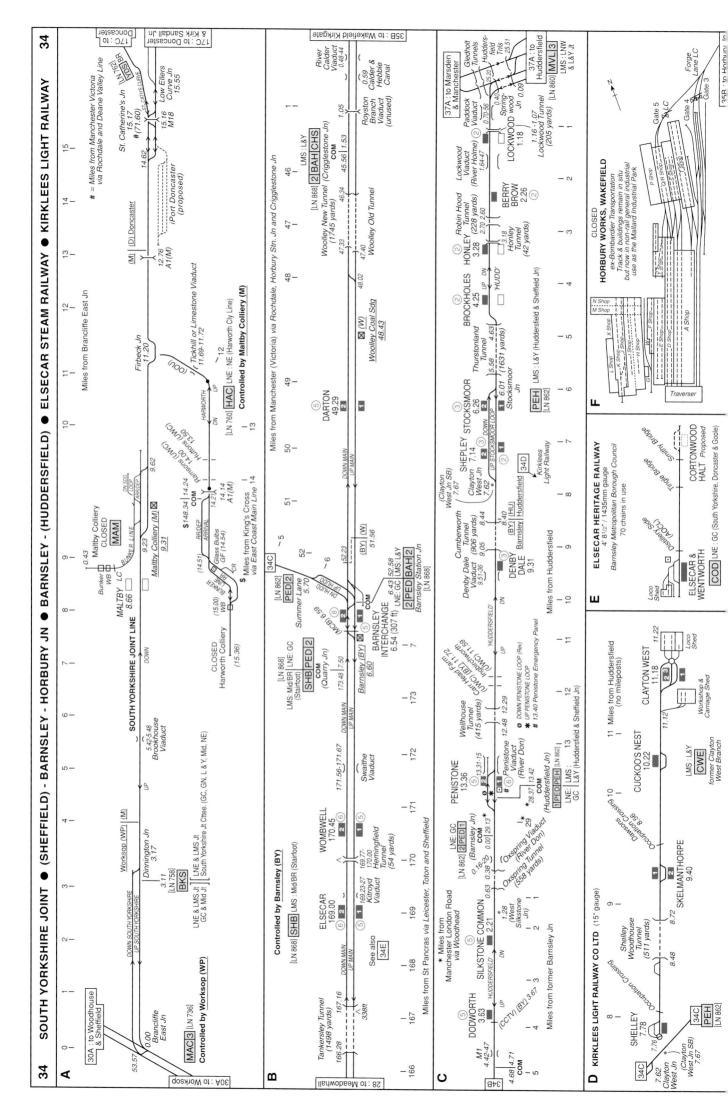

(DONCASTER) - WAKEFIELD - (LEEDS) ● HORBURY JN - WAKEFIELD - CASTLEFORD ● MONK BRETTON ● PONTEFRACT - CASTLEFORD

A

35B

Wintersett

171.19   171.07

Controlled by York (L)

FITZWILLIAM 169.15
168.61 [LN 836] DOL1

MOORTHORPE 11.29
Footpath (R/G) 11.25
Moorthorpe Jn 11.24
[LN 846] SKM [LN 882]

SOUTH ELMSALL 164.48
South Elmsall (UWC) 164.01

South Kirkby Jn
USK = UP SOUTH KIRKBY
DSK = DOWN SOUTH KIRKBY
165.74 (L) York (FE) Ferrybridge
166.00 South Kirkby Jt
LMS & LNE Jt [LN 882]

32A : to Swinton

Hemsworth Loops
167.31 UP DONCASTER

168.09 168.11

Miles from King's Cross

Doncaster (D) (L)
161.28 York (Leeds Ardsley)
Adwick Jn 160.65

ADWICK 159.72 Carcroft Jn
160.08 160.14
[LN 836] DOL1
Carcroft Jn
UP SKELLOW
160.57 CJS
Skellow Jn 0.61
SKA [LN 882]

Miles from King's Cross via Carcroft Jn

Arksgate (8) (UWC) 158.10
DOWN LEEDS 158.60 HABD
UP LEEDS

BENTLEY (S. Yorks) 157.47
(CCTV) 157.52
[LN 101] ECM1

17D : to York
18A : to Stainforth Jn
17C/32B : to Scunthorpe

HJB [LN 766] LNE : GC (Doncaster Avoiding Line)
32A : to Mexborough
Cock Hill
(CCTV) 156.52
156.50 156.36
DN MAIN
156.00 UP MAIN
DOWN SLOW
UP SLOW
Marshgate Jn
157.50 157.52
Controlled by Doncaster (D)
2.31 2.64
[LN 752] DOW LNE : GC
17C : to Doncaster

B

40A : to Milford Jn

Controlled by Ferrybridge (FE)
(L) York
PONTEFRACT BAGHILL 4.31
[LN 836] DOL1 LNE : GN & GC Jt (West Riding & Grimsby Jt)

River Went 7.57
Miles from Burton Salmon
Baghill HABD 6.70
DOWN PONTEFRACT
UP PONTEFRACT
5.60

[LN 804] SMJ 2 LMS & LNE Jt
Swinton & Knottingley Jt (Mid, NE)

Controlled by York (L)
(D) Doncaster (L)
0.00 0.22

Controlled by York (L)
Wrenthorpe Sdgs
Balne Lane
WAKEFIELD WESTGATE 175.65
175.36 175.32
Viaduct
[LN 854] MVN 2 LNE : GN & GCJt
LMS : L&Y
Manchester & Leeds
DOWN L&Y SLOW/FAST
UP L&Y SLOW
UP L&Y FAST
WESTGATE CURVE
47.48 47.35 47.20
SANDAL & AGBRIGG 174.05
Chevet Viaduct 179.47

Controlled by York (L)
[LN 836] DOL1 LNE : GN & GCJt
Shay Lane Viaduct 172.54-60
173 —
Miles from St Pancras via Leicester, Toton & Barrow Hill

River Calder Viaduct
[LN 874] MEW [LN 874]
LNE : NE (York & North Midland)
DOWN METHLEY
UP METHLEY

22.04 Whitwood Jn (CD)
0.01
Castleford (MCB) 21.22

CASTLEFORD 20.76
[LN 836] 1 (L) York
20.39 (NIRU) Castleford East Jn
21.02 21
DOWN Castleford West Jn
CUTSYKE
Cutsyke Jn 2.61 CPM 1 59.00
(CJ) 59.01

Controlled by Castleford (CD)
[LN 854] NOC LNE : NE (York & North Midland)
186.15 DOWN NORMANTON
LINE 1 NORTH
LINE 1 SOUTH
186.05 UP L&Y
Altofts Jn 23.57
186.00 M62 185.63

WAKEFIELD EUROPORT
DB Cargo
Crane Sdgs
W. Euro. GSP
L1N
LRL LRN
CR
TERMINAL LINE
LRL = LOCO RELEASE LINE

NORMANTON 185.11 100 ft
UP MID.
DOWN MIDLAND
185.73
184.63 (K) (CD)
Footpath LC (R/G)
[LN 872] TJC 3 LMS : Mid (North Midland)
Calder Viaduct 186.53-68
Goose Hill GF
Goose Hill Jn 50.31 184.56
[LN 854] MVN TJC 3 LMS : L&Y
(dormant from Oakenshaw Jn)
Miles from Man. Victoria via Rochdale
184.65

Turners Lane Jn 48.33
48.28 Calder Bridge Jn
[LN 870] CTL LMS : L&Y
[LN 882] WAG1 LMS : L&Y
River Calder Viaduct
48.48 48.50
48.00
DN TURNERS LA CURVE
UP T LA CURVE
Oakenshaw Jn 48.76 Oakenshaw West Jn
49.33 WAG1
Crofton Jn 48.56
49.41
Crofton Depot Bombardier
Fuel Point
CW
Shed
Crofton Old Stn No. 1 (UWC) 50.28 50.36
Crofton East Jn 183 04 (UWC) 50.25
OSC LMS Mid BR
50.23 50.28

Controlled by Wakefield Kirkgate (K)
[LN 882] WAG1 LMS : L&Y
(Wakefield, Pontefract & Goole)

STREETHOUSE 52.15
Red Lane (MG) 52.27
(CCTV) 52.11
WAG1 2 1

FEATHERSTONE 53.71
Sportsfield (UWC) 54.12
(CCTV) 1 2

40A : to Milford Jn
Controlled by Ferrybridge (FE)
(L) York
PONTEFRACT BAGHILL 4.31

GLASSHOUGHTON
58.20 (MG) 57.76
Woodman Lane (UWC) 58.00
M62 57.76

Miles from Manchester Victoria & Wakefield Kirkgate, via Rochdale & Wakefield Kirkgate, reverse at Pontefract Monkhill 56.39 and increase to Cutsyke Jn

Prince of Wales (P) 56.67
Parkside Farm (UWC) — 57
(MCB) 56.66
Wakefield Kirkgate (CJ) 59.00
Prince of Wales (K) (P)
Pon W. Jn (P)
Pon.W.Jn

PONTEFRACT TANSHELF 55.64
55.42
56.43 56.36
DN GOOLE UP GOOLE
DN SDG
DOWN GDS

PONTEFRACT MONKHILL 56.40
(FE) 1
WAG1 LMS : L&Y (Wakefield, Pontefract & Goole)

Controlled by Wakefield Kirkgate (K)
LMS : L&Y (Wakefield, Pontefract & Goole)
WAG1 [LN 882]

40A : to Knottingley & Goole

Miles from Manchester Victoria via Rochdale

WAKEFIELD KIRKGATE 47.62
THRO 47.48
Platforms 1 2 3
Up Freight Sdgs
Westgate South Jn 47.43
Wakefield Kirkgate West Jn 47.43
Wakefield Kirkgate East Jn 47.68
[LN 850] WWK LNE : GN
WVK 47.62
Wakefield Sdgs Hanson
Down Sdgs Engrs
Down Sdgs
WAREHOUSE RD.
Bottom Sdg 2
Top Sdgs

Miles from Manchester Victoria via Rochdale
Healey Mills (HM) 44.02
Horbury Jn (HJ) 45.38
Horbury Stn Jn 45.47 45.41
Horbury Sdgs
Bombardier (Closed)
34F
[LN 886] MKB LMS : Mid
Monk Bretton Ardagh Glass Ltd
Hopper
175.78 MONK BRETTON LOOP
Monk Bretton Jn GF 45.00
[LN 886] TJC 3 LMS : Mid (North Midland)
dormant from 166.60 (Swinton Jn. South : 32A) to 175.78 and from 181.75 to 184.56
[LN 868] CHS LMS : L&Y
River Calder Viaduct 0.44-0.48
Calder & Hebble Canal 0.59
former DOWN MIDLAND
former UP MIDLAND (Royston) DN
173 —
Miles from St Pancras via Leicester, Toton & Barrow Hill
Hare Park Jn 181.70 181.72
DOWN DONCASTER
UP DONCASTER 175.19
PRISON SDG
DPL SDG
DOL1 [LN 836] LNE : GN & GCJt
Chevet Viaduct 179.47

* = (K) 47.69
Ø = [LN 850] WWK LNE : GN
= Wakefield Kirkgate West Jn 47.43
§ = Wakefield Kirkgate East Jn 47.68
$ = LNE : GN & GCJt

a = Oakenshaw S. Jn
b = Oakenshaw Farm (UWC) 49.25
c = OAKENSHAW
UP MIDLAND

37B : to Healey Mills & Huddersfield

35A

171.73 171.70
DN DON UP DON
DN DROFTON
UP DROFTON
Crofton 49.40 50.36

35A

35

October 2016

© Copyright TRACKmaps. No reproduction without permission

(WAKEFIELD) - LEEDS ● LEEDS ● LEEDS - HORSFORTH ● LEEDS - METHLEY JUNCTION ● LEEDS - (CHURCH FENTON) ● MIDDLETON RAILWAY

A

Leeds former stations:
'Wellington' (platforms 1-6) LMS : Mid
'New' (through platforms) LMS (Mid) & LNE (NE) Jt

PLATFORMS
approximate sections (45) shown (Throughout Accommodation)

Indicate directions of travel
SG = Signals Gantry
L3624-26 = Signal numbers
Indicate directions of travel for which signals apply

1	(14)	10	(5)
2	(12)	11	(18)
3	(4)	12	(15)
4	(7)	13	(5)
5	(10)	14	(4)
6	(14)	15	(11)
7	(5)	16	(11)
8	(17)	17	(5)
9	(13)		

Controlled by York (L)
LEEDS : 115ft
(from Doncaster, Marshgate Jn)|LN 836|(to Leeds, Neville Hill Jn)

NEVILLE HILL DEPOT (NL)
TMD & Coaching Stock 18.40
NEVILLE HILL UP SIDINGS : *DB Cargo*
A = Armley Group (7) coaches 1-7
F = Freight Traffic (9) 1-9
M = Marsh Lane Group (8) coaches 1-8
For full details see 41A

e = Neville Hill West Jn 18.74

Neville Hill West Jn 18.18

Miles from Selby South Jn

Hunslet East

Marsh Lane Sdgs

Richmond Hill Tunnel (118 yards)

London Kings Cross 185.70

mean of through platforms

River Aire 185.69

Leeds & Liverpool Canal

Controlled by York (L)

Leeds Midland Road: Freightliner Loco and Vehicle Depot

Cemex Hunslet East: Ready Mix Concrete Discharge Point

Klocckner Metals UK

Leeds (Stourton) Freightliner Terminal

Stourton Jn

Woodlesford

Methley Jn

Calder Viaduct

MIDDLETON PARK 1.26

B

Controlled by York (CF)

CROSS GATES 16.11

GARFORTH 13.23

EAST GARFORTH 12.56

MICKLEFIELD 10.69

Miles from Selby South Jn

Controlled by York (CF)

C

HEADINGLEY 2.11

HORSFORTH 4.61

Bramhope Tunnel (2 miles 241 yards)

Miles from Leeds, Wortley Jn

D

MIDDLETON RAILWAY TRUST
4' 8½" / 1435mm gauge

MOOR ROAD (LEEDS)

Moor Road LC
Beza Road LC
Tulip Street LC

Resource Centre
Shed works

LEEDS HISTORICAL NOTES
The area has been subjected to reduction, rationalisation and restoration of facilities.
The complexity of pre-grouping lines and stations has been omitted but the following is a brief guide only.
The former 'GN' route **DOL** continued from Copley Hill West Jn via Holbeck West Jn to the former Leeds Central terminus.
The former 'Midland' routes **TJC** and **ELN** remain with a triangular junction giving access to and from former Leeds Wellington Street (present area of platforms 1-6)
The former 'LNW' route **MDL** followed current routes to Leeds New Station
The former 'NE' route **HUL** shared Leeds New Station

BURLEY PARK 1.27

Headingley Tunnel (70 yards)
Kirkstall Viaduct (River Aire, etc)
Armley Jn

Harrogate (LH)
[Skelton Jn & Armley Jn]

Kirkstall Loops
Wortley Jn
Wortley W. Jn
Wortley S. Jn

Copley Hill East Jn
Copley Hill West Jn

Holbeck

Whitehall West Jn 185.25
Whitehall East Jn 185.28
Leeds West Jn 185.45

Farnley Viaduct formerly LNW (BR.NE)
Engine Shed Jn 195.20
Holbeck Depot Jn

Whitehall Road Jn
HOLBECK DEPOT
Whitehall Spur
Stoneblower Line
On-track Machine Workshop

Outwood 178.26
to Wakefield
to Dewsbury & Huddersfield
to Bradford
to Shipley

a = Miles from former Leeds, Wortley Jn (196.06 Mid)
b = Miles from London, St Pancras via Toton, Barrow Hill & Cudworth
c = Miles from former Holbeck South Jn (185.26 GN)
d = Miles from Manchester Victoria via Stalybridge
e = Miles from London, King's Cross via Doncaster

HEBDEN BRIDGE / MARSDEN - MIRFIELD - (LEEDS) / HEALEY MILLS

This page is a TRACKmaps railway track schematic diagram for the Hebden Bridge / Marsden – Huddersfield – Mirfield – (Leeds) / Healey Mills area, containing numerous station, junction, tunnel and viaduct labels with mileages.

Selected labels include:

- HEBDEN BRIDGE (HB) 23.55
- MYTHOLMROYD 24.68, Mytholmroyd Viaduct 24.60
- SOWERBY BRIDGE 28.51, Sowerby Bridge Tunnel (657 yards), Sowerby Viaduct 28.20
- BRIGHOUSE 34.31
- MIRFIELD 39.20, Mirfield Viaduct (River Calder)
- DEIGHTON 27.60
- HUDDERSFIELD 25.60, Huddersfield Viaduct spans 1-47, Huddersfield Tunnels (696 yards)
- MARSDEN 18.59, Standedge Tunnel (3 miles, 66 yards)
- SLAITHWAITE 21.19, Slaithwaite Viaduct, Golcar Viaduct 22.50, Milne Viaduct 23.50
- Bradley Tunnel (132 yards), Bradley Colne Viaduct
- Heaton Lodge East Jn 37.48, Heaton Lodge South Jn
- Bank House Tunnel (214 yards), Copley Viaduct, River Calder Viaduct
- Greetland, Elland Tunnel (420 yards)
- MORLEY 38.24, Morley Tunnel (1 mile, 1609 yards)
- COTTINGLEY 40.02, Churchwell Viaduct
- BATLEY 35.09, Batley Viaduct 34.60
- DEWSBURY 33.62, Jack Lane Viaduct 34.20
- RAVENSTHORPE 32.28, Thornhill LNW Jn
- HEALEY MILLS YARD (N/RU), Healey Mills (HM) 42.64
- HORBURY Station Jn 44.02, Storrs Hill
- 'CALDER VALLEY LINE'

Directions: to Todmorden and Manchester, to Stalybridge and Manchester, to Halifax, to Wakefield Kirkgate, to Barnsley, to Leeds, to York.

'LNW' miles in brackets.

© Copyright TRACKmaps. No reproduction without permission

October 2016

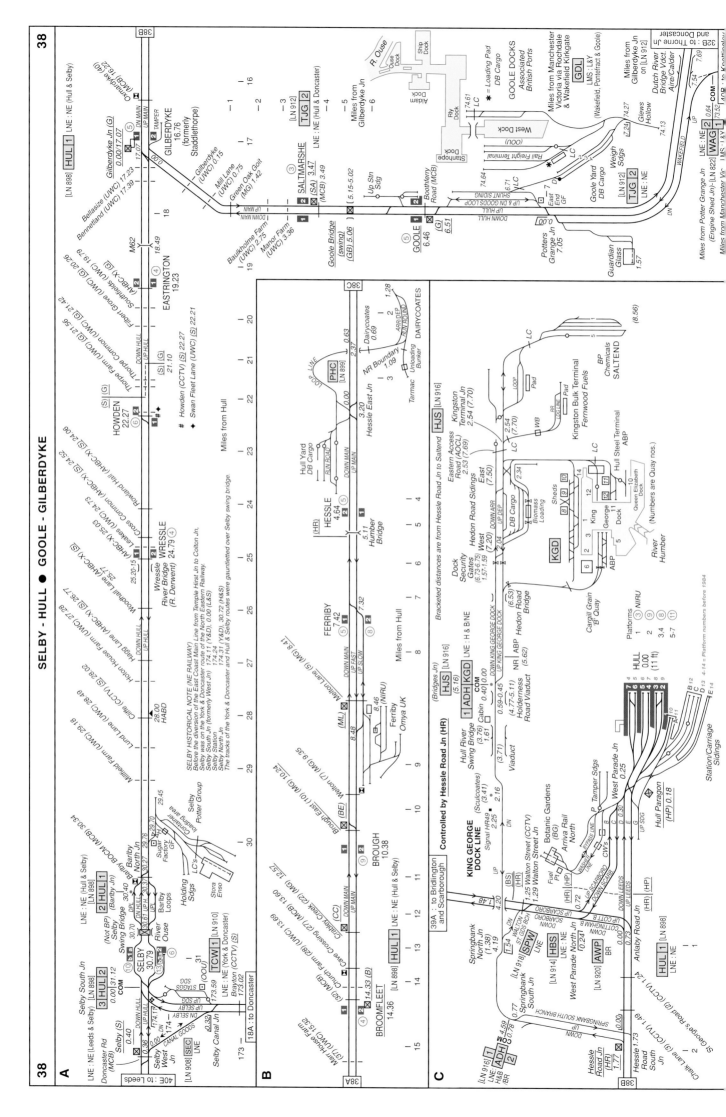

SELBY – HULL ● GOOLE – GILBERDYKE

(HULL) - BRIDLINGTON - FILEY - SEAMER ● (YORK) - SCARBOROUGH

A

38C: to Hessle Road Jn

(Cottingham Jn) 2.11

1.48

4.20

[LN 916] 38C : to Saltend
1 ADH/HJS

[HR] (HR) Hessle Road
[BS]

38C: to Hull

Miles from Hull

Thwaite Gates (4) (CCTV) [BS] 3.63
COTTINGHAM 3.77
Holtby (UWC) 4.17
Pillwood Farm (UWC) 5.00
5

Atkinsons (UWC) 4.72
Roadside (UWC) 5.14
Wainess (UWC) 5.28

England Springs (UWC) 6.51
Ashworth's (19) (UWC) 7.07
Flemingate (22) (UWC) 7.57
Halfway House (UWC) 6.02

Beverley Parks (19) (AHBC-X) 5.14

Fleming (22) (MCB) 8.02
Cherry Tree (24) (CCTV) [BS] 8.16
BEVERLEY 8.20
Beverley North (25) (CCTV) 8.39

Molescroft Grange (27) (UWC) 9.39
Park Cottage (31) (UWC) 10.14
Burnfields (30) (UWC) 10.69

ARRAM 11.16
(35) (AHBC-X)

Lockington (39) (AHBC-X) 12.24
Scorborough (38) (AHBC-X) 12.74
Beswick (40) (AHBC-X) 13.53
Kilnwick (42) (AHBC-X) 14.01
Watton (43) (AHBC-X) 14.44
Abbey Farm (45) (UWC) 15.04

HUTTON CRANSWICK 16.21
Cranswick (50) (AHBC-X) 16.18

Hutton (51) (UWC) 16.73
Low Green Farm (55) (UWC) 17.29

[LN 914] HBS LNE : NE Hull & Selby (Bridlington)

B

Driffield (59) (MCB) 19.28
DRIFFIELD 19.38
Station Road (61) (CCTV) 19.34
Wansford Road (61) (CCTV) 19.54
18.76-78 (D)

Trout Beck Bridge

Buckton Lane (AHBC) 35.16

345ft

Meadow Gates (62) (UWC) 20.00
Chicken Farm (UWC) 20.69
(AHBC-X) (D) 21.32
Medwell Lane (D) 21.58
NAFFERTON 21.44
Black Carr (72) (UWC) 22.06
Outgates Farm (74) (UWC) 22.35
(D) (UWC) 22.76
Millgredale (76) (UWC) 23.34
Lowthorpe (78) (AHBC-X) 23.54
LOWTHORPE 23.64
Mill Farm (77) (UWC) 23.48

Thornholme (UWC) 26.61
Manor Farm (UWC) 26.40
Harpham (83) (UWC) 25.10
Burton Agnes (84) (AHBC-X) 25.45
BURTON AGNES 25.45
Hasthorpe (UWC) 27.25

Carnaby (AHBC-X) 28.52

FLAMBOROUGH 33.31
Flamborough (AHBC) 33.31
Sewerby (BN) 32.35
Bempton Sands Lane (UWC) 34.19

Bridlington Quay (CCTV) (BN) 31.06
Bridlington (BN) 30.58
BRIDLINGTON 30.72 35ft
30.49
30.30
DEL (NIRU) UEL
DEL = DOWN EXCURSION LINE
UEL = UP EXCURSION LINE

[LN 914] HBS LNE : NE Hull & Selby (Bridlington)

[LN 914] HBS LNE : NE York & N. Midland (Bridlington)

UP & DN BRIDLINGTON

C

BEMPTON 34.43
(AHBC) (BN)

Royal Oak (AHBC-X) 43.04
Lowfield No.2 (UWC) 42.89
Royal Oak Farm (UWC) 42.49

HUNMANBY 41.53
Hunmanby Jn 41.47
Burton (24) (UWC) 41.51
Hunmanby Sands Ln (ABCL-X) 41.72

Grange Farm (UWC) 45.36
Misson (AHBC) 45.41

East Lea (UWC) 45.07
FILEY 44.30
Filey Jn 44.49

Cayton (AHBC) 48.19
Grove Farm (UWC) 49.06
Gristhorpe (MG) 46.39
Lebberston Road (UWC) 46.72

Seamer South Jn 49.77
Seamer West 50.43 38.66
[LN 880] YMS
39E
UM DM
39E

LNE : NE York & N. Midland

[LN 914] HBS LNE : NE (York & North Midland (Bridlington))

Bridlington Seamer (SR) (BN)

D

Miles from York

MALTON 21.12
20.77
21.20
(7) (M)

Huttons Ambo-River Bridge

18.33-38

Kirkham Abbey (88) (MG) 15.01
Howsham (82) (UWC) 12.32
Crambeck (UWC) 16.75
Portandella Farm (UWC) 19.12
High Farm (99) (UWC) 21.50
Mill Garth (UWC) 21.70
Wistow (99) (MCB) 21.32
Waitgate (99) (UWC) 22.32

15.65 (Castle Howard)

(K) (BH)

a = Green Farm (73) (UWC) 11.72
b = Brisby's (76) (UWC) 12.17
c = Newcombes (85) (UWC) 13.65
d = Kilby's (114) (UWC) 24.53

Foston Gates (67) (UWC) 10.20
Flaxton (61) (AHBC-X) [S] 9.21
Common Road (MCB) [S2] 7.52
Flaxton Moor (55) (UWC) 8.28

Thornton (UWC) 9.40

Howsham (82) (UWC) 12.32
Manor Farm (UWC) 13.38
Low Grange (84) (UWC) 14.05
Oakdale (86) (UWC) 14.49

Barton (72) (MCB) 10.74
Plain Moor (77) 11.77
Manor Farm (Barton) (74) 11.48
Barr Farm (BN) 38.63
Scagglethorpe Grange (111) (UWC) 23.63
Norton Parks (107) (UWC) 22.46
Marr House Farm (UWC) 23.89
Birdsall Estates (110) (UWC) 24.14
Lilac Farm (115) (UWC) 24.72

(M) 21.20

Norton Parks (106) (UWC) 22.78
Malton (98) (UWC) 22.35

LNE : NE (York & North Midland (York & Scarborough))
[LN 880] YMS

19 : to York

E

SCARBOROUGH 42.06 (157ft)
1 2 3 4 5
Platforms 1 (14) (7) / 4 (5) (7) / 2 (9) / 3 (9)

SCW
Carriage Sdgs
Excursion Sidings

DOWN SCARBOROUGH
UP SCARBOROUGH

Seamer West Jn
Meads Lane (BW) 38.47
SEAMER 39.14
39.17 (SR) (YS)
Seamer South Jn 49.77
39C : to Hull
(6) 39.17 (SR) (YS)

Pasture Lane (UWC) 38.20
30.43
12

UB = UP BRIDLINGTON
DB = DN BRIDLINGTON

Robin's Bottom Plantation (UWC) 36.40
Gannon Hall (UWC) 33.62
Ganton (AHBC-X) 33.03
Long Plantation (UWC) 34.08

Willerby Carr (UWC) 35.22
Ganton (MG) 35.69
Birmingham (UWC) 35.62
Jacksons (BS) 34.24

Hertford River

Weaverthorpe (MG) 32.68
Jacksons (UWC) 33.03
Westerdale (UWC) 32.09
Cousins (AHBC-X) 31.00
Grange Farm (UWC) 31.56
(W) (M)

West Heslerton (AHBC-X) 29.74
East Heslerton (AHBC-X) 30.32
Heslerton Station (AHBC-X) 29.32
Sand Lane (UWC) 30.52

Knapton (AHBC-X) (M) 28.19
Elm Tree Farm (UWC) 27.41
Wilkinsons (UWC) 27.75

Ivy Lea Farm (M) 25.42
High Scampston (UWC) 25.72
Low Scampston (UWC) 25.19
Rillington (AHBC-X) 26.54

[LN 880] YMS LNE : NE (York & North Midland (York & Scarborough))

Miles from York

October 2016

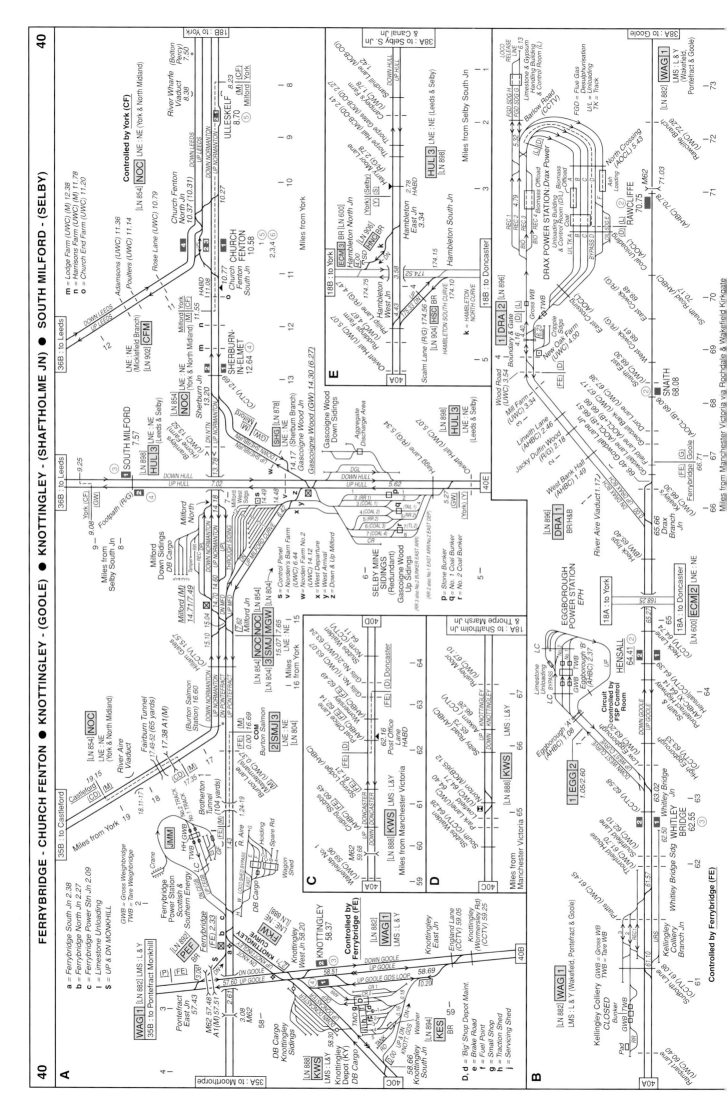

(LEEDS) - ILKLEY / KEIGHLEY / BRADFORD ● (LEEDS) - BRADFORD - HALIFAX

October 2016

© Copyright TRACKmaps. No reproduction without permission

A

A

41 : to Shipley & Leeds

* Miles from St. Pancras *via* Ilkley

SKIPTON
Platforms
1 ⑤
2 ⑩
3/4 (9D/7L)

Controlled by York (L)

STEETON &
SILSDEN 215.04
Thompsons 214.31

Raws (UWC) 216.10
Eastburn (UWC) 215.55
Kildwick (CCTV) 216.52
216.60 Kildwick HABD

Miles from St. Pancras *via* Cudworth & Keighley

CONONLEY
218.20
Shady Lane (UWC) 218.52

Pettys No.1 (UWC) 218.60

UP SHIPLEY MAIN
DOWN SHIPLEY MAIN

Haw Bank Tunnel (220 yds) 220.77-221.07
(Embsay Jn)

42C : to Embsay

220.60
220.71
Keighley Road Viaduct 222.24
222.27

0.00 220.64
COM 2 SKS 1 221* 221 222*
[LN 930]
Broughton Road CS North Arriva Rail DOWN BAY
Up Sdgs STABLING SDG
CW 2B DOWN
2B 2A 3 b 2 b 3 a
SKIPTON Skipton South Jn 221.00
221.21 CW SS DN
UP SHIPLEY FAST
DN SHIPLEY SLOW
221.33 Skipton Middle Jn
221.60 222.68 (222.54*) BCH
221.68 Skipton North Jn DN
Skipton North Jn for Colne

1 SKW TJC 3 LMS : Mid (Leeds & Bradford Extension)
(former Skipton North Jn for Colne)
[LN 922]

LMS : Mid (North Western)
LMS : Mid (North Western)

RYLSTONE
(Swinden Quarry)
Tarmac
NR Bdy 6.50
Loading Bunker Bunker No.1 Line RR No.2 Line RR No.3 Line
Loading Shute
Wagon/Pilot Shed

GRASSINGTON OR SWINDEN BRANCH
LMS : Mid (Yorkshire Dales)

Rylstone 5.17
Flyston (UWC)

4 ⑤
GARGRAVE
224.79
1
Gargrave HABD (York) 225.72
(H) River Aire 225.04
(H) (L) River Aire 225.66-63
2 (L) Hellifield York

Niffany Viaduct (River Aire) 223.03-06
Marshalls (UWC) 222.18
Niffany (UWC) 222.50

Leeds & Liverpool Canal

DOWN SHIPLEY MAIN

Bell Busk Viaduct (River Aire) 227.45-42
5534ft
Switches Farm (UWC) 230.06
230.00
[NW 9901] [LN 922]
229.40

7.09

LNW LINE

4 : 33C : to Hellifield
41 : to Shipley & Leeds
41 : to Hellifield

B THE KEIGHLEY AND WORTH VALLEY LIGHT RAILWAY LTD   4' 8½" / 1435mm gauge

OXENHOPE 4.70
Exhibition Shed
Running Shed footpath CS Works 4.76
LC's
4.60 Loop Yard GF

HAWORTH 3.54
Loco Shed
4.10 Top Points GF
3.75 Bottom Points GF
Haworth LOOP (OOU) GS 4

Mytholmes Viaducts River Worth
3.03 3.14
3.09 3.19 3.23
Mytholmes Tunnel (75 yds)
3
3

OAKWORTH 2.67
Oakworth Crossing 2.67
GS

2.02
Crossing (Occupation)
2.21 Damems Jn
DAMEMS 2.00
2

Skibeden PW Sdg
219.30
Ingrow Tunnel (150 yds) (River Worth)
INGROW WEST 1.24
1.42
1.35
Crane Sdg
Bahamas Locomotive Society Shed

1
River Worth 0.15
(G.N.Jn) 0.59
West GF KEIGHLEY 0.09
North GF
Derailer GF Derailer Sdg GF
SB 0.12 (OOU) 0.15

LMS : Mid KWV

a = Keighley Stn. 212.22
b = original Keighley Stn. 212.18
(0.00 for Worth Valley Branch)

41 : to Shipley & Leeds
TJC 3
212.06
211.74)
⑩
-0.10
212.22
a b
212.18
⑪ N
b a
220.49
Bow Bridge GF
220.60
Bow Bridge Loop

EMBSAY
220.25
1
2
Dock
(Embsay Station)
Vintage Carriages Trust Shed

C EMBSAY & BOLTON ABBEY STEAM RAILWAY : Yorkshire Railway Museum Trust   4' 8½" / 1435mm gauge

42A : to Rylstone
(Embsay Jn)
220.64
[LN 930]
42A : to Skipton

BOLTON ABBEY 216.66
(Former Guiseley SB)
THE DUKE'S SDG 1 216.56
2 3
Coal & Water
217
DOWN
Engineers'
217.70 Draughton Sdg

HAWORTH 3.54 Loco Shed

HOLYWELL HALT 219.00
Miles from St. Pancras *via* Ilkley

218.45
Stoneacre Loop S&T

LMS : Mid SKI

Damems Jn 219

D NENE VALLEY RAILWAY   4' 8½" / 1435mm gauge

Miles from Blisworth

47
Railworld
46.78
PETERBOROUGH
NENE VALLEY
46.70
46.66
Wharf Road 46.52
2 1
46.56
16A ↗ York 47.08
15D
London
FCM 1
LNE : GN
FOM
Old Great North Road (MCG) 40.56

ORTON MERE
45.32 (Longueville Jn)
45.53
45.26 1
45.24
Footpath 45.24
Girdle Lane (Open) 44.58
1.47

FERRY MEADOWS 44.34
Ham Lane (AOCL) 44.12
S&T

Lynch River Bridge (R. Nene) 43.43
Horse 43.40
Footpath 43.46

Splash Dyke Viaduct 42.60
Station Road (Open) 41.74
41.77 (Castor)

TOM LMS : LNW
River Nene 40.58
40.56
40.52 3
40.63
Civil Engr 40.72
WANSFORD 40.52
C&W
1 2
5

Wansford Tunnel (616 yards)
40.27
Loco Shed
39.79
39.72
YARWELL JUNCTION 39.55
39.48

E BEAMISH NORTH OF ENGLAND OPEN AIR MUSEUM   4' 8½" / 1435mm gauge

N

Electric Tramway 2.27km (track 2.29km) 550v dc.
Tram stop distances in Miles and Chains
0 100 200 300 metres

ROWLEY
Pit
Goods Shed
Coal & lime drops
Store
The Town 0.57
LC
LC
LC

Tram Depot & Workshop
LC
Foulbridge 1.10
LC
LC

Narrow Gauge System (2')
Beamish Colliery Junction
Screens
BEAMISH COLLIERY
Loco Shed
Colliery Sidings
Drift Mine Railway (2')
Entrance 1.33 / 0.00 COM
Pockerley Bottom 0.19
Pockerley Wagonway (see below)
LC
LC
LC
LC
Loco Transfer Facility

Pockerley Wagonway (1820's)
4' 8½" / 1435mm gauge
Approx 240 metres

A

4 : 29C : to Kingmoor & Gretna Jn / Dumfries & Glasgow

Alt: 67ft
CARLISLE
69.09/0.00

COLLIER LANE SDG

Carlisle North Jn

UP MAIN

DN

M

Carriage Sidings

High Wapping Sidings

27.56

[NW 4001] WCM1 CGJ7

Carlisle (CE)

Bog Jn 0.44

(Forks Jn) 0.29

1.12

0.25

1.00

69

SCG MCG LMS:M&C [NW 4025]

UP M&C GOODS
DOWN M&C GOODS

UP MAIN
DOWN MAIN

4 : 32C : to Dalston

Currock Jn
26.74

Currock Yard
Currock, Currock Wagon Shops
0.00

[NW 4033] CBC3 LMS : M&C

Miles from Maryport

Upperby Jn
68.23

Miles from Lancaster 68

Upperby Bridge Jn
67.59 (Lancaster & Carlisle)

[NW 4001] CGJ7 LMS : LNW

UCJ LMS : LNW

4 : 29B : to Oxenholme & Carnforth

UP THROUGH GOODS
DOWN THROUGH GOODS

DOWN GOODS LOOP

THROUGH GOODS

RR SDG

0.00
0.38
0.40
0.16

Wagon Repair GF

On-track machines Sdg

[NW 4023] ULR LMS : LNW

[NW 9901] NGB

NEC2 [LN 682] LNE : NE (Newcastle & Carlisle)

59.49 London Rd Jns
59.45

0.00
0.34

Petteril Bridge Jn
59.26

London Road Sdgs

Carlisle, Petteril Bridge: LMS : Mid

UP NEWCASTLE
DOWN NEWCASTLE

UP MIDLAND
DOWN MIDLAND

Upperby & St. Nicholas

UCJ [NW 4021] LMS : LNW

Upperby Yard GF
0.11

307.12
307

SHUNT NECK

DN & UP NCTLE
UP NEWCASTLE GDS
DOWN NEWCASTLE GDS

58.00 Carlisle (CE) | Corby Gates (CG)
58.10

Carlisle (CE) LNW

M6 1
M6 58

M6 305.77

[NW 9901] SAC LMS : Mid

CUMWHINTON 304.11

SETTLE & CARLISLE LINE

4 : 34C : to Appleby

Miles from St Pancras via Cudworth and Keighley

57
306
305
304
303

303.40

Scotby (UWC) 57.16

WETHERAL 55.76

Wetheral Viaduct (River Eden) 55.72-64

Corby Gates (CG) 55.54

MCB Corby Gates

Corby Viaduct (Glenwiley) 55.48-42

Broadwath (AHBC-X) 54.62

(Heads Nook) 54.20

HABD Wetheral (CE)
56.73

How Mill (AHBC-X) 52.66

CG

Upper Denton (UWC) 44.66
Upper Denton West (UWC) 44.34
Denton Village (MG) 44.01
Denton Farm (UWC) 43.85
Denton School (AHBC-X) 43.23

Hightown Farm (UWC) 45.38
Lane Head (MG) 45.34

Gelt Viaduct 51.29-25

51.47

Baron House (UWC) 41.36
Long Byre (AHBC-X) 41.05
Blenkinsop Footpath 40.19

BRAMPTON (Cumbria)
49.21

Brampton Fell (MG) 50.10

BF

Naworth (AHBC-X) 47.67

Milton Village (MCB) 48.60

[LN 682] NEC2 LNE : NE (Newcastle & Carlisle)

Miles from Newcastle

47   48   49   50   51   52   53   54   55   56   57   58   59   60.02
68.55
68.6
68.73
68.73

43B

B

Low Row (LR) 46.19

(494 ft) MOB (MG) 46.24

Denton Mains Farm (UWC) 44.18

[LN 682] NEC2 LNE : NE (Newcastle & Carlisle)

Miles from Newcastle

39   40   41   42   43   44   45   46   47

43C

43B

C

HALTWHISTLE 37.17 405 ft (HW)
37.20

Haltwhistle Signal Box (listed)
(Haltwhistle Jn) 37.10

Whitchester Tunnel (202 yards)
35.79-70
35.62

Melkridge Sdgs
Greengates (UWC) 35.35

35.10

(HW) 34.08
(HW) 38.27

BARDON MILL 32.29

Haugh Gatehouse 33.40

(BM) (UWC)
32.41

[LN 682] NEC2 LNE : NE (Newcastle & Carlisle)

Miles from Newcastle

33   34   35   36   37   38   39

43B

21C : to Blaydon & Newcastle

D

MARYPORT & CARLISLE LINE

SOUTH TYNEDALE RAILWAY

ALSTON 0.02 875 ft

(A) 0.05

Carriage Works
RR
Carriage GF

Shield Well GF
C. Sdgs

Alston MPD (52C)

Holms

Carriage Shed

GILDERDALE 1.38

Gilderdale Viaduct (51) 1.44-48

Tyne Viaduct (57) 0.42-44

KIRKHAUGH 2.23

South GF 2.23
North GF

Whitley Viaduct (48) 2.03

Dock

LINTLEY HALT 3.21

RR

Extension to Slaggyford (1 mile) proposed

3.35 end of line
(part of former branch from Haltwhistle to Alston)

2' 0" gauge

LNE : NE ALN 2

0.00
1
2
3

E

HAYDON BRIDGE 28.32 (HB)

Lipwood (UWC) 29.12
Willow Gap (UWC) 29.48
Lipwood Viaduct (South Tyne) 30.23-19

Ridley Hall, South Tyne Viaduct 31.50-45

West Mill Hills (UWC) 27.63
East Mill Hills (UWC) 27.35
Gossenholme (UWC) 26.17
Allonside (UWC) 27.24
Cossgates (UWC) 25.08
Fourstones Farm (UWC) 24.32
Fourstones Stn (UWC) 24.62
Moss Cottages (UWC) 23.79
Quality (UWC) 23.68
Warden (AHBC-X) 23.54
Warden Bridge (River Tyne)
Warden (UWC) 23.20

HEXHAM 20.66

Spiral (UWC) 21.60
(Border Counties Jn) 21.76

Tyne Green (UWC) 21.30

MIDDLE ROAD 20.53 (H, HM)
UP 20.42

Freight Sdgs DB Cargo

Thrie Green (UWC) 21.30

Wylie Haugh (UWC) 19.34
Disson Haugh (UWC) 18.36
Devils Water West 18.57
Dissin (AHBC-X) 19.20

CORBRIDGE 17.59

Farnley Haugh (UWC) 16.48
17.08
16.72

Cutting Vice Tunnel

RIDING MILL 15.35

[LN 682] NEC2 LNE : NE (Newcastle & Carlisle)

Miles from Newcastle

15   16   17   18   19   20   21   22   23   24   25   26   27   28   29   30   31   32

43C

43

October 2016

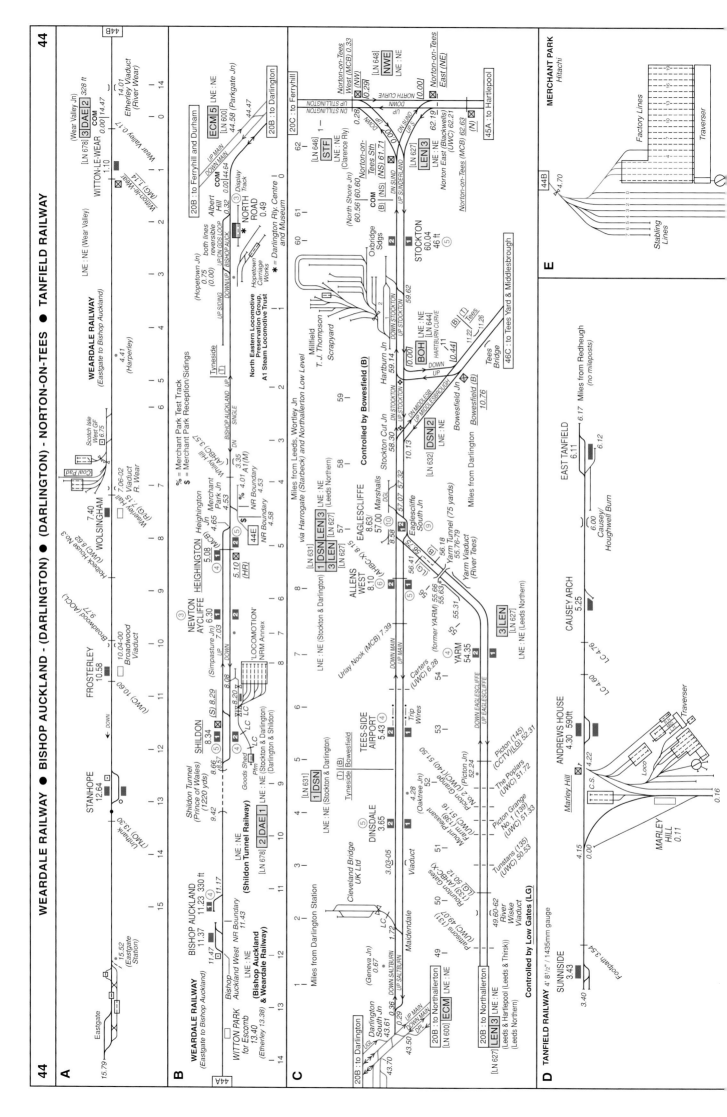

44 WEARDALE RAILWAY ● BISHOP AUCKLAND - (DARLINGTON) ● (DARLINGTON) - NORTON-ON-TEES ● TANFIELD RAILWAY 44

NORTON-ON-TEES - HARTLEPOOL - SUNDERLAND - SEABURN

A

45B

Crimdon Dene Viaduct

75.36-47

Controlled by Ryhope Grange (NS)

[LN 627] LEN 3 LNE : NE (Leeds Northern)

DOWN MAIN
UP MAIN

Miles from Leeds, Wortley Jn via Harrogate (Starbeck) and Northallerton low level

Lancaster Road Jn
72.20
72.50

72.73

JDR Cables

Hartlepool Docks PD Ports

73.20

Hartlepool South Works
Tata Steel   20 inch Pipe Mill
1.66

2.08
42 inch Pipe Mill
84 inch Pipe Mill

Church Street (CCTV) 71.40
2 4
1 7

HARTLEPOOL
71.55
17ft

HLD LNE : NE

Stranton Jn
71.14
71.12

Greatham Ryhope
(GM) Grange (NS)
(Leeds Northern)

[LN 627] LEN 3 LNE : NE (Stockton & Hartlepool)

Cliff House Jn
70.02
DN CLIFF HOUSE LP
UP CLIFF HOUSE LOOP

[LN 627] LEN 3 LNE : NE (Leeds Northern)

DOWN MAIN
UP MAIN

SEATON CAREW
69.36 69
0.70
0.62
2
6 Seaton Snook
69.41 Seaton Carew Jn

[LN 656] 1 POC2
SOT LNE : NE

0.00 Seaton Snook Jn
[LN 656]

Graythorpe (AOCL) 0.25

Port (Port Clarence Branch)
Clarence Jn 3.05 3.08 3.25 Phillips Loop
Port Clarence GF

Seal Sands Biofuel Refinery
Greenergy
Ldg Gantry
SD
North Tees (AOCL) 4.71
(OOU) 5.01
4.18

(former Greatham Creek Branch)
5.21
BASF run-round loop
1.22
Rohm Haas (AOCL) 1.42
Monsanto Sdg Jn 1.43
Monsanto (AOCL) 1.46
0.00 Seal Sands Branch Jn 0.12
ICI Brinefield (open) 0.39
NEEB (open) 0.52
North/South (open) 0.71

Simon Storage South (Propylene)
1.52
Biofuels (open) 1.74
SS Chemicals (AOCL) 2.11
Phillips No.2 (AOCL) 2.16
Phillips No.3 (AOCL) 2.22
2.23

Simon Storage (OOU) North
Seal Sands Storage 0.06
Seal Sands Road (AOCL) 0.05
0.00 Seal Sands run-round loop
2.42
2.44

[LN 652] SES LNE : NE

Billingham Jn
64.47 7
63.69

Billingham (MCB) 62.60
[LN 627]
Norton-on-Tees
62.63
LEN 3
(N) (B)
[Mo (62.60)]

[LN 652] 1 POC1
LNE : NE (Clarence Rly)

BILLINGHAM
Greatham (MCB) 67.28
Greatham 67.29
(GM)
GREATHAM
67.52 67.32
Hartlepool Power Stn
British Energy
Nuclear Electric Division
Unloading/Loading Bay
LS
Belasis Lane (BL)
1.04
1.13
1.08 0.00
1.08 1.13
0.00
West LC 1.51
(Haverton Hill)
DOWN
(Haverton Hill) 2.02
DOWN
1.38 (open)

Seaton-on-Tees
Cowpen Lane (AHBC-X) 65.44
Greatham Viaduct 66.41-43

P.W. Sdg
Haverton Hill Exchange Sidings

HAH

Phillips Sdg
3.25
Phillips Sdg
Jn 3.25

0.54 Haverton Hill South Jn

Teesside EfW Plant
SITA UK
(Planned Rail Connection)

Haverton Hill: East Grid

LC 1.24

(OOU)

44C : to Stockton/Ferryhill

B

Controlled by Ryhope Grange (NS)

Miles from Leeds, Wortley Jn via Harrogate (Starbeck) and Northallerton low level

Castle Eden Viaduct
(Easington)
80.33
180 ft

78.15-26 78.44 (Horden)

Blackhills Farm (UWC) 78.78

[LN 627] LEN 3 LNE : NE (Leeds Northern)

Hawthorn Dene Viaduct
81.67-72

Dawdon Dene Viaduct
83.31-37
Dawdon Jn 84.11
1.65
1.36 NR/Port of Seaham
UP
Polka Sdg
6
2
1
SEAHAM
84.49
SEA LNE : NE

Seaham Harbour Victoria Group
DB Cargo and Tarmac
1.08
Under Track Unloading
Cargo Durham Warehouse
Pad

Hall Dene (MCB) 85.42

(RG) Ryhope Grange
(NS) Ryhope Grange

former Muirton/Hawthorn Washery Branch
OOU
No.1
No.3 RB1
No.2
Ryhope Grange Sdgs

Ryhope Grange (RG, NS)
87.63
87.47 0.00
DN MAIN
UP MAIN
(T) Tyneside
88.60

Grangetown (open) 0.30
[LN 662] HNB
LNE : NE
(Londonderry)
HENDON BRANCH

[LN 627] LEN 3
LNE : NE
(Londonderry)

89.06 711 yds 127 yds
89.36 89.39-45
DN SUN UP SUN

No. 5 SDG
RR
ARRIVAL
No. 18
No. 19
1.07
1.33
0.79
Londonderry Sdgs

NR PSA
Hendon
1.53
1.64

§ = Combined Bi-directional 3/4 in separate designated platforms. Station covered by 'Umbrella' from 89.51 to 89.64

= Queen Alexandra Bridge River Wear Vdct 89.77-90.11

o = Monkwearmouth Jn

[LN 627] LEN 3 LNE : NE (Brandling Jn) Controlled from Tyneside (T)

SOUTH HYLTON
3.17
3.13
3.20
6
1

NETWORK RAIL
(Metro trains only)

PALLION
1.67
4
[LN 628]
NEK
2
MILLFIELD
1.01
3
2
UNIVERSITY
0.44
3
2
PARK LANE
0.21
3
2
DN S HYLTON
UP S HYLTON

§
SUNDERLAND
89.60
89.56
0.17
0.44
0.00
3 2 1
92ft
Sunderland North End 89.71
89.64
89.49 89.51
0.00
Sunderland South End Jn
Sunderland South Tunnels

STADIUM OF LIGHT
90.48 3
2
1
SEABURN
91.32 3
1
ST PETERS
90.08 90.20
2
#
1
90.00

Corporation Quay
2.39
crane
LC
LC
2.17
Swing Bridge
2.04
LC
2.00
2.49

Hudson Dock
Loco Shed

River Wear

Sunderland South Dock
Port of Sunderland Authority

46A : to Newcastle

45A

46A : to Newcastle

45

© Copyright TRACKmaps. No reproduction without permission

October 2016

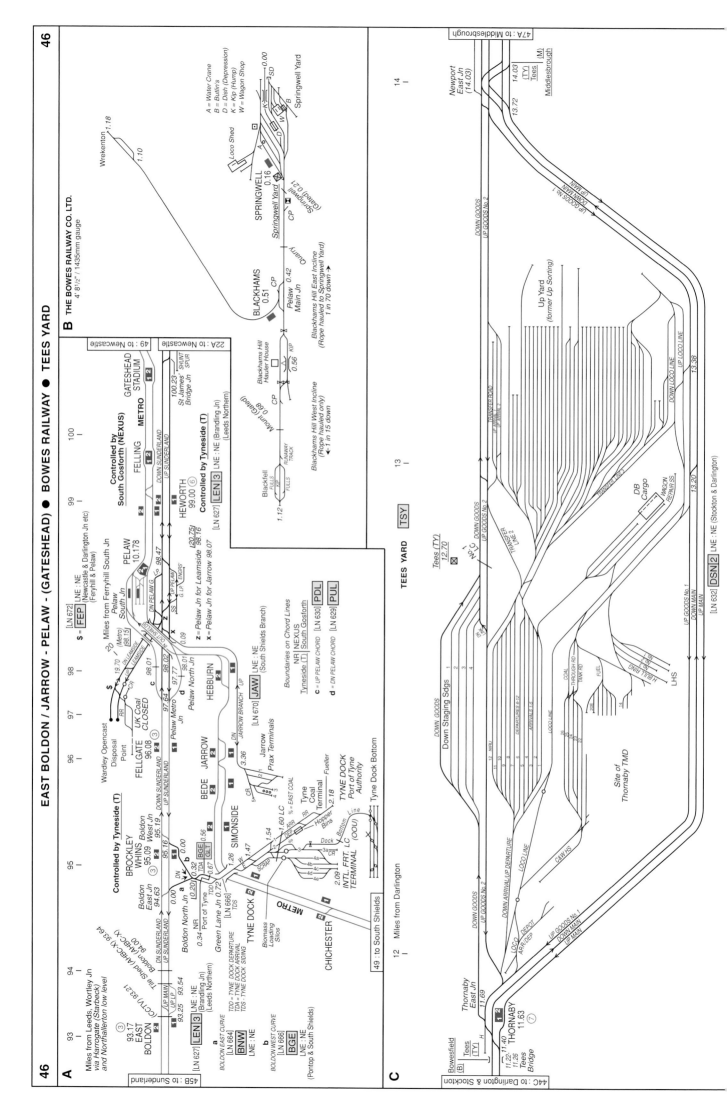

EAST BOLDON / JARROW - PELAW - (GATESHEAD) ● BOWES RAILWAY ● TEES YARD

MIDDLESBROUGH - REDCAR / NUNTHORPE

A

Ovens

REDCAR COKE OVENS
SSI (UK)
Closed

Coke - Ovens

LC
Loading Bank

Raw Ore Stocks
Buried
Loading Pad (OOU)

Conveyor
Pad

Limestone
Coal
Raw Coal Stocks

REDCAR ORE TERMINAL
Redcar Bulk Terminals
Blended Ore Stocks

LC

Bunkers
Wagon Loading Control Room
Bunkers
Pad Coke LC Redcar SSI
WBS
SB (OOU)
CR

REDCAR BLAST FURNACE

REDCAR WORKS
SSI UK
(Closed)

Pad - Coke
LC
(OOU) IN
ARRIVAL DEPARTURE (OOU) OUT
ARR DEP ORE DEP

REDCAR MINERAL TERMINAL
Redcar Bulk Terminals
Blended Coal Stocks

Bunkers

Sidings
1-3 ICL (UK) Cleveland Potash
4-6 Tees Dock Freightliner Terminal

Tees Dock Freightliner Terminal

TEES DOCK
PD Ports

LC
LC

ICL (UK) (Cleveland Potash)
THPA LINE
M
CRIPPLES
LC

Steel Export Terminal
M = Maintenance Shed

LC LC LC LC LC

20.25
20.13 20.50
Tod Point Jn
NR Redcar
20.05
Redcar Ore Terminal Jn 20.10
0.56
0.58 Sembcorp 0.59
NR
NR LC LC

HOT METAL RAILWAY

BRITISH STEEL REDCAR ③ 20.56
❷
❶
1.03

[LN 632] 2 DSN 3
LNE : NE (Stockton & Darlington / Middlesbrough & Redcar)
COM 21.72 22.16
21

48A : to Saltburn

Iron Plating
Iron Area

East Gate Mount (open) 1.34
Boundary Road North (open)
Northway (open)
Eastway (open)
LC

ICI Wilton Jn 0.00/1.38
Outwards Sdgs
Inwards Sdgs (OOU)
ARRIVAL
DEPARTURE
COAL LINE
[LN 640]
OUTWARD INWARD
LS
Coal Access 2.07
Coal
North Gate (open) 2.24
Wilton 11 EtW CR P CR
SITA Sembcorp Marcroft

Wilton International - Semcorp Utilities UK

Freightliner Terminal LC (Gated) 2.61

CLOSED Cleveland (Wilton) Freightliner Terminal

Coal Hopper
Coal Line
0.70

Control Tower
Iron Granulation Shop
LACKENBY STEELWORKS
Repair Shop
Loco Shed (OOU)

[LN 638] WCI 20
Shell Jn 0.00 19.32
Lackenby No.4 Grid
Lackenby No.3 Grid
WILTON BRANCH
DOWN MAIN
UP MAIN

Teesside Beam Mill
British Steel - (Greybull Capital)
Coil Plate Mill
Export Bay
Comcast Plant
BOS Plant
Torpedo & Ladle Repair Shop

DOWN GOODS
UP GOODS
DOWN MAIN
UP MAIN
PD NR

19
Grangetown (G) Jn
18.65
18.75
18.51
Slag Rd (TMO) 18.67
SSI NR
LC

GRANGETOWN 18.41
British Steel (Greybull Capital) and SSI (UK) Lackenby Works Middlesbrough (Part Closed)
LC

[LN 636]
BEAM MILL LINE
18.34

Miles from Darlington
18

SOUTH BANK COKE WORKS
SSI (UK) *Closed*
Ovens
Beam Mill Jn 18.03
DOWN GOODS
UP GOODS
DOWN MAIN
UP MAIN

❶ SOUTH BANK ④ 17.40
South Bank Jn 17.31
[LN 632] DSN 2
LNE : NE (Stockton & Darlington)

former BS Coke Ovens Line
OOU
DOWN
UP
16.37 (Inner Jn Eston Branch)
16.06 (MCB)

❶ MIDDLESBROUGH ⑩ 15.00

B

North Sea Supply Base
Wharf - A.V. Dawson
Dent's Wharf / A.V. Dawson
Wagon Repair/ Paint Shop
Ayrton Terminal - A.V. Dawson
Depot Road LC
ASST = Automotive Steel Storage Term.
Tees Riverside Intermodal Park A.V. Dawson
Warehouse
Middlesbrough Goods Yard A.V. Dawson
Cobra Railfreight

Forty Foot Rd LC
ASST FASST
SALT RD Pad
WB Marcroft
z
a
RH SHUNT LINE
MARSH BRANCH
IN LINE
OUT LINE
DOWN GOODS
DOWN MAIN
UP MAIN

a = Ayrton Sidings
t = Tank loading
z = Under Track Unloading Facility

Newport East Jn 14.03
13.73
[LN 632] DSN 2
14.71 (M)
Tees (T) (M)
LNE : NE (Stockton & Darlington)

46C : to Tees Yard & Thornaby

15 16 17 18

❷ b ❶ a
West End Dk
14.65 14.71 (M)
14.03 (T) (M)
MIDDLESBROUGH 15.00 ⑩
47B

MIDDLESBROUGH
15.00
28 ft
❷ b ❶ a (M) 14.65 14.71
Carriage Sdgs
DOWN GOODS
UP GOODS
DOWN MAIN
UP MAIN
15.18 15.23
Engrs 0.00
= Cargo Fleet Rd (CCTV) (M) 0.14
⑩

Whitehouse 15.76 (W)
(16.06) MCB
CARGO FLEET

UP NUNTHORPE SINGLE
DN

Guisborough Line
16.06
16

Controlled by Middlesbrough (M)

JAMES COOK UNIVERSITY HOSPITAL ④ ⑤ 2.01
MARTON (formerly ORMESBY) ④ 2.56
2
3
4
GYPSY LANE 3.60
Marton Lane (ABCL) 3.62
NUNTHORPE ④ 4.25 287 ft
Morton Lane (MCB) 4.27
UP & DN LOOP 4.31
Morton Carr (AOCL+B) 4.68 UP LOOP
(Nunthorpe Jn) 5.30
Morton Grange Farm No.4 (UWC) 5.50
5
6

Nunthorpe to Whitby
No Signalman Token with RemoteToken Stations (RTS)

[LN 634] MBW 1
LNE : NE (Stockton & Darlington & Guisborough & Middlesbrough & Ayrton Branch
and Ayrton Branch

48B : to Whitby

47A
47B

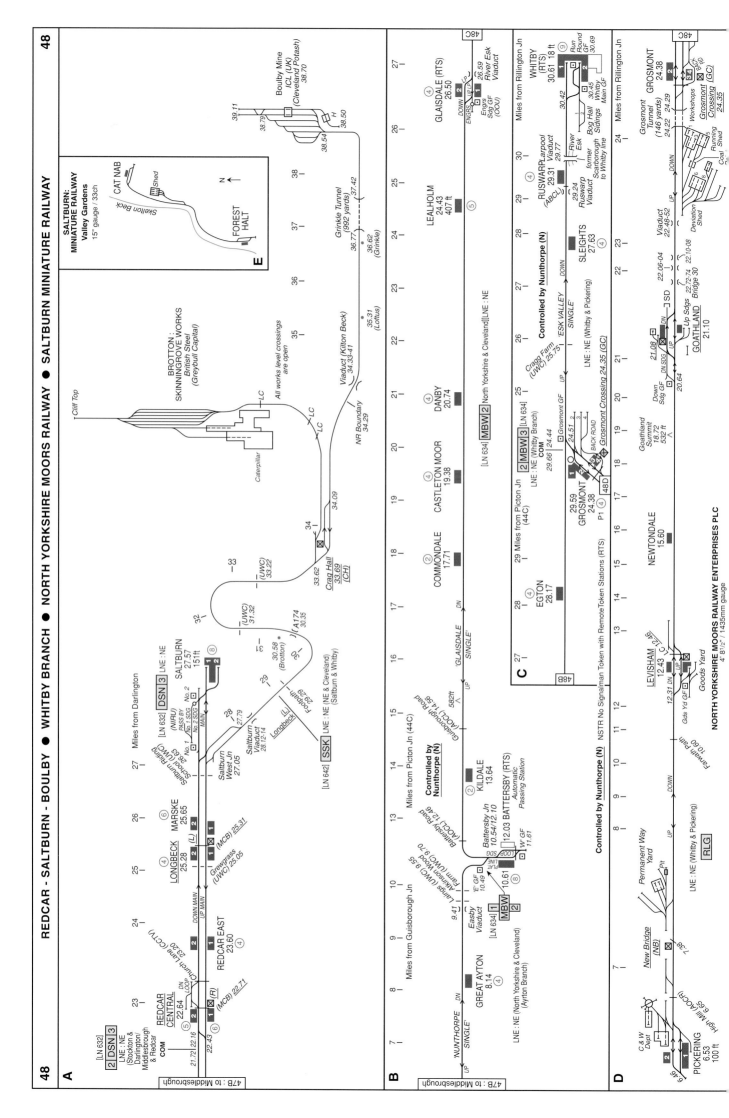

TYNE & WEAR PASSENGER TRANSPORT EXECUTIVE METRO (NEXUS) ● NORTH TYNESIDE STEAM RAILWAY

All distances on this page are metric;
station distances are from point of origin.
28 metres north of Gosforth South Junction.

Electrification at 1500V dc

4' 8½" / 1435mm gauge

M ✕

WHITLEY BAY 11.959
MONKSEATON 10.918
CULLERCOATS 12.698
SDG LOOP
WEST MONKSEATON 9.657
Footpath (Murton)
TYNEMOUTH 14.631
Emergency Over-run
SOUTH SHIELDS 21.972
CHICHESTER 20.653
TYNE DOCK 19.297
Tyne Dock Tunnel 170m
46A: Boldon
46A: Port of Tyne
46A: Jarrow Oil Terminal
SIMONSIDE 18.008
BEDE 17.300
NORTH SHIELDS 16.459 (Bay 16.552)
North Shields Tunnel 719m
Crossgate Viaduct 233m
Hylton Street Permanent Way Depot
Preston Refuge Siding (aka 'Bagnall's Siding')
MEADOW WELL 17.792
PERCY MAIN 18.396
PERCY MAIN
Stephenson Railway Museum
MIDDLE ENGINE LANE
NORTH TYNESIDE STEAM RAILWAY 4' 8½" / 1435mm gauge 1mile 62chains
HOWDON 19.708
HADRIAN ROAD 21.157
Willington Viaduct (319m)
Limekiln Road HGV Crossing
WALLSEND 22.276
JARROW 16.144 15.681
15.400
HEBBURN 13.376
14.987 13.612
South Drive Crossing (FP)
Reyrolles 12.182
Bill Quay Jn 11.243
NR 97.77 Pelaw Metro
NR 98.01 Pelaw Flyover 33.5m
a = DOWN PELAW CHORD
z = UP PELAW CHORD
46A: to Sunderland
46A: to Wardley
46A: to Newcastle
Pelaw North Jn
Pelaw South Jn
IN SHIELDS
OUT SHS
Pelaw Sidings
PELAW 10.178
FELLING 8.245
HEWORTH 9.283
GATESHEAD STADIUM 7.093
GATESHEAD 5.937
Greensfield Tunnel Mouth
Queen Elizabeth II Bridge (352m)
River Tyne
Forth Banks Tunnel Mouth
WALKERGATE 24.058
Shields Rd Tunnel 75m
CHILLINGHAM ROAD 24.896
Byker Tunnel 550m
BYKER 26.011
Byker Viaduct (815m)
Ouse Burn
Stoddart Street Sdgs
MANORS 27.648
former JESMOND BR Station 2.898
MANORS SPUR (1235m)
SHIELDS IN / OUT
214m
ST JAMES 28.731
MONUMENT 4.060/28.290
CENTRAL STATION 4.577
HAYMARKET 3.548 Prudhoe St
JESMOND 2.760
Jesmond Jn 2.586
WEST JESMOND 1.550
ILFORD ROAD 0.790
LONGBENTON 1.223
SOUTH GOSFORTH 0.125
Point of origin : 0 km
Stoneyhurst Road
NORTHUMBERLAND PARK 6.660
SHIREMOOR 7.721
23C : to Bedington
OUT LOOP IN LOOP
NETWORK RAIL
PALMERSVILLE 4.928
Benton (North) Jn 4.24/0.00
22B : to Morpeth
22B : to Newcastle
Footpath 5.552
BENTON 2.869
Benton East GF
FOUR LANE ENDS 2.092
Gosforth East Jn 0.610
REGENT CENTRE 1.186
Gosforth Depot (see inset)
Gosforth Middle Jn
Gosforth South Jn
Control Centre
Gosforth West Jn 1.046
AVOIDING LINE
Christon Rd
WANSBECK ROAD 2.125
KENTON IN / OUT
FAWDON 2.660
KINGSTON PARK 4.091
BANK FOOT 4.842
Fawdon Lane (AOCL)
Brunton Lane (AOCL)
Station Road (AOCL)
CALLERTON PARKWAY 7.157
Woolsington Bridleway
Callerton Lane (AOCL)
AIRPORT 8.162 8.228
continued above / continued below

GOSFORTH DEPOT
Cheswick Drive Crossing AVOIDING LINE (1245m)
Depot Panel
EAST DEP / EAST REC
Gosforth East Jn 0.610
To Gosforth South Jn
WEST REC / HEADSHUNT
Top Shed CW
OIL NECK
Christon Rd IN / OUT
Gosforth Middle Jn
Gosforth West Jn 1.046

October 2016

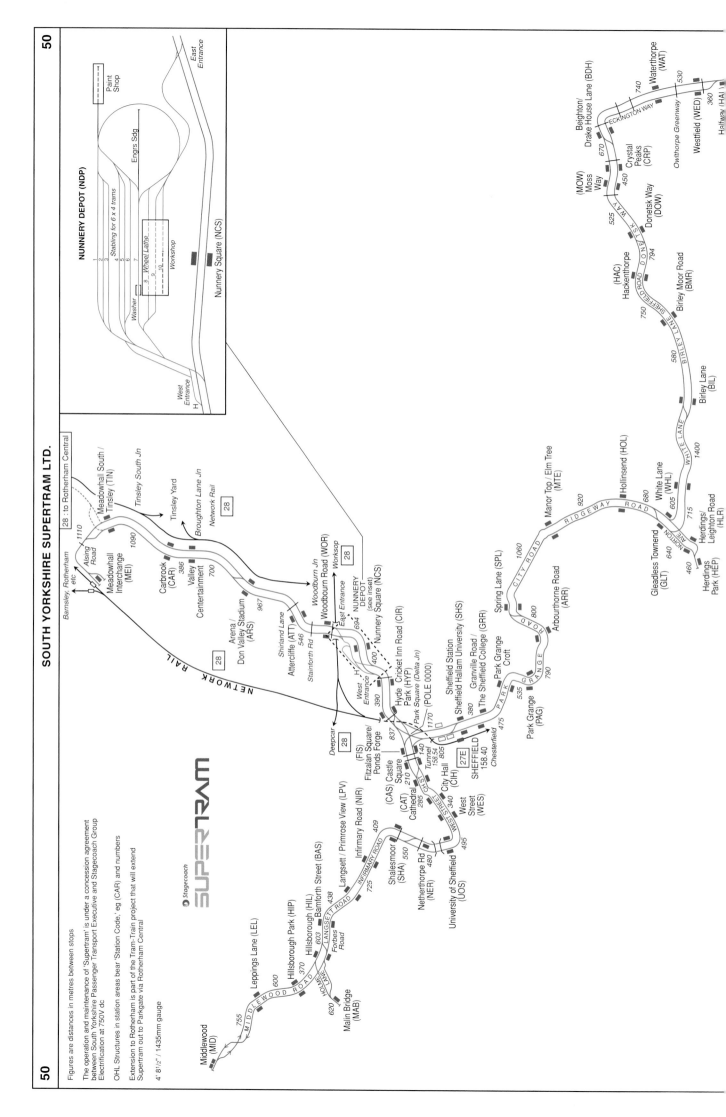

SOUTH YORKSHIRE SUPERTRAM LTD.

Figures are distances in metres between stops

The operation and maintenance of 'Supertram' is under a concession agreement between South Yorkshire Passenger Transport Executive and Stagecoach Group
Electrification at 750V dc

OHL Structures in station areas bear 'Station Code,' eg (CAR) and numbers

Extension to Rotherham is part of the Tram-Train project that will extend Supertram out to Parkgate via Rotherham Central

4' 8½" / 1435mm gauge

Stagecoach SUPERTRAM

NUNNERY DEPOT (NDP)

Paint Shop

East Entrance

Engrs Sdg

1
2
3
4   Stabling for 6 x 4 trams
5
6
7
Washer   8   Wheel Lathe
9
10   Workshop

West Entrance

Nunnery Square (NCS)

28 : to Rotherham Central

Barnsley, Rotherham etc

Alsing Road

Meadowhall South / Tinsley (TIN)

Tinsley South Jn

Tinsley Yard

Broughton Lane Jn

Network Rail

1110

Meadowhall Interchange (MEI)

1090

Carbrook (CAR)   386

Valley Centertainment   700

Arena / Don Valley Stadium (ARS)   967

Attercliffe (ATT)   546   Shirland Lane

Stainforth Rd   Woodburn Jn

Woodbourn Road (WOR)   694

NUNNERY DEPOT (see inset)   400

Nunnery Square (NCS)

East Entrance

Worksop

28

28

NETWORK RAIL

28

Deepcar

West Entrance (Delta Jn)   390

Hyde Cricket Inn Road (CIR)

Park Square (Delta Jn)

(POLE 0000)

1170

837

Sheffield Station
Sheffield Hallam University (SHS)

Granville Road / The Sheffield College (GRR)   380

Park Grange Croft

Spring Lane (SPL)

920

Manor Top / Elm Tree (MTE)

RIDGEWAY   ROAD

680

Hollinsend (HOL)

CITY   ROAD   1060

Arbourthorne Road (ARR)

800

PARK   GRANGE   ROAD

Park Grange (PAG)   535

790

475

Chesterfield

27E

SHEFFIELD
158.40

158.54

City Hall (CIH)

Tunnel   805

140

Fitzalan Square / Ponds Forge (FIS)

210

(CAS) Castle Square

(CAT) Cathedral   285

WEST STREET   340

West Street (WES)   495

University of Sheffield (UOS)

Netherthorpe Rd (NER)   480

Shalesmoor (SHA)   550

INFIRMARY ROAD   725

Infirmary Road (NIR)   409

Langsett / Primrose View (LPV)

LANGSETT ROAD   438

Forbes Road   603

Bamforth Street (BAS)

Hillsborough (HIL)   370

Hillsborough Park (HIP)

600

Leppings Lane (LEL)

755

MIDDLEWOOD ROAD

HOLME LANE   620

Malin Bridge (MAB)

Middlewood (MID)

Spring Lane (SPL)

Gleadless Townend (GLT)   640

NORTON   AVENUE

715

Herdings / Leighton Road (HLR)   460

Herdings Park (HEP)

White Lane (WHL)   605

WHITE LANE   1400

Hollinsend (HOL)

Birley Lane (BIL)

580   BIRLEY LANE

Birley Moor Road (BMR)

750   SHEFFIELD ROAD   794

(HAC) Hackenthorpe

DONETSK   WAY

525

(MOW) Moss Way

450   Donetsk Way (DOW)

Crystal Peaks (CRP)

670

ECKINGTON WAY

Beighton / Drake House Lane (BDH)

740

Waterthorpe (WAT)

530

Owlthorpe Greenway

Westfield (WED)

360

Halfway (HAI)

Index

This index covers practically all the named locations relating to the National Network which appear on the maps to assist the reader in their search. Stations are listed in capitals, signal boxes with their codes and level crossings with their type. Some BW and FP crossings in the maps have been carried to the index together with some road and motorway bridges, but not all. Locations of now-defunct assets are given in brackets. Other public service lines, light rail, heritage lines, narrow gauge and other private lines are indexed by their line name and key stations only.

Billingham-on-Tees SB (B) 45A
BINGLEY 41
Bingley Tunnel 41
Binnington LC (UWC) 39E
Biofuels LC (open) 45A
Birdsall Estates LC (UWC) 39D
Birtley Jn 21B
BISHOP AUCKLAND 44B
BISHOP AUCKLAND
(Weardale Railway) 44B
BISHOPS STORTFORD 11B
Bishops Stortford Carriage Sidings 11B
Bishops Stortford Up Loop GF 11B
(Bishopsgate Jn) 2A
(Bishopsgate Low Level) 2A
Bishopsgate Tunnel 2A
Black Bank LC (AHBC-X) 13C
Black Bush LC (AHBC) 13C
Black Carr Jn 17C
Black Carr LC (UWC) 39B
Black Horse Drove LC (R/G) 12A
Black Mill LC 6C
(Blackhall Rocks) 45B
BLACKHAMS (Bowes Rly) 46B
Blackhills Farm LC (UWC) 45B
BLACKHORSE ROAD 10B
Blackstock LC (UWC) 9A
Blankney (Metheringham Moor Lane)
LC (MCB-OD) 26B
Blankney Estates LC (UWC) 26B
Blaxhall LC (AOCL+B) 9A
BLAYDON 21B
(Blaydon Jn) 21B
Blaydon SB (B) 21B
Blenkinsop LC (FP) (R/G) 43B
Blockmore LC (UWC) 12C
Blofield Hall LC 9A
Bloss LC (UWC) 9A
Blotoft LC (MCB-OD) 25B
Blue Gowts LC (MCB-OD) 24D
Blundeston LC (UWC) 8
Boat House LC (UWC) 21C
Bog Hall LC (UWC) 20C
Bog Hall Sidings 48C
Bog Jn (Carlisle) 43A
Boldon East Jn 46A
Boldon LC (AHBC-X) 46A
Boldon North Jn 46A
Boldon West Jn 46A
Bole LC (UWC) 30B
Bollo Lane LC (CCTV) 1A
BOLTON ABBEY (Embsay &
Bolton Abbey Rly) 42C
(Bolton Percy) 40A
BOLTON-UPON-DEARNE 32A
Bolton-upon-Dearne LC (FP) (R/G) 32A
BOND STREET (Crossrail) 2D
Bonsall Lane LC (MG) 30C
Bootham LC (AHBC-X) 19
Bootham Stray LC (UWC) 19
Boothferry Road LC (MCB) 38A
Booth's No. 1 LC (UWC) 18A
(Border Counties Jn) 43E
Boreham Viaduct 5C
Boroughbridge Road LC (CCTV) 20B
Boss Hall Jn 9A
BOSTON 25C
Boston & Spilsby Road LC (AHBC-X) 26D
Boston Docks 25C
Boston Swing Bridge 25C
Botanic Gardens (BG) 38C
Botany Bay LC (CCTV) 17A
Bothal Viaduct (River Wansbeck) 22B
BOTTESFORD 25A
Bottesford LC (UWC) 25A
Bottisham Road LC (AHBC) 11C
Bottom Hall Viaduct 41
(Boughton) 29A
Boughton Brake Tunnel 29A
Boughton Jn 29A
Boulby Mine 48A
Boultham Crossing LC (CCTV) 26A
Boultham Jn 26B
Bound Green C.S. GF 14B
Boundary Road North (open) 47B
Bounds Green TMD (BN) 14B
BOW CHURCH (DLR) 3A
Bow Depot 2B
Bow Depot Jn 2B
Bow East 2B
Bow Jn 2B
Bow Road 2B
BOWES PARK 24A
Bowes Park Jn 24A
Bowesfield Jn 44C
Bowesfield SB (B) 44C
Bowling Tunnel 41
Boyes LC (UWC) 20B
Bradbury LC (UWC) 20C
Bradfield LC (R/G) 9B
BRADFORD FORSTER SQUARE 41
BRADFORD INTERCHANGE 41
Bradford Interchange 'A' GF 41
Bradley Hall Farm No. 1 LC (UWC) 37A
Bradley Jn 37A
Bradley Tunnel 37A
Bradley Wood Jn 37A
Bradway Tunnel 27E
Bragbury Jn 24B
BRAINTREE 5D
BRAINTREE FREEPORT 5D
Bramfield LC (ABCL) 8
Bramhope Tunnel 18C
BRAMLEY 41
Bramleys (Home Farm) LC (UWC) 40A
BRAMPTON (Cumbria) 43A
BRAMPTON (Suffolk) 8
Brampton Fell LC (MG) 43A
Brampton Fell SB (BF) 43A
BRAMPTON HALT (Bure Valley Rly) 7D
Brampton LC (AOCL+B) 8
Bramwith Road LC (AHBC) 18A
Brancliffe East Jn 30A
BRANDON 13A
Brandon LC (MCB-OD) 13A
Branston & W. Cross Roads Tunnel 26B
Bratts Black House LC (UWC) 9A
Brayford Jn 26B
Brayford LC (CCTV) 26B
Brayton Jn 18A
Brayton LC (CCTV) 18A
Brent Curve 1A
Brent Curve Jn 1A
Brent Sidings (Willesden) 1A
BRENTFORD 1A
BRENTWOOD 5B
BRESSINGHAM STEAM MUSEUM 7F
Brewery Lane LC (MCB-OD) 25B
Brewster Lane LC (AOCL+B-X) 26D
Breydon Access (24) LC (UWC) 8
Breydon Access (51) LC 8
(Breydon Jn) 8
Breydon Sluice LC (UWC) 8
Brick House Crossovers 5C
Brick Kiln LC (UWC) 9A
Bridge 2314 (Twenty Foot River) 13C
Bridge 357 (Norwich) 7A
Bridge 47 (York) 19
Bridge C (Finsbury Park) 14A
Bridge Jn (Doncaster) 17C
(Bridges Jn (Hull)) 38C
BRIDLINGTON 39B
Bridlington Quay LC (CCTV) 39B
Bridlington SB (BN) 39B
BRIGG 30C
Brigg LC (MG) 30C
Brigg SB (B) 30C
BRIGHOUSE 37A
BRIGHTSIDE (disused) 28
Brightside Station Jn 28
BRIMSDOWN 10B
Brimsdown LC (CCTV) 10B
Brinkley Road LC (AHBC) 11C
Brinsworth St LC (CCTV) 28
Brisby's LC (UWC) 39D
Britannia Farm LC (UWC) 8
British Steel Coal Terminal
(Immingham) 31B
British Steel Ore Terminal
(Immingham) 31B
BRITISH STEEL REDCAR 47B
Broad Road LC (UWG) 8
Broad Street Tunnel 28
Broadfield Lane LC (CCTV) 25C
Broadwath LC (AHBC-X) 43A
BROCKFORD (Mid-Suffolk Light Rly) 12E
BROCKHOLES 34C
BROCKLESBY (disused) 31A
Brocklesby East Jn 31A
Brocklesby West Jn 31A
BROCKLEY WHINS 46A
BROMLEY-BY-BOW (LUL) 3A
Brompton LC (AHBC-X) 20B
BRONDESBURY 1A
BRONDESBURY PARK 1A
(Brookfields SB) 11C
Brookhouse Viaduct 34A
BROOKMANS PARK 15A
Broom Hill Viaduct 9A
BROOMFLEET 38B
Broomfleet LC (MCB) 38B
Broomfleet SB (B) 38B
Broomston LC (UWC) 17B
Brotherton Tunnel 40A
(Brotton) 48A
BROUGH 38B
Brough East LC (MG) 38B
Brough East SB (BE) 38B
Broughton Lane Jn 28
Broughton No. 1 GF 29A
Broughton No. 2 GF 29A
Broughton Road CS 42A
Browick Road LC (AHBC-X) 13B
Browns LC (UWC) 30B
BROXBOURNE 11A
Broxbourne 'A' GF 11A
Broxbourne Jn 11A
BRUCE GROVE 10B
Brumfields LC (UWC) 39A
BRUNDALL 8
BRUNDALL GARDENS 8
Brundall Jn SB (BL) 8
Brundall LC (MG) 8
Brunton Lane LC (AOCL) (Metro) 49
Bryants LC (UWC) 13A
BUCKENHAM 8
Buckenham LC 8
Buckton Lane LC (AHBC) 39C
Bullpit Lane LC (CCTV) 16C
Bungalow Lane LC (R/G-X) 7A
BURE VALLEY RAILWAY 7D
BURES 5E
Burgess Drove LC (UWC) 11C
(Burley Jn) 41
BURLEY PARK 36A
BURLEY-IN-WHARFEDALE 41
Burn Lane LC (MCB-OD) 18A
BURNHAM-ON-CROUCH 10A
Burnt House Drove LC (AHBC-X) 13C
Burnt House LC (UWC) 8
Burrs Road LC (CCTV) 6A
Burston LC (AHBC-X) 6C
Burtey Fen LC (MCB-OD) 24D
BURTON AGNES (disused) 39B
Burton Agnes LC (AHBC-X) 39B
Burton Lane (Mastermans) LC (UWC) 40A
(Burton Lane Jn) 19
Burton Lane No. 1 LC (AHBC) 25C
Burton Lane No. 2 LC (AHBC) 25C
Burton Salmon 40A
(Burton Salmon Station) 40A
BURY ST. EDMUNDS 12D
Bury St. Edmunds SB (BY) 12D
Bury St. Edmunds Yard 12D
Bury Street Jn 10B
BUSH HILL PARK 10B
Buslingthorpe LC (AHBC-X) 27A
Butterswood LC (ABCL-X) 31B
Butterthwaite Lane LC (UWC) 28
Butterwell Disposal Point 22B
Butterwell GF 'A' 22B
Butterwell GF 'C' 22B
Butterwell Jn 22B
Butterwell SB (B) 22B
BUXTON (Bure Valley Rly) 7D
BYKER (Metro) 49
Byker Tunnel (Metro) 49
Byker Viaduct (Ouse Burn) (Metro) 49
Bystable Lane LC (MGH-Key) 31B
Bytham Viaduct 16B

C

Cadmore Lane LC (UWC) 11A
Cadwell 15B
Calder & Hebble Canal Viaduct
(Horbury) 34B
Calder Bridge Jn 35B
Calder Viaduct (Altofts) 35B
CALEDONIAN ROAD AND
BARNSBURY 1A
Callerton Lane LC (AOCL) (Metro) 49
CALLERTON PARKWAY (Metro) 49
Calverley Viaduct (River Aire) 41
Cam Farm LC (UWC) 24C
Cambois LC (TMO) 23C
CAMBRIDGE 11C
Cambridge Carriage Sidings 11C
Cambridge Chord 11B
Cambridge Depot (CA) 11C
CAMBRIDGE HEATH 10B
Cambridge Jn (Hitchin) 15B
CAMBRIDGE NORTH 11C
(Cambridge North (Mill Road Jn)) 11C
Cambridge Reception Sidings 11C
Cambridge SB (CA) 11C
Cambridge South Jn 11C
Camden Jns 1A
CAMDEN ROAD 1A
Camden Road Central Jn 1A
Camden Road East Jn 1A
Camden Road Incline Jn 1A
Camden Road Tunnels 1A
Camden Road West Jn 1A
Camden Viaduct 1A
Campbell Road 3A
Campey's Farm LC (UWC) 40E
Camps LC (UWC) 11A
Canal Bridge Viaduct (Thorne) 32B
Canal Tunnels 1A
CANARY WHARF (Crossrail) 2D
Canklow 28
CANNING TOWN DLR) 2C
Cannons Mill Lane LC (R/G-X) 11B
CANONBURY 1B
Canonbury Tunnel 14A
Canonbury West Jn 1B
CANTLEY 8
Cantley LC (MWG) 8
Cantley SB (C) 8
Capenters Road Curve 2B
Carcroft Jn 35A
Cargill Grain 'B' Quay (Hull) 38C
CARGO FLEET (disused) 47B
Cargo Fleet Road LC (CCTV) 47B
CARLISLE 43A
Carlisle North Jn 43A
Carlisle SB (CE) 43A
Carlisle South Jn 43A
Carlton Emergency Crossovers 16C
Carlton Gatebox 17A
Carlton LC (CCTV) 17A
Carlton Loops 16C
Carlton Road Jn 1A
Carnaby LC (AHBC-X) 39B
Carpenters Road North Jn 2B
Carpenters Road South Jn 2B
Carr 17C
Carr Head Farm LC (UWC) 34C
Carr Lane LC (UWC) 17C
Carters LC (UWC) 44C
Casefield LC (UWC) 5E
Castle Eden Viaduct 45B
CASTLE HEDINGHAM
(Colne Valley Rly) 4D
Castle Hills Jns 20B
(Castle Howard) 39D
Castle Sidings GF 22A
CASTLEFORD 35B
Castleford East Jn 35B
Castleford LC (MCB) 35B
Castleford SB (CD) 35B
Castleford West Jn 35B
(Castles Jn (Newcastle)) 22A
CASTLETON MOOR 48B
Cat Lane LC (UWC) 18D
CAT NAB (Saltburn Rly) 48E
(Catcliffe Jn) 28
Catcliffe Viaduct 28
CATTAL (formerly Goldsborough) 18D
Cattal LC (MG) 18D
Cattal SB (C) 18D
Cattawade Viaduct 6A
CAUSEY ARCH (Tanfield Rly) 44D
Cave Crossing LC (Gatebox) (MCB) 38B
Cayton (AHBC) 39C
Cedar Jn 1A
(Cemetery SB) 14B
Central FLT (Felixstowe) 9A
CENTRAL STATION
(NEWCASTLE) (Metro) 49
CHADWELL HEATH 5A
CHAFFORD HUNDRED 3B
Chain Bridge LC (AHBC) (March) 13C
Chain Bridge LC (RC) (Blaydon) 21B
Chalk Lane LC (CCTV) 38C
CHALKWELL 3C
(Chaloner Whin Jn) 18B
Channelsea North Jn 2B
Channelsea South Jn 2B
Chantry Road LC (RC) 9A
Chapel Farm LC (UWC) 31B
CHAPEL ROAD (East Suffolk Light Rly) 7C
Chapel Road LC (MCG) 8
CHAPELTOWN 28
Chapeltown Viaduct 28
CHAPPEL & WAKES COLNE 5E
Chappel Viaduct 5E
Charlestown Viaduct (River Aire) 41
CHATHILL 23A
Chathill Crossovers 23A
Chathill LC (CCTV) (R/G) 23A
Cheal Road LC (MCB-OD) 24D
CHELMSFORD 5C
Chelmsford Lower Yard 5C
Chelmsford Viaducts 5C
Chequers Lane LC (CCTV) 4A
Cherry Hinton Bypass LC (CCTV) 11C
Cherry Hinton High Street LC (CCTV) 11C
Cherry Holt LC (AHBC-X) 24D
Cherry Tree LC (CCTV) 39A
Cherry Willingham LC (AHBC-X) 27A
Cherryholt LC (UWC) 30B
CHESHUNT 11A
Cheshunt Jn 11A
Chester Moor Viaduct 21A
CHESTERFIELD 27E
Chesterfield Down Sidings 27E
Chesterfield North Jn 27E
Chesterfield South Jn 27E
CHESTER-LE-STREET 21A
Chester-le-Street Viaduct 21A
Chesterton Jn 11C
Chesterton Jn LC (CCTV) 11C
Chesterton Jn Yard 11C
Cheswick Drive LC (Metro) 49
Chettisham LC (AHBC-X) 13C
Chevet Viaduct 35B
Chevington LC (CCTV) 23A
Chevington North Crossovers 23A
CHICHESTER (Metro) 49
Chicken Farm LC (UWC) 39B
CHILLINGHAM ROAD (Metro) 49
Chillingham Road Jn 22A
CHINGFORD 10B
Chingford Country End Sidings 10B
Chingford London End Sidings 10B
Chippenham Jn 12D
Chippenham Jn SB (CM) 12D
Chitts Hill LC (CCTV) 5E
Chivers LC (AHBC-X) 13A

Location	Code
HACKNEY WICK	1B
HADDISCOE	8
HADLEY WOOD	15A
Hadley Wood North Tunnels	15A
Hadley Wood South Tunnels	15A
HADRIAN ROAD (Metro)	49
Hagg Lane LC (AHBC-X) (Wressle)	38A
Hagg Lane LC (R/G)	
(Gascoigne Wood)	40A
HAGGERSTON	1B
Haisthorpe LC (UWC)	39B
Hales Street LC (AHBC-X)	6C
HALESWORTH	8
Halfway House LC (UWC)	39A
Halfway sign (ECML)	20A
HALIFAX	41
Halifax Jn	6A
Halifax SB (H)	41
Halvergate LC (UWC)	8
Hambleton East Jn	40E
Hambleton North Curve	18B
Hambleton North Jn	18B
Hambleton South Curve	18B
Hambleton South Jn	18B
Hambleton West Jn	40E
Hamiltons LC (UWC)	27A
HAMMERTON	18D
Hammerton LC (MG)	18D
Hammerton Road LC (MCG)	18D
Hammerton SB (H)	18D
(Hammerton Street Jn)	41
Hammerton Street Loop	41
HAMPSTEAD HEATH	1A
Hampstead Heath Tunnel	1A
(Hampstead Road Jn)	1A
Hampstead Tunnel	1A
Hanson Aggregates Terminal	
(Dagenham)	4A
Hansons LC (UWC)	26C
Harbrough Jn	31A
HARDINGHAM (Mid-Norfolk Rly)	13B
Hardmead LC (UWG)	11A
Hare Park Jn	35B
Harford Bridges	13B
Hargham No. 1 LC (AHBC)	13B
Hargham No. 2 LC (UWC)	13B
HARLESDEN	1A
Harlesden Jn	1A
HARLING ROAD	13B
Harling Road LC (MCB-OD)	13B
HARLOW MILL	11A
Harlow Mill Aggregates Terminal	11A
Harlow Mill GF	11A
Harlow Mill Yard	11A
HARLOW TOWN	11A
Harlow Town GF	11A
HAROLD WOOD	5B
Harpham LC (UWC)	39B
HARRINGAY	14B
HARRINGAY GREEN LANES	1B
Harringay Jn	14B
Harringay Park Jn	1B
Harringay Viaduct	14B
Harrisons Farm LC (UWC)	40A
HARROGATE	18C
Harrogate SB (H, LH)	18C
Harry Moor Lane LC (R/G)	40E
Harston LC (AHBC)	24C
Hartburn Jn	44C
HARTLEPOOL	45A
Hartlepool Docks	45A
Hartlepool Power Station	45A
Hartlepool South Works	45A
Hartley LC (AHBC)	23C
Harts Drove LC (R/G)	13C
HARWICH INTERNATIONAL	9B
Harwich Refinery	9B
HARWICH TOWN	9B
Harworth Colliery	34A
Haslingfield Road LC (Open)	24C
Hassingham Bridge	8
HATFIELD	15A
HATFIELD & STAINFORTH	32B
Hatfield & Stainforth Up Yard	32B
Hatfield Lane LC (UWC)	32B
Hatfield Main Colliery	32B
HATFIELD PEVEREL	5C
Hatson LC (UWC)	12B
Haugh Gardens LC (UWC)	43C
Haughley Jn	6B
Haughley LC (AHBC)	6B
Hauxton LC (AHBC)	24C
HAVENHOUSE	26D
Havenhouse LC (AHBC-X)	26D
(Haverton Hill)	45A
Haverton Hill East Grid	45A
Haverton Hill Exchange Sidings	45A
Haverton Hill South Jn	45A
Haw Bank Tunnel	42A
Hawks LC (UWC)	12C
HAWORTH (KWV Rly)	42B
Hawthorn Bank LC (CCTV)	24D
Hawthorn Dene Viaduct	45B
Haxby Road LC (CCTV)	19
Haxby Station LC (CCTV)	19
Haxey & Epworth GF	17B
Haxey LC (CCTV)	17B
HAYDON BRIDGE	43E
Haydon Bridge LC (MG)	43E
Haydon Bridge SB (HB)	43E
Hayes LC (UWG)	24C
Hayfields LC (UWC)	17C
HAYMARKET (Metro)	49
Haywards LC (AOCL+B)	9A
Haywood Jn	18A
Haywood LC (CCTV)	18A
HEADINGLEY	36C
Headingley Tunnel	36A
(Heads Nook)	43A
Healey Mills 'A' Jn	37B
Healey Mills 'B' Jn	37B
Healey Mills 'C' Jn	37B
Healey Mills 'D' Jn	37B
Healey Mills SB (HM)	37B
Healey Mills Yard	37B
HEALING	31A
Heath Farm LC (UWC)	8
Heath No. 59 LC (MG)	13B
Heathrow HEX Depot	1A
(Heaton)	22A
Heaton Carriage Sidings	
Control Tower	22A
Heaton GSP	22A
Heaton Lodge East Jn	37A
Heaton Lodge Jn	37A
Heaton Lodge South Jn	37A
Heaton North Jn	22A
Heaton South Jn	22A
Heaton Traction & Rolling Stock	
Maintenance Depot	22A
HEBBURN (Metro)	49
HEBDEN BRIDGE	37A
Hebden Bridge SB (HB)	37A
Hebdons LC (UWC)	20B
Heck Ings LC (BW)	40B
Heck Lane LC (CCTV)	40B
Heck Sidings	18A
HECKINGTON	25C
Heckington LC (MG)	25C
Heckington SB (HN)	25C
Hedon Road Bridge	38C
Hedon Road Sidings	38C
Heeley	27E
HEIGHINGTON	44B
Heighington Jn	44B
Heighington LC (MCB)	44B
Heighington SB (HR)	44B
Helpston Jn	16B
Helpston LC (MCB)	16B
Hemingfield Tunnel	34B
Hemsworth Loops	35A
Henderson Quay	31B
Hendon Branch (Sunderland)	45B
HENSALL	40B
Hensall LC (CCTV)	40B
Henwick Hall LC (MCB-OD)	18A
Hepscott Jn	23C
Hepscott LC (AHBC)	23C
Herries Road Viaduct	28
Herries Road Viaduct (5 Arches)	28
HERTFORD EAST	11A
HERTFORD NORTH	24A
Hertford River Bridge (Seamer)	39E
Hertford Up Sidings	24A
Hertford Viaduct	24A
Heslerton Station LC (AHBC-X)	39E
Hessay LC (MG)	18D
Hessay WD GF	18D
HESSLE	38B
Hessle East Jn	38B
Hessle Road Jn SB (HR)	38C
Hessle Road South Jn	38C
Hethersett GF	13B
Hett Mill LC (CCTV)	20C
HEWORTH (interchange with Metro)	46A
HEWORTH (Metro)	49
HEXHAM	43E
Hexham SB (H, HM)	43E
Hexthorpe Goods Jn	32A
Hexthorpe Jn	32A
Hexthorpe Up West Sidings	17C
Heyworth LC (MCB-OD)	18A
Hiams Fen House LC (UWC)	13A
Hibaldstow LC (AHBC-X)	30C
Hickleton HABD	32A
High Eggborough LC (CCTV)	40B
High Farm LC (UWC)	39D
High Ferry Lane LC (AHBC)	26D
High Ferry LC (AHBC)	26D
High Level Bridge (Newcastle)	22A
High Level Bridge Central Jn	22A
High Level Bridge Jn	22A
High Marnham	29C
High Meads Enclosure	2B
High Meads Jn	2B
High Scampston LC (AHBC-X)	39E
High Street Bridge (Stratford)	2B
(High Street Jn (Gateshead))	22A
High Street LC (CCTV) (Lincoln)	26B
High Street LC (Pig's Bay)	3E
High Wapping Sidings	43A
HIGHAMS PARK	10B
Highams Park LC (CCTV)	10B
HIGHBURY & ISLINGTON	1B
HIGHBURY & ISLINGTON	
(Moorgate Lines)	14A
Highbury Vale Jn	14A
Highdyke	16B
Highgate Road Viaduct	1A
Highover Farm LC (UWC)	24C
Hightown Farm LC	43B
Hilgay LC (AHBC)	12A
Hillam Gates LC (CCTV)	40A
Hillings Road LC (UWC)	8
Hinxton LC (AHBC)	11B
Hipperholme Tunnel	41
Hirst Lane LC (Gatebox)	23C
HITCHIN	15B
Hitchin 'A' GF	15B
Hitchin 'B' GF	24C
Hitchin Down Yard	15B
Hitchin East Jn	24C
Hitchin North Jn	15B
Hitchin Plant Maintenance Depot	15B
Hitchin South Jns	15B
Hitching Up Yard	15B
Hitchs No. 12 LC (UWC)	12C
Hobhole Bank Bridleway LC	26D
Hobhole Bank LC (UWC)	26D
Hochkings LC (UWC)	26C
Hockham Road LC (R/G-X)	13B
HOCKLEY	10A
Hockley LC (R/G-X)	6A
Hoe Street Tunnel	10B
Hogs Croft LC (UWC)	11B
Hogwell LC (UWC)	10A
Holbeck Depot	36A
Holbeck Depot Jn	36A
Holbeck Jn	36A
Holderness Road Viaduct	38C
Holdingham Lane LC (UWC)	25B
Holgate Depot	19
Holgate Jn	19
Holgate Reception Sidings	19
Holloway Jns	14A
Holme Green LC (R/G)	15C
Holme LC (CCTV)	15D
Holme Lode LC (CCTV)	15D
Holme Road LC (UWC)	12B
Holmes Chord	28
Holmes Jn LC (CCTV)	28
HOLT (North Norfolk Rly)	8
Holtby LC (UWC)	39A
Holton Gatehouse LC (AHBC-X)	27A
Holton-le-Moor LC (MCB)	27A
Holton-le-Moor SB (H)	27A
HOLYWELL HALT	
(Embsay & Bolton Abbey Rly)	42C
Holywell LC (ABCL)	23C
HOMERTON	1B
(Honington Jn)	25A
Honington LC (AHBC-X)	25A
HONLEY	34C
Honley Tunnel	34C
Hook Moor Farm LC (UWC)	32B
(Hopetown Jn)	44B
Hopetown Works	44B
Hopperton Grange LC (UWC)	18D
Hopperton Old Station LC (UWC)	18D
Horbury Jn GF	35B
Horbury Jn SB (HJ)	35B
Horbury Sidings	35B
Horbury Station Jn	37B
Horbury Works	34F
(Horden)	45B
HORNBEAM PARK	18C
HORNCHURCH (LUL)	3B
Horns Bridge	27E
HORNSEY	14B
Hornsey Aggregates Terminal	14B
Hornsey Carriage Sdgs	14B
Hornsey EMU Depot (HE)	14B
Hornsey Maintenance Shed	14B
Hornsmill Viaduct (River Lea)	24A
Horse Fen LC (UWC)	12C
Horsemoor LC (AHBC-X)	13C
HORSFORTH	36C
Hoton House Farm LC (UWC)	38A
Hough Lane LC (AHBC-X)	
(Honington)	25A
Hough Lane LC (FPG) (Claypole)	16C
(Hougham)	16C
HOVETON & WROXHAM	8
How Mill LC (AHBC-X)	43A
Howard No. 1 LC (UWC)	30B
HOWDEN	38A
HOWDEN (Metro)	49
Howden LC (CCTV)	38A
Howdon Lane LC (AOCL) (Metro)	49
Howley Park LC (BW)	37B
Howsham LC (AHBC-X) (Lincs)	27B
Howsham LC (Gatebox) (MG)	
(Kirkham Abbey)	39D
HS1 Viaduct (Kings Cross)	14A
Hubbards LC (UWC)	9C
HUBBERTS BRIDGE	25C
Hubberts Bridge LC (MG)	25C
Hubberts Bridge SB (HB)	25C
HUDDERSFIELD	37A
(Huddersfield Jn)	34C
Huddersfield SB (HU)	37A
Huddersfield Tunnels	37A
Huddersfield Viaduct	37A
Hudson Dock (Sunderland)	45B
HULL	38C
Hull Dock Security Gates	38C
Hull Docks	38C
Hull Paragon SB (HP)	38C
Hull River Swing Bridge	38C
Hull Station Sidings	38C
Hull Steel Terminal	38C
Hull Yard	38B
Humber Bridge (Hessle)	38B
Humber International Terminal	31B
Humber Refinery	31B
Humber Road Jn	31B
(Humber Road LC)	31B
Humber Sea Terminal	31B
Humber Terminals (Grimsby)	31C
HUMBERSTON NORTH SEA LANE	
(Cleethorpes Coast Light Rly)	27D
HUNMANBY	39C
Hunmanby Jn	39C
Hunmanby LC (ABCL-X)	39C
Hunmanby Sands Lane (ABCL-X)	39C
Hunslet Down Sidings	36A
Hunslet East	36A
Hunslet South Jn	36A
Hunslet Station Jn	36A
Hunters LC (UWC)	8
HUNTINGDON	15C
Huntingdon Down Sidings	15C
Huntingdon North Jn	15C
Huntingdon South Jn	15C
Hunwick Jn	6A
Hurn Lane LC	25C
(Hutton Bonville Feeder Stn)	20B
HUTTON CRANSWICK	39A
Hutton LC (AHBC-X)	39A
Huttons Ambo River Bridge	39D
Huttons LC (UWC)	34A
HYKEHAM	26A
Hykeham LC (AHBC-X)	26A
Hylton Street Depot (Metro)	49
HYTHE	6A
Hythe Jn	6A
Hythe LC (CCTV)	6A

I

Location	Code
IAWS LC (Open)	31B
ICI Brinefield LC (Open)	45A
ICI Wilton Jn	47B
Ickles Viaduct	28
Ickleton Mill Lane LC (UWG)	11B
Ickleton Road LC (CCTV)	11B
ILFORD	5A
Ilford (Aldersbrook) Flyover	5A
Ilford Carriage Inspection Shed	5A
Ilford Depot Country End Jn	5A
Ilford Depot London End Jn	5A
Ilford EMU Depot (IL)	5A
Ilford Paint Shop	5A
ILFORD ROAD (Metro)	49
Ilford Shop A	5A
Ilford Yard Sidings	5A
ILKLEY	41
Immingham Bulk Terminal	31B
Immingham C & W	31B
Immingham Dock	31B
Immingham East Jn	31B
Immingham East Storage	31B
Immingham Freight Terminal Sidings	31B
Immingham Reception Sidings	31B
Immingham Reception Sidings SB (IR)	31B
Immingham TMD	31B
Immingham Token Exchange Point	31B
Immingham West Jn SB (IW)	31B
Ingate Street LC (ABCL)	8
INGATESTONE	5C
Ingatestone LC (MCB)	5C
Ingbirchworth LC (UWC)	34C
Ingrave Summit	5B
INGROW WEST (KWV Rly)	42B
(Inner Jn Eston Branch)	47B
Intermodal Terminal (Purfleet)	4A
Intwood LC (AHBC-X)	13B
iPort Doncaster	34A
IPSWICH	6B
Ipswich (or Stoke) Tunnel	6A
Ipswich Goods Jn	6B
Ipswich Stabling Point (IP)	6B
Ipswich Upper Yard	6B
Ipswich West Bank	6A
Ipswich Yard	6B

Ivy Farm LC (R/G) 24C
Ivy Lea Farm LC (UWC) 39E

J

Jack Lane Viaduct 37B
Jacksons LC (UWC) 39E
Jacky Duffin Wood LC (R/G) 40B
JAMES COOK UNIVERSITY HOSPITAL 47B
Jaques Hall LC (UWG) 9B
JARROW (Metro) 49
Jarrow Oil Terminal 46A
Jefferies (R/G-X) 4B
JESMOND (former BR, disused) 49
JESMOND (Metro) 49
Jesmond Jn (Metro) 49
Jetty Avenue LC (UWC) 9A
Jiggs Lane LC (FPG) 15B
Joan Croft Emergency GSP 18A
Joan Croft Jn 18A
Johnsons LC (UWC) 25B
Jubilee Carriage Sdgs (Norwich) 7A
Junction Road Jn 1A
Jurgens LC (MCB) 4A
Jurgens Long Siding 4A

K

Keadby Canal Bridge 33A
Keadby Canal LC (Gatebox) (MCB) 33A
Keadby River Bridge (River Trent) 33A
Kealey's LC (UWC) 40B
Kebwood Lane LC (UWC) 33C
Keepers Lane LC (UWC) 9A
KEIGHLEY 41
KEIGHLEY & WORTH VALLEY LIGHT RAILWAY LTD 42B
KEIGHLEY (KWV Rly) 42B
Keighley Road Viaduct 42A
Keighley Sdg GF 41
Keighley Station Jn 41
Kelby Lane LC (AHBC-X) 25A
KELLING HEATH PARK (North Norfolk Rly) 8
Kellingley Colliery 40B
Kellingley Colliery Branch Jn 40B
(Kelloe Access Line Jn) 20C
KELVEDON 5C
Kemp LC (UWC) 8
KENNETT 12D
Kennett Aggregates Terminal 12D
Kennett GF 12D
KENSAL GREEN 1A
Kensal Green Jn 1A
Kensal Green Tunnels 1A
KENSAL RISE 1A
Kent House Farm LC (UWC) 18C
KENTISH TOWN 1A
Kentish Town Jn 1A
Kentish Town Viaduct 1A
KENTISH TOWN WEST 1A
Kersey No. 1 LC 3C
Kersey No. 7 LC 3C
Kesteven LC (MCB-OD) 26C
Keswick LC (AHBC-X) 13B
Kettleby LC (AHBC) 30C
Kettlestring Farm LC (UWC) 19
KEW BRIDGE 1A
Kew Curve 1A
Kew East Jn 1A
KEW GARDENS 1A
KILBURN HIGH ROAD 1A
Kilburn High Road Bridge 1A
Kilburn Loop 1A
Kilby's LC (UWC) 39D
KILDALE 48B
Kildwick HABD 42A
Kildwick LC (CCTV) 42A
(Killamarsh) 27E
Killingholme 31B
Killingworth Bridleway LC 22B
Killingworth LC (CCTV) 22B
Kiln Lane LC (AHBC-X) (Ely) 12A
Kiln Lane LC (AOCL) (Immingham) 31B
Kilnhurst 32A
Kilnwick LC (AHBC-X) 39A
Kilton Beck Viaduct 48A
KIMBERLEY PARK (Mid-Norfolk Rly) 13B
King Edward Bridge 22A
King Edward Bridge East Jn 22A
King Edward Bridge North Jn 22A
King Edward Bridge South Jn 22A
King George Dock (Hull) 38C
Kings College LC (UWC) 33C
King's Cross East Sidings 14A
Kings Cross SB (K) 14A
KING'S CROSS, LONDON 14A
Kings Dyke LC (MCB) 13C
Kings Dyke SB (K) 13C
Kings LC (UWG) 11B
KING'S LYNN 12B
King's Lynn Carriage Sidings 12B
(King's Lynn Harbour Jn) 12B
King's Lynn Jn 12B
King's Lynn SB (KL) 12B
King's Lynn Yard 12B
Kings Sdgs GF 12C
Kingston Bulk Terminal (Hull) 38C
Kingston Farm LC (UWC) 9A
KINGSTON PARK (Metro) 49
Kingston Terminal Jn 38C
KIRBY CROSS 6A
KIRK SANDALL 32B
Kirk Sandall Jn 32B
Kirkby Laythorpe LC (AHBC) 25C
Kirkham Abbey LC (MG) 39D
Kirkham Abbey SB (K) 39D
KIRKHAUGH (South Tynedale Rly) 43D
KIRKLEES LIGHT RAILWAY CO LTD 34D
KIRKSTALL FORGE 41
Kirkstall Forge Viaduct (River Aire) 41
Kirkstall Loops 36A
Kirkstall Viaduct (River Aire) 36A
Kirton Lane LC (CCTV) 32B
Kirton Lime Sidings SB (KL) 30C
KIRTON LINDSEY 30C
Kirton Tunnel 30C
Kisby LC (UWC) 13C
Kitroyd Viaduct 34B
KIVETON BRIDGE 30A
KIVETON PARK 30A
Kiveton Park LC (MCB) 30A
Kiveton Park SB (KS) 30A
Klondyke Yard 19
Knapton LC (AHBC-X) 39E
KNARESBOROUGH 18C
Knaresborough LC (MG) 18C
Knaresborough SB (K) 18C
Knaresborough Tunnel 18C
Knaresborough Viaduct 18C
KNEBWORTH 15B
Knodishall LC (TMO) 9A
KNOTTINGLEY 40A
Knottingley (Wormersley Road) LC (CCTV) 40A
Knottingley Depot (KY) 40A
Knottingley East Jn 40A
Knottingley Sidings 40A
Knottingley South Jn 40A
Knottingley West Jn 40A

L

Laburnum Farm LC (UWC) 18D
Lackenby Steel Works 47B
Ladysbridge LC (UWG) 5E
LAINDON 3B
Laings LC (UWC) 48B
(Laisterdyke East Jn) 41
(Laisterdyke West Jn) 41
Laisterdyke Yard 41
Lakenham 6C
Lakenham Viaduct 6C
LAKENHEATH 13A
Lakenheath LC (MCB-OD) 13A
Lakenheath No.8 LC (R/G) 13A
LAKESIDE CENTRAL (Cleethorpes Coast Light Rly) 27D
Lamarsh School Lane LC (UWC) 5E
Lamesley Crossover 21B
Lancaster Road Jn 45A
Landing Lane Bridge 19
Landspring Dyke LC (UWC) 8
Lane Head LC (Gatebox) 43B
Langford LC (AHBC) 26A
Langley Jn Aggregates Terminal 15B
Langley Jns 15B
Langley Moor Viaduct 20C
Langley South Jn 15B
Langley South Jn 24B
Langwith Jn (Shirebrook) 29A
LANGWITH WHALEY-THORNS 29A
Langworth LC (MCB) 27A
Langworth SB (L) 27A
Langworth Viaduct 27A
Larpool Viaduct 48C
Laundry Lane LC (AOCL+B) 11C
Lawsons LC (UWC) 25B
LEA BRIDGE 10B
Lea Bridge Road Viaduct 10B
Lea Jn 2B
Lea Valley Viaduct 10B
Leakes LC (UWC) 38A
LEALHOLM 48B
Leasingham Moor LC (MSL-X) 25B
Lebberston Road LC (Gatebox) (MG) 39C
LEEDS 36A
Leeds & Liverpool Canal (Gargrave) 42A
Leeds & Liverpool Canal (Leeds) 36A
Leeds (Stourton) FLT 36A
Leeds East Jn 36A
Leeds Midland Road 36A
Leeds West Jn 36A
Leeman Road Yard (York) 19
LEEMING BAR (Wensleydale Rly) 20D
LEIGH-ON-SEA 3C
LEISTON (disused) 9A
Leiston Station LC (TMO) 9A
Leonards LC (UWC) 12C
Letchworth EMU Carriage Servicing Depot 24C
LETCHWORTH GARDEN CITY 24C
Leverton LC (AHBC-X) 30B
Levington No.6 Gates LC (AHBC) 9A
LEVISHAM (NYMR) 48D
Lexden Viaduct 5E
Ley Street Yard Sidings 5A
LEYBURN (Wensleydale Rly) 20D
Leys Summit 15D
LEYTON MIDLAND ROAD 3A
LEYTONSTONE HIGH ROAD 3A
Lightcliffe Tunnel 41
Lilac Farm LC (UWC) 39D
Limbs No. 1 LC (UWC) 29A
Lime Kiln LC (AOCL+B) (Woodbridge) 9A
Limekiln Road LC HGV LC (Metro) 49
Limestone Viaduct 34A
LINCOLN CENTRAL 26B
Lincoln Road LC (MCG) (Enfield) 10B
Lincoln SCC (WS,SL,LG,BL,NL) 26B
LINCOLNSHIRE WOLDS RAILWAY 27C
Lindsell LC (R/G) 15C
Lindsey Refinery 31B
Lindsey Refinery Control Tower 31B
LING FARM HALT (Bressingham) 7F
Lingwood LC (MCG) 8
LINTLEY HALT (South Tynedale Rly) 43D
Linwith Lane LC (AHBC) 40B
Lipwood LC (UWC) 43E
Lipwood Viaduct (South Tyne) 43E
Lismore Circus Umbrella Tunnel 1A
Lissingley LC (AHBC-X) 27A
Litlington LC (AHBC) 24C
(Little Bytham) 16B
Little Hayes LC (UWC) 10A
Little London LC (MCB-OD) 31A
Little Mill Crossovers 23A
Little Mill LC (CCTV) 23A
Little Ouse Viaduct 13A
Little Steeping LC (AHBC-X) 26D
Littlebury Tunnel 11B
Littlefield Lane LC (MCB-OD) 31A
LITTLEPORT 12A
Littleport (Footpath) (R/G) 12A
Littleport Bypass (AHBC-X) 12A
Littleport LC (MCG) 12A
Littleport SB (L) 12A
Littlewood Viaduct 29A
Littleworth LC (MCB-OD) 24D
LIVERPOOL STREET (Crossrail) 2D
Liverpool Street IECC (L) 2A
LIVERPOOL STREET, LONDON 2A
LIMEHOUSE 3A
LINGWOOD 8
Lloyds & Martin LC (UWG) 12A
Lock Gate Mill LC (UWC) 8
Lockington LC (AHBC-X) 39A
LOCKWOOD 34C
Lockwood Tunnel 34C
Lockwood Viaduct (River Holme) 34C
Locomotion, NRM Annex 44B
Lodge Farm LC (UWC) (Honington) 25A
Lodge Farm LC (UWC) (Sherburn-in-Elmet) 40A
(Loftus) 48A
Lolham LC (CCTV) 16B
London End Jn (Shoeburyness) 3C
LONDON FIELDS 10B
London Gateway 4B
London Gateway Rail Control Centre (LG) 4B
London Road (Ipswich) 6B
London Road Jns (Carlisle) 43A
London Road LC (ABCL) (Beccles) 8
London Road LC (AHBC) (Spalding) 24D
London Road LC (TMO) (Boston) 25C
London Road Sidings 43A
London Road Viaduct (Sheffield) 27E
London Tunnel 1 (Stratford Portal) (HS1) 2B
London Tunnel 2 (Dagenham Portal) (HS1) 4A
London Tunnel 2 (Stratford Portal) (HS1) 2B
LONDON, FENCHURCH STREET 3A
LONDON, KING'S CROSS 14A
LONDON, LIVERPOOL STREET 2A
Londonderry Sidings 45B
Long Bridge Viaduct 11A
Long Byre LC (AHBC-X) 43B
Long Drain LC (UWC) 8
Long Lane LC (CCTV) 20B
Long Plantation LC (UWC) 39E
LONGBECK 48A
Longbeck LC (MCB) 48A
Longbeck SB (L) 48A
LONGBENTON (Metro) 49
Longhirst LC (CCTV) 22B
Longlands Jn 20B
Longlands Tunnel 20B
Loversall Carr Jn 17C
Loversall Jn 17C
Low Eggborough LC (UWC) 40B
Low Ellers Curve Jn 17C
Low Farm LC (UWC) 8
Low Fell Jn 21B
Low Fell Royal Mail Tyneside 21B
Low Gates Goods Yard 20B
Low Gates LC (MCB) 20B
Low Gates SB (LG) 20B
Low Green Farm LC (UWC) 39A
LOW MOOR 41
Low Row LC (MCB) 43B
Low Row SB (LR) 43B
Low Scampston LC (AHBC-X) 39E
Low Street LC (CCTV) 4B
LOWESTOFT 8A
Lowestoft Harbour 8A
Lowestoft SB (L) 8A
Lowfield LC (UWC) 40D
Lowfield No.2 LC (UWC) 39C
LOWTHORPE (disused) 39B
Lowthorpe LC (AHBC-X) 39B
Lucker LC (CCTV) 23A
Lucks Road LC (AHBC-X) 24D
LUDBOROUGH (Lincolnshire Wolds Rly) 27C
Lund Lane LC (UWC) 38A
Lymn Bank LC (AOCL+B-X) 26D
Lynemouth Power Station 23C
Lynemouth SB 23C
Lynemouth Smelter 23C
Lynemouth Works LC (AOCL) 23C

M

M1 Bridge (Ardsley) 36A
M1 Bridge (Dodworth) 34C
M1 Bridge (Garforth) 36B
M1 Bridge (Holbeck) 36A
M1 Bridge (Kiverton) 30A
M1 Bridge (Treeton) 28
M1 Bridge (Woodlesford) 36A
M1 Viaduct (Tinsley) 28
M11 Bridge (Elsenham) 11B
M11 Bridge (Foxton) 24C
M11 Bridge (Stansted Mountfitchet) 11B
M11 Spur Bridge (Great Chesterford) 11B
M18 Bridge (Bessacarr) 17C
M18 Bridge (Rossington) 17C
M18 Bridge (St. Catherines Jn) 17C
M180 Bridge (Elsham) 33C
M25 Bridge (Crews Hill) 24A
M25 Bridge (Harold Wood) 5B
M25 Bridge (Ockendon) 3B
M25 Bridge (Theobalds Grove) 10B
M25 Bridge (Waltham Cross) 10B
M25 Bridge (West Horndon) 3B
M4 Bridge (Kew East Jn) 1A
M6 Bridges (Pettril Bridge) 43A
M62 Bridge (Ardsley) 36A
M62 Bridge (Brighouse) 37A
M62 Bridge (Eastrington) 38A
M62 Bridge (Ferrybridge) 40A
M62 Bridge (Glasshoughton) 35B
M62 Bridge (Heck) 18A
M62 Bridge (Knottingley) 40C
M62 Bridge (Normanton) 35B
M62 Bridge (Rawcliffe) 40B
M621 Bridge (Cottingley) 37B
M621 Bridge (Geldard Road) 36A
M621 Bridge (Holbeck) 36A
Magdalen Road LC (MCB) 12B
Magdalen Road SB (MR) 12B
Maidendale 44C
Mallard Board July 1938 16B
MALTBY (disused) 34A
Maltby Colliery 34A
Maltby Colliery SB (M) 34A
Malting Lane LC (AHBC-X) 25B
Maltings LC (UWC) (Woodbridge) 9A
Maltings LC (UWG) (St. Margarets) 11A
MALTON 39D
Malton LC (MCB) 39D
Malton SB (M) 39D
MANEA 13C
Manea LC (MCB) 13C
Manea SB (M) 13C
MANGAPPS (Mangapps Farm) 10C
MANGAPPS FARM RAILWAY MUSEUM 10C
MANNINGTREE 6A
Manningtree East Jn 9B
Manningtree North Jn 6A
Manningtree South Jn 6A
Manningtree South Jn LC (CCTV) 6A
Manor Farm (112) LC (UWC) (Rillington) 39D
Manor Farm Crambe LC (UWC) 39D
Manor Farm LC (UWC) (Barton) 39D
Manor Farm LC (UWC) (Burton Agnes) 39B
Manor Farm LC (UWC) (Langworth) 27A
Manor Farm LC (UWC) (Saltmarshe) 38A
Manor Farm LC (UWC) (Strensall) 19
MANOR PARK 5A
Manor Sidings 4A
Manor Way LC (CCTV) (Rainham) 4A
Manor Way LC (UWC) (Tilbury) 4B
MANORS 22A
MANORS (Metro) 49
Mansfield Road LC (CCTV) 30B
Manston LC (R/G) 36B

Manton Wood Jn 30A
Manton Wood Siding 30A
MARCH 13C
March Down Yard 13C
March East Jn 13C
March East Jn LC (MCB) 13C
March East SB (ME) 13C
March South Jn LC (MCB) 13C
March South SB (MS) 13C
March Up Yard 13C
March West Jn 13C
March Whitemoor Jn 13C
Marchey's House Jn 23C
Marchey's House LC (MCB) 23C
Marchey's House SB (MH) 23C
Mares Close LC (UWC) 23C
Margaretting LC (R/G-X) 5C
MARKET RASEN 27A
Market Rasen LC (FP) (R/G) 27A
Market Rasen Viaducts 27A
Markham Summit 17A
MARKS TEY 5E
Marks Tey GF 5E
Marks Tey Jn 5E
Marks Tey Sand Terminal 5E
MARLEY HILL (Tanfield Rly) 44D
Marr House Farm LC (UWC)
(Broomfleet) 38B
Marr House Farm LC (UWC) (Malton) 39D
MARSDEN 37A
(Marsh East Jn) 31A
Marsh Lane Jn 36A
Marsh Lane LC (AHBC) (Immingham) 31C
Marsh Lane Sidings (Leeds) 36A
Marsh Lane Viaduct 36A
(Marsh North Jn) 31A
Marsh West Jn 31A
(Marshall Meadows) 23B
Marshalls LC (UWC) 42A
Marshes LC (UWC) 8
Marshgate Jn 17C
Marshgate Sidings 17C
Marshmoor 15A
MARSKE 48A
Marston Moor LC (Gatebox) 18D
Martin Road LC (UWC) 26B
Martins LC (UWC) 12A
MARTON (formerly ORMESBY) 47B
Marton Carr LC (AOCL+B) 47B
Marton Lane LC (ABCL) 47B
MARYLAND 2B
Maryland East Crossovers 2B
Masborough (Station North) Jn 28
Masborough Sorting Sdgs South Jn 28
(Masborough Station South Jn) 28
Masons LC (UWC) 26C
Masserellas LC 18A
Matt Pitts Lane LC (AOCL+B-X) 26D
Maud Foster LC (AHBC) 25C
Maxey LC (CCTV) 16B
Maypole Rasen LC (UWC) 27A
Mead Lane LC (FP) (R/G-X) 11A
Meadow Croft Farm LC (UWC) 31B
Meadow Gates LC (UWC) 39B
MEADOW WELL (Metro) 49
MEADOWHALL INTERCHANGE 28
Meads Lane LC (UWC) 39E
Meardsall LC (UWC) 26A
Medge Hall LC (Gatebox) (MG) 32B
MELDRETH 24C
Meldreth Road LC (AHBC) 24C
Melkridge Siding 43C
Mellis LC (AHBC-X) 6C
MELTON (SUFFOLK) 9A
Melton Lane LC (MG) 38B
Melton Lane SB (ML) 38B
Melton LC (Suffolk) (AOCL+B) 9A
Melton Sewage LC (UWC) 9A
MENSTON 41
Merchant Park 44E
Merchant Park Jn 44B
Merchant Park Test Track 44B
Merrings LC (UWG) 4B
METHERINGHAM 26B
Methley Jn 36A
Methley North LC (R/G) 36A
Methringham Up Siding 26B
Metro Tunnel 22A
METROCENTRE 21B
MEXBOROUGH 32A
Mexborough (East) Jn 32A
MICKLEFIELD 36B
Micklefield Jn 36B
Mickley LC (R/G) 21C
Middle Drove LC (R/G) 13C
MIDDLE ENGINE LANE (N.T.S.R.) 49
Middlemere LC (AHBC) 12C
Middlesborough Carriage Sidings 47B
Middlesborough SB (M) 47B
MIDDLESBROUGH 47B
Middlesbrough Goods Yard 47A
Middleton LC (ABCL) 9C
MIDDLETON PARK (Middleton Rly) 36D
MIDDLETON RAILWAY TRUST 36D
MIDDLETON TOWERS (disused) 12B
Middleton Towers LC (TMO) 12B
Middleton Towers Sand Terminal 12B
(Midland Jn (Dewsbury)) 37B
MID-NORFOLK RAILWAY 13B
MID-SUFFOLK LIGHT RAILWAY 12E
Mile End (Devonshire Street) 2B
Mile End LC (AHBC-X) (Shippea Hill) 13A
Milford Down Sidings 40A
Milford Jn 40A
Milford North 40A
Milford SB (M) 40A
Milford West Sidings 40A
Milford West Sidings Control Panel 40A
Mill Drove LC (AHBC-X) 12C
Mill Farm LC (UWC) (Drax) 40B
Mill Farm LC (UWC) (Lowthorpe) 39B
Mill Garth LC (UWC) 39D
Mill Green LC (CCTV) 24D
Mill Lane (UWC) 38A
Mill Lane Jn 41
Mill Lane Jn SB (M) 41
Mill Race Jn 28
Millfield 44C
MILLFIELD (Metro) 45B
Millfield Farm LC (UWC) 38A
Millmoor 28
Mills Exchange Sidings (Scunthorpe) 33A
Milne Viaduct 37A
Milner Royd Jn 37A
Milner Royd Jn SB (MR) 37A
Milton Estates No. 1 LC (UWC) 24D
Milton Fen LC (AHBC) 11C
Milton Village LC (Gatebox) (MCB) 43A
Mineral Quay (Immingham) LC (TMO) 31B
Mineral Quay Sidings (Immingham) 31B
Mingledale LC (UWC) 39B
MIRFIELD 37A
Mirfield East Jn 37A
Mirfield Viaduct (River Calder) 37A
MISTLEY 9B
Mistley LC (Footpath) (R/G) 9B
Mistley Up Sdg GF 9B
Mitre Bridge Curve 1A
Mitre Bridge Jn 1A
Mitre Bridge LC (CCTV) 1A
Moat Hills LC (CCTV) 17C
Molescroft Grange LC (UWC) 39A
Molewood Jn 24A
Molewood Tunnel 24A
Monk Bretton 35B
Monk Bretton Loop 35B
MONKSEATON (Metro) 49
Monkwearmouth Jn 45B
Monsanto LC (AOCL) 45A
Monsanto Siding Jn 45A
Montfichet Road Bridge 2B
MONUMENT (Metro) 49
Moody Lane LC (AOCL)
(West Marsh Jn) 31C
Moor Lane LC (UWC) 33C
MOOR ROAD (LEEDS)
(Middleton Rly) 36D
Moorends Farm LC (UWC) 32B
Moores LC (UWC) 11C
MOORGATE 14A
Moorgate Tunnel 14A
MOORTHORPE 32A
Moorthorpe Jn 32A
Moorthorpe LC (FP) (R/G) 32A
Moortown LC (AHBC-X) 27B
MORLEY 37B
Morley Tunnel 37B
MORPETH 22B
Morpeth Jn 22B
Morpeth North Jn 22B
Morpeth North LC (CCTV) 22B
Morpeth SB (M) 22B
Morston Hall No. 5 Gates LC (AHBC) 9A
(Mortimer Street Jn) 1A
Mortimer Street Viaduct 1A
Morton Grange Farm No. 4 LC (UWC) 47B
Moss Cottages LC (UWC) 43E
Moss LC (MCB-OD) 18A
Moulton LC (AHBC-X) 6C
Mount Bures LC (ABCL) 5E
Mount Pleasant Farm LC (UWC) 44C
Mountains LC (UWC) 25A
Mountnessing Jn 10A
Mucking LC (AHBC) 4B
Munceys LC (UWC) 12C
MURTON PARK
(Derwent Valley Light Railway) 19B
Museum GF
(Chappel & Wakes Colne) 5E
Muskham Viaduct 16C
Muston LC (AHBC) 39C
MYTHOLMROYD 37A
Mytholmroyd Viaduct 37A

N

NAFFERTON 39B
Nafferton LC (AHBC-X) 39B
Nairns LC (UWC) 11C
NATIONAL RAILWAY MUSEUM 19
National Railway Museum (Great Hall) 19C
National Railway Museum (South Hall) 19
Navarino Road Jn 1B
Naworth LC (AHBC-X) 43A
NCB Terminal (Immingham) 31B
NEASDEN 1A
Neasden Curve 1A
Neasden Freight Terminal 1A
Neasden Jn SB (NJ) 1A
Neasden South Jn 1A
NEEB LC (Open) 45A
NEEDHAM MARKET 6B
Nene Carriage Sidings (Peterborough) 16A
NENE VALLEY RAILWAY 42D
Nether Lane LC (AHBC-X) 39B
Nether Poppleton LC (AHBC) 18D
Neville Hill Depot (NL) 41A
Neville Hill East Jn 36A
Neville Hill Up Sidings 36A
Neville Hill West Jn 36A
NEW BARNET 15A
New Barnet Down Sidings 15A
New Barnet South Crossovers 15A
New Barnetby LC (MCB-CCTV) 30C
New Bedford River Viaduct 13C
New Bridge (Lakenheath) LC (UWC) 13A
NEW CLEE 31A
New Cut LC (UWC) (Malton) 39D
New Cut LC (UWC) (Reedham) 8
New Earswick LC (UWC) 19
New England North 16A
New England Sidings (West Yard) 16A
New Furnace Tunnel 41
NEW HOLLAND 31B
New Holland Bulk Services 31B
New House Farm LC (UWG) 5D
New Inn Farm (UWC) 18D
New Inn LC (Immingham) (Open) 31B
New Kew Jn 1A
New Moor LC (AOCL) 23C
New Oak Farm LC (UWC) 40B
NEW PUDSEY 41
New Pudsey Tunnel 41
NEW SOUTHGATE 14B
New Swinton Curve 32A
New York Farm LC (UWC) 18C
NEWARK CASTLE 26A
Newark Castle LC (MCB-CCTV) 26A
Newark Crossing 26A
Newark Crossing East Jn 26A
Newark Crossing South Jn 16C
NEWARK NORTH GATE 16C
Newark South Jn 16C
Newark Up Sidings 16C
NEWCASTLE 22A
Newcastle East Jn (Castle Jn) 22A
Newcastle South Jn 22A
Newcastle West Jn 22A
Newcombe's LC (UWC) 39D
Newham LC (CCTV) 23A
Newmans LC (UWC) 10A
NEWMARKET 11C
NEWPORT (Essex) 11B
Newport East Jn 46C
Newport Viaduct 11B
Newsham LC (MCB) 23C
Newsham North Jn 23C
Newsham SB (N) 23C
Newthorpe LC (UWC) 36B
NEWTON AYCLIFFE 44B
Newton Flotman LC (AHBC-X) 6C
(Newton Hall) 20C
NEWTONDALE (NYMR) 48D
Niffany LC (UWC) 42A
Niffany Viaduct (River Aire) 42A
No. 13 LC (UWC) (Brundall) 8
No. 132 LC (UWC) (Blotoft) 25B
No. 134 LC (UWC) (Blotoft) 25B
No. 135 LC (UWC) (Blotoft) 25B
No. 161 LC (UWC) (Alnmouth) 23A
No. 162 LC (UWC) (Alnmouth) 23A
No. 176 LC (East Tilbury) 4B
No. 18 LC (UWC) (Sibsey) 26D
No. 193 LC (R/G) (Tweedmouth) 23B
No. 2 LC (UWC) (Brundall) 8
No. 22 LC (UWC) (St. James Deeping) 24D
No. 23 LC (UWC) (Acle) 8
No. 24 LC (UWC) (St. James Deeping) 24D
No. 26 LC (UWC) (Buckenham) 8
No. 28 LC (UWC) (Healing) 31A
No. 29 LC (UWC) (Great Coates) 31A
No. 30 LC (UWC) (Cantley) 8
No. 30 LC (UWC) (Sibsey) 26D
No. 316 LC (UWC) (Saxilby) 26C
No. 319 LC (UWC) (Saxilby) 26C
No. 35 LC (Market Rasen) 27A
No. 36 LC (UWC) (Sleaford) 25C
No. 42 LC (UWC) (Spalding) 24D
No. 43 Gate LC (CCTV)
(London Gateway) 4B
No. 50 LC (UWC) (Spalding) 24D
No. 52 LC (UWC) (Spalding) 24D
No. 53 LC (UWC) (Haddiscoe) 8
No. 54 LC (UWC) (Haddiscoe) 8
No. 56 LC (UWC) (Haddiscoe) 8
No. 58 LC (UWC) (Somerleyton) 8
No. 59 LC (UWC) (Somerleyton) 8
No. 6 LC (UWC) (Ancaster) 25A
No. 66 LC (FP) (R/G) (St. Neots) 15C
No. 67 LC (UWC) (Somerleyton) 8
No. 68 LC (Market Rasen) 27A
No. 71 LC (FP) (R/G) (St. Neots) 15C
No. 72 LC (UWC) (Oulton Broad North) 8
No. 75 LC (UWC) (Spalding) 24D
No. 76 LC (UWC) (Spalding) 24D
No. 82 LC (R/G) (Thirsk) 20A
No. 85 LC (UWC) (Spalding) 24D
No. 89 LC (R/G) (Thirsk) 20A
No. 93 LC (Hartford Bridge) 13B
Noblethorpe LC (MG) 18A
Norden Farm No. 2 LC (UWC) 40A
Norden's Barn Farm LC (UWC) 40A
Nordic Steel Terminal 31B
Normanby Park GF 33B
NORMANTON 35B
Normanton LC (AHBC-X) (Bottesford) 25A
Normanton LC (FP) (R/G) 35B
NORTH BAY RAILWAY (Scarborough) 19A
North Blyth 23C
North Carr LC (MCB-OD) 17B
North Cove LC (UWC) 8
North Crossing LC (AOCL) 40B
North Drain Viaduct 24D
NORTH ELMHAM (Mid-Norfolk Rly)
(disused) 13B
NORTH FAMBRIDGE 10A
North Fen LC (AHBC-X) 13C
North FLT (Felixstowe) 9A
North Gate LC (open) 47B
North Green LC (AOCL+B) 9C
North Kelsey LC (AHBC-X) 27B
North Lincoln Jn 33A
North London Incline 1A
North London Line Viaduct 14A
NORTH NORFOLK RAILWAY 8
North Pole Depot (NP) 1A
North Pole Jn 1A
North Pole Reception Sidings 1A
North Pole Transfer Sidings 1A
NORTH ROAD (Darlington) 44B
North Sea Supply Base Wharf 47A
North Seaton LC (Gatebox) (MCB) 23C
North Seaton Viaduct 23C
NORTH SHIELDS (Metro) 49
North Shields Tunnel (Metro) 49
(North Shore Jn) 44C
NORTH STATION (Southend Pier) 3D
North Tees LC (AOCL) 45A
NORTH THORESBY
(Lincolnshire Wolds Rly) 27C
NORTH TYNESIDE STEAM RAILWAY 49
NORTH WALSHAM 8
North Walsham Terminal 8
NORTH WEALD (Epping Ongar Rly) 4C
North Woolwich Portal 2C
NORTH YORKSHIRE MOORS
RAILWAY 48D
North/South Access LC (Open) 45A
NORTHALLERTON 20B
Northallerton East Jn 20B
Northallerton High Jn 20B
Northallerton Low Jn 20B
Northallerton Tunnel 20B
Northallerton Up Sidings 20B
NORTHALLERTON WEST
(Wensleydale Rly) 20D
Northfleet Hope Terminal 4B
Northorpe LC (MG) 30C
Northorpe SB (N) 30C
NORTHUMBERLAND PARK 10B
NORTHUMBERLAND PARK (Metro) 49
Northumberland Park LC (CCTV) 10B
Northway LC (open) 47B
Norton East (Blackwells) LC (UWC) 44C
Norton LC (Gatebox) (MCB) 40D
Norton Marsh LC (UWC) 8
Norton Parks LC (UWC) 39D
Norton-on-Tees East Jn SB (NE) 44C
Norton-on-Tees LC (MCB) 44C
Norton-on-Tees SB (N) 44C
Norton-on-Tees South Jn SB (NS) 44C
Norton-on-Tees West Jn LC SB (NW) 44C
Norton-on-Tees West LC (MCB) 44C
Norwell Lane LC (CCTV) 16C
NORWICH 7A
Norwich Road (Salhouse)
LC (AHBC-X) 8
Norwood Junction 21B
Norwood LC (MG) (Shirebrook) 29A
Norwood Road LC (AHBC) 13C
Nottingham Branch Jn (Grantham) 16C
Nunnery Depot (Supertram) 50
Nunnery Jn (Sheffield) 28
Nunnery Main Line Jn 28
NUNTHORPE 47B
(Nunthorpe Jn) 47B
Nunthorpe LC (MCB) 47B
Nunthorpe SB (N) 47B
Nursery LC (UWG) 6A

O

Oakbutts LC (UWC) 19
Oakcliffe LC (UWC) 39D
Oakenshaw Farm LC (UWC) 35B
Oakenshaw Jn 35B
Oakenshaw South Jn 35B
OAKLEIGH PARK 14B
(Oaktree Jn) 44C
Oakwood Farm LC (R/G) 18D
OAKWORTH (KWV Rly) 42B
OCKENDON 3B
(Octagonal SB) 25C
(Offord & Buckden) 15C
Offord LC (CCTV) 15C
Old Bedford River Viaduct 13C
Old Hall Mill LC (UWC) 8
(Old Haltwhistle SB) 43C
OLD HEATH (Mangapps Farm) 10C
Old Jn LC (UWC) 31A
Old Kew Jn 1A
Old Lady LC (UWC) 8
Old Leake LC (AHBC-X) 26D
Old Oak Common East Jn 1A
Old Oak Common Sidings 1A
Old Oak Common West Jn 1A
(Old Oak Jn) 1A
Old Oak Sidings (Willesden) 1A
OLD STREET 14A
Old Trent Dyke Viaduct 26A
Old Trent Road LC (MCB) 26C
OLLERTON (disused) 29A
Olympia Park Jn 2B
One Mile Bridge 7A
ONGAR (Epping Ongar Rly) 4C
Orient Way Depot (OW) 10B
ORTON MERE (Nene Valley Rly) 42D
(Orwell) 9A
Osterfen LC (CCTV) 16C
(Otterington) 20A
OULTON BROAD NORTH 8
Oulton Broad North Jn 8
Oulton Broad North LC (MCB) 8
Oulton Broad North SB (OB) 8
OULTON BROAD SOUTH 8
Oulton Broad Swing Bridge SB & GF 8
Ouse Dock (Goole) 38A
Ouseburn Viaduct 22A
Ouston Crossovers 21A
Outgates Farm LC (UWC) 39B
OUTWOOD 36A
Owlett Hall LC (UWC) 40A
Owston Grange Farm No. 1 (UWC) 18A
Ox Pasture Lane LC (FPG) 26B
Oxbridge Sidings 44C
OXENHOPE (KWV Rly) 42B
Oxmardyke LC (Gatebox) (MCB) 38A
Oxmarsh LC (MG) 31B
Oxmarsh SB (OX) 31B
Oxspring Tunnel 34C
Oxspring Viaduct (River Don) 34C

P

PADDINGTON (Crossrail) 2D
Paddock Viaduct 34C
(Padnal) 13A
(Palace Gates) 14B
Palgrave LC (AHBC-X) 6C
PALLION (Metro) 45B
PALMERS GREEN 24A
Palmers No. 142 LC (UWC) 13A
PALMERSVILLE (Metro) 49
Palmersville LC (FP) (Metro) 49
PANNAL 18C
(Pannal Jn) 18C
Pardon Mill LC (FP) 11A
Park Cottage LC (UWC) 39A
Park Drain LC (CCTV) 17B
Park House Farm LC (UWC) 23C
PARK LANE (Metro) 45B
Park Lane Jn 22A
Park Lane LC (BW) (Theobalds Grove) 10B
Park Lane LC (UWC) (Askern) 40D
Park Lane LC (UWC) (Wymondham) 13B
Park Lane Sdgs (Darlington) 20B
Park Road LC (CCTV) (Spalding) 24D
Park Sidings (Boston) 25C
Parkeston Carriage Sidings 9B
Parkeston Container Terminal 9B
Parkeston East LC (CCTV) 9B
Parkeston Goods Jn 9B
Parkeston New Yard 9B
Parkeston SB (P) 9B
Parkeston Tip Sidings 9B
Parkeston West LC (MCB) 9B
Parkeston Yard 9B
Parkgate Jn (Rotherham) 28
(Parkgate Jn) (Darlington) 44B
Parkside Farm LC (UWC) 35B
Parrots No. 22 LC (UWC) 13A
Parrots No. 23 LC (UWC) 13A
Parvins No. 81 (R/G) LC 20A
Pasture Lane LC (BW) 39E
Pasture Road LC (ABCL) 31B
Pasture Street LC (MCB-OD) 31A
Pattisons LC (UWC) 44C
Peakirk LC (UWC) 24D
Peascliff Crossovers 16C
Peascliff Tunnel 16C
PEASHOLM (North Bay Rly) 19A
Peckfield LC (BW)(UWC) 36B
PEGSWOOD 22B
PELAW (Metro) 49
Pelaw Jn 46A
Pelaw Metro Jn 46A
Pelaw North Jn 49
Pelaw Sidings (Metro) 49
Pelaw South Jn 49
Pelham Street Jn 26B
Pemberton LC (UWG) 11C
PENISTONE 34C
Penistone Emergency Panel 34C
Penistone Road Bridge (Sheffield) 28
Penistone Viaduct (River Don) 34C
PERCY MAIN (Metro) 49
PERCY MAIN (N.T.S.R) 49
PETERBOROUGH 16A
(Peterborough East) 16A
Peterborough East Jn 16A
Peterborough GBRf Depot 16A
PETERBOROUGH NENE VALLEY (Nene Valley Rly) 42D
Peterborough North Depot 16A
Peterborough SB (P) 16A
Peterborough Virtual Quarry 16A
Petteril Bridge 43A
Petteril Bridge Jn 43A
Pettys No. 1 LC (UWC) 42A
Philip Lane LC (R/G) 40E
Phillips No. 2 LC (AOCL) 45A
Phillips No. 3 LC (AOCL) 45A
Phillips Siding Jn 45A
Phillips Siding Jn GF 45A
PICKERING (NYMR) 48D
Picton Grange No. 1 LC (UWC) 44C
Picton Grange No. 2 LC (UWC) 44C
(Picton Jn) 44C
Picton LC (CCTV) 44C
Pig's Bay (Qinetiq) 3E
Pile Sdgs GF 22A
Pilgrim St Crossover 22A
Pilleys Lane LC (AHBC) 25C
Pillwood Farm LC (UWC) 39A
Pilmoor) 20A
Pipers Wood Summit 17A
Pitmore Viaduct 5E
PITSEA 3B
Pitsea Hall LC (CCTV) 4B
Pitsea Jn 3B
Plain Moor LC (UWC) 39D
PLAISTOW (LUL) 3A
Plantation LC (UWC) 8
Plants LC (R/G) 16B
Platts LC (UWC) 40B
Plawsworth Viaduct 21A
Pleasants LC (R/G) 12A
Plessey Crossovers 22B
Plessey Road LC (AOCL) 23C
Plessey Viaduct 22B
Pockerley Wagonway (Beamish Museum) 42E
Polka Siding 45B
Pond Street LC (UWG) 8
PONDERS END 10B
Ponsbourne Tunnel 24A
PONTEFRACT BAGHILL 35A
Pontefract East Jn 40A
PONTEFRACT MONKHILL 35B
PONTEFRACT TANSHELF 35B
Pontefract West Jn 35B
(Poole Street) 14A
Pools LC (R/G-X) 13A
Poplar Drove LC (UWC) (Ely) 12C
Poplar Drove LC (UWC) (Littleport) 12A
Poplar Farm LC (MCB-OD) 13B
(Poplar Jn) 1A
POPPLETON 18D
Poppleton LC (MG) 18D
Poppleton SB (P) 18D
Pork Lane LC (AHBC) 6A
(Port Clarence) 45A
Port Clarence GF 45A
Port Clarence Jn 45A
Port Jn 4B
Port of Blyth LC (TMO) 23C
Port of Parkeston Quay 9B
Portobella Farm LC (UWC) 39D
Post Office Lane HABD 40C
Post Office Lane LC (AHBC) 40C
Potland Burn Disposal Point 23C
Potland LC (AOCL) 23C
Potteric Carr Jn 17C
POTTERS BAR 15A
Potters Bar Tunnels 15A
Potters Grange Jn 38A
Poulters LC (UWC) 40A
Pratts LC (UWC) 8
Preston Manor LC (UWC) 20C
Preston Refuge Siding (Metro) 49
PRIMROSE HILL (disused) 1A
Primrose Hill Jn 1A
Primrose Hill Tunnels 1A
Prince of Wales LC (MCB) 35B
Prince of Wales SB (P) 35B
PRINCE REGENT (DLR) 2C
Priory View / Whitehouse LC (UWC) 8
Prison Siding (Wakefield) 35B
PRITTLEWELL 10A
PRUDHOE 21C
Prudhoe LC (MCB) 21C
Prudhoe SB (PE) 21C
Prudhoe Street (Metro) 49
PUDDING MILL LANE 2B
Pudding Mill Lane Jn (future) 2E
Pudding Mill Lane Portal (future) 2E
Pumphouse LC (UWC) 25B
PURFLEET 4A
Purfleet Deep Wharf 4A
Purfleet LC (CCTV) 4A
Purfleet Long Siding 4A
Purfleet Long Siding Jn North 4A
Purfleet Long Siding Jn South 4A
Purfleet Thames Terminal 4A
Pushpole LC (UWC) 31A
Pyewipe Jn 26B
Pyewipe Road LC (MG) 31C
Pyewipe Road SB (P) 31C

Q

Quadring LC (AHBC-X) 25B
Quality LC (UWC) 43E
Quarrington LC (AHBC) 25A
Quarry Hill Jn 36A
(Quarry Jn) 34B
Queen Adelaide Bridge (Ely) 13A
Queen Adelaide LCs (AHBC-X) (Ely) 12A
Queen Alexandra Bridge (Sunderland) 45B
Queen Elizabeth Bridge 4A
Queen Elizabeth Dock (Hull) 38C
Queen Elizabeth II Bridge (Metro) 49
QUEENS PARK 1A
Queens Park Depot (LUL) 1A
Queens Park Jn (LUL) 1A
Queens Road (Sheffield) 27E
(Queens Road Jn) 31B
Queen's Road Tunnel 10B

R

Rackheath Road LC (AHBC-X) 8
Rail Service Centre (Scunthorpe) 33A
Railway Dock (Goole) 38A
Rainbow Bridge Viaduct (River Don) 32A
RAINHAM 4A
Rainham Creek Bridge 4A
Rainham Creek Viaduct (HS1) 4A
Rainham LC (CCTV) 4A
Rampart Lane LC (UWC) 40B
Ramsey Road LC (AHBC) 13C
Ramsons LC (UWC) 34A
Ranelagh Road LC (MCG) 6B
Ranskill Emergency Crossovers 17A
Ranskill Gatebox 17A
Ranskill LC (MCB) 17A
Ranskill Loops 17A
(Raskelf) 20A
Rat Hole Lane LC (UWC) 30B
RAUCEBY 25A
Rauceby LC (MCH) 25A
Rauceby SB (RY) 25A
RAVENSTHORPE 37B
Rawcliffe Branch LC (UWC) 40B
Rawcliffe LC (AHBC) 40B
RAWCLIFFE 40B
Raws LC (UWC) 42A
RAYLEIGH 10A
Reading Lane Jn 10B
Reasby Manor LC (UWC) 27A
Rectory Farm LC (UWG) 24C
RECTORY ROAD 10B
Rectory Road LC (Diss) (AHBC-X) 6C
Red Barns Tunnel 22A
Red Cap Lane LC (ABCL) 25C
Red House Farm LC (UWC) (Newsham) 23C
Red House Farm LC (UWC) (Wickham Market) 9A
Red Lane LC (MG) 35B
Redbourn Yard (Scunthorpe) 33A
REDCAR CENTRAL 48A
Redcar Coke Ovens 47B
REDCAR EAST 48A
Redcar LC (MCB) 48A
Redcar Mineral Terminal 47B
Redcar Ore Terminal 47B
Redcar Ore Terminal Jn 47B
Redcar SB (R) 48A
Redcar Steel Works 47B
REDMIRE (Wensleydale Rly) 20D
Redmoor LC (AOCL) 13C
REEDHAM (Norfolk) 8
Reedham Accomodation LC (UWC) 8
Reedham High LC (UWC) 8
Reedham Jn SB (RJ) 8
Reedham Occupation LC (UWC) 8
Reedham Swing Bridge 8
Reedham Swing Bridge SB (RB) 8
Reedham Viaduct 8
Reepham LC (CCTV) 27A
REGENT CENTRE (Metro) 49
Regent Oil LC (TMO) 31B
Regent Street LC (CCTV) 6B
Regent's Canal Bridge (Bow) 2B
Regent's Canal Bridge (Cambridge Heath) 10B
Regents Canal Bridge (Limehouse) 3A
Relly Mill Viaduct 20C
Rendlesham Viaduct 24A
Renishaw Slitting Mill LC (UWC) 27E
Renwick Road Jn 4A
RETFORD (HL) 17A
RETFORD (LL) 30B
Retford North 17A
Retford South Jn 17A
Retford Western Jn 17A
Reyrolles Jn (Metro) 49
Richies LC (UWC) 18A
RICHMOND 1A
Richmond Hill Tunnel 36A
Richmond SB (GB) 1A
RIDING MILL 43E
Ridley Hall, South Tyne Viaduct 43E
Ridleys Sdg (Immingham) 31B
Rigton LC (MCB-CCTV) 18C
Rillington LC (AHBC-X) 39E
Ripple Lane 4A
Ripple Lane East Jn 4A
Ripple Lane Exchange Sidings 4A
Ripple Lane West Jn 4A
Ripple Lane West Yard 4A
River Aire Bridge (Ferrybridge) 40A
River Aire Bridge (Leeds) 36A
River Aire Bridge (Temple Hirst) 18A
River Aire Viaduct (Drax) 40B
River Aire Viaduct (Fairburn) 40A
River Aire Viaduct (Gargrave) 42A
River Aire Viaduct (Saltaire) 41
River Aln Viaduct 23A
River Bank LC (UWC) 26C
River Blyth Bridge 8
River Board LC (UWC) 8
River Calder Bridge (Healey Mills) 37B
River Calder Bridge (Mirfield) 37A
River Calder Viaduct (Horbury) 34B
River Calder Viaduct (Milner Royd) 37A
River Calder Viaduct (Turners Lane) 35B
River Calder Viaduct (Whitwood) 35B
River Calder Viaducts (Greetland) 37A
River Cam Bridge (Cambridge North) 11C
River Cam Viaduct (Foxton) 24C
River Can Viaduct 5C
River Chelmer Viaduct 5C
River Coquet Viaduct 23A
River Derwent Viaduct 21B
River Devon Viaduct 26A
River Don & Navigation Viaduct (Kirk Sandall) 32B
River Don Bridge (Conisbrough) 32A
River Don Viaduct (Doncaster) 17C
River Don Viaduct (Hexthorpe) 32A
River Esk Viaduct (Glaisdale) 48B
River Fynn Viaduct 9A
River Great Ouse Bridge (Ely) 12A
River Great Ouse Bridges (Downham Market) 12A
River Idle Viaduct (Retford) 17A
River Lea Bridge (Bow) 2B
River Lea Bridge (Bromley-by-Bow) 3A
River Lea Bridge (Lea Jn) 2B
River Meden Bridge (Welbeck) 29A
River Nene Bridge (Peterborough) 16A
River Nene Viaduct (Peterborough) 16A
River Nidd Bridge (Hammerton) 18D
River Roding Bridge (Barking) 3A
River Rother Viaduct 28
River Ryton Viaduct 30A
River Skerne Viaduct (Aycliffe) 20C
River Skerne Viaduct (Darlington) 20B
River Stour Viaduct 6A
River Ter Viaduct 5C
River Thames Bridge (Kew) 1A
River Trent Viaduct (Gainsborough) 26C
River Waveney Viaduct 6C
River Went Viaduct (Pontefract) 35A
River Wharfe Viaduct (Ulleskelf) 40A
River Wiske Viaduct (Rounton) 44C
River Wissey Viaduct 12A
River Worth Viaduct 41
Riversdale Farm LC (UWC) 19
Riverside Freight Depot (Norwich) 7A
(Riverside Jn) 22A
Roadside LC (UWC) 39A
Robarts 1 LC (UWG) 11A
Robarts 3 LC (UWG) 11A
Robbery Lane Viaduct 15B
Roberts Road Depot (Doncaster) 17C
Robin Hood Tunnel 34C
Robin's Bottom Plantation LC (UWC) 39E
Robinson LC (UWC) 31B
Robinson Road LC (TMO) 31B
Robinsons LC (UWC) 26B

ROCHFORD 10A
Rohm Haas LC (AOCL) 45A
Romanby Road LC (CCTV) 20B
ROMFORD 5B
Romford Engineer's Depot 5B
Romford Jn 5B
Romford London End Jn 5B
Romford ROC 5B
Rookery No. 1 LC (UWC) 10A
Rose Lane LC (UWC) (Attleborough) 13B
Rose Lane LC (UWC) (Church Fenton) 40A
(Rossington) 17A
Rossington Colliery Jn 17C
Rossington Emergency Crossovers 17C
Rossington GSP 17C
Rossington LC (CCTV) 17A
ROTHERHAM CENTRAL 28
Rotherham Central Jn 28
Rotherham Main LC 28
ROTHERHAM MASBOROUGH (disused) 28
Rotherham Steel Terminal 28
Roudham Hall Road LC (UWC) 13B
ROUGHTON ROAD 8
(Roughton Road Jn) 8
Roundabout Drove LC (UWC) 12C
(Roundham Jn) 13A
ROUNDHOUSE HALT (Barrow Hill) 28A
Roundwood Chord 32A
Roundwood Exchange Sidings 32A
Roundwood Steel Works 32A
Rounton Gates LC (AHBC-X) 44C
Routes LC (R/G) 9A
Rowland Hall LC (AHBC-X) 38A
ROWLEY (Beamish Museum) 42E
Rowston LC (MCB-OD) 25B
Roxby Gullet 33B
Roxton Siding LC (MCB-OD) 31A
Royal Border Bridge 23B
Royal Mint St. Jn 3A
Royal Oak Farm LC (UWC) 39C
Royal Oak LC (AHBC-X) 39C
Royal Oak Portal 2D
ROYAL VICTORIA (DLR) 2C
Royal Victoria Portal 2C
ROYDON 11A
Roydon LC (CCTV) 11A
Roydon Lock LC (UWG) 11A
ROYSTON 24C
Royston Branch Viaduct 34B
(Royston Jn) 35B
Ruckholt Road Bridge 10B
Ruckholt Road Jn 10B
Ruddings Farm LC (UWC) 40E
(Runton East Jn) 8
Rushey Moor LC (UWC) 40D
Rushey Sidings LC (AHBC-X) 30B
RUSKINGTON 25B
Ruston's Tip LC (R/G) 26B
RUSWARP 48C
Ruswarp LC (ABCL) 48C
Ruswarp Viaduct 48C
Rye Hill Farm LC (UWC) 31A
RYE HOUSE 11A
Rye House Aggregates Terminal 11A
Ryhope Grange SB (RG, NS) 45B
Ryhope Grange Sidings 45B
Rylstone 42A
Rylstone LC (TWO) 42A
Ryther Viaducts 18B

S

(S & D Crossing) 20B
Sadlers LC (FPS) 11A
St. Catherine's Jn 17C
(St. Dunstans) 41
St. Georges Road (Hull) LC (CCTV) 38C
St. Germans LC (AHBC) 12B
ST. JAMES (Metro) 49
St. James Bridge Jn (Gateshead) 22A
St. James Deeping LC (MCB-OD) 24D
St. James Jn (Goods) 17C
St. James Jn (Passenger) 17C
ST. JAMES STREET 10B
ST. MARGARETS 11A
St. Margarets LC (CCTV) 11A
ST. NEOTS 15C
St. Neots North Jn 15C
St. Neots South Jn 15C
(St. Quentin Park) 1A
SALHOUSE 8
SALTAIRE 41
SALTBURN 48A
SALTBURN MINATURE RAILWAY 48E
Saltburn No. 1 GF 48A
Saltburn No. 2 GF 48A
Saltburn Riding School LC (UWC) 48A
Saltburn Viaduct 48A
Saltburn West Jn 48A
Saltend 38C
Salterhebble Down & Up Tunnels 37A
SALTMARSHE 38A
Saltmarshe LC (MCB) 38A
Saltmarshe SB (S) 38A
Salvation Army Colony No. 2 LC 3C
Sand Bank Jn 17C
Sand Lane LC (UWC) 39E
SANDAL & AGBRIGG 35B
Sandfords Farm LC 10A
Sandhill Lane LC (MCB-OD) 40E
Sandhill LC (AHBC-X) 12A
SANDY 15C
Sandy Down Sidings 15C
Sandy Lane LC (UWC) 13B
Sandy North Jn 15C
Sandy South Jn 15C
Santon Foreign Ore Branch LC 33A
Santon LC (Norfolk) (AHBC-X) 13A
Santon Ore Mining LC (UWC) 33A
SAWBRIDGEWORTH 11A
Sawbridgeworth LC (CCTV) 11A
Sawston LC (CCTV) 11C
Sawston LC (UWC) 11C
SAXILBY 26C
Saxilby LC (MCB-OD) 26C
SAXMUNDHAM 9A
Saxmundham Jn 9A
Saxmundham Road LC (TMO) 9A
Saxmundham SB (ES) 9A
Scagglethorpe Grange LC (UWC) 39D
SCALBY MILL (North Bay Rly) 19A
Scalm Lane LC (R/G) 18B
SCARBOROUGH 39E
Scarborough Bridge (York) 19
Scarborough Bridge Jn 19
Scarborough Carriage Sidings 39E
School Corner LC (UWC) 23C
School Lane LC (FPG) 17A
Scopwick LC (MCB-OD) 26B
Scorborough LC (AHBC-X) 39A
Scotby LC (UWG) 43A
Scothern LC (AHBC-X) 27A
Screener LC (UWC) 30C
Scremerston LC (CCTV) 23B
Scrooby LC (UWC) 17A
SCRUTON (Wensleydale Rly) 20D
(Sculcoates) 38C
SCUNTHORPE 33A
Scunthorpe SB (S) 33A
Scunthorpe West Jn 33A
Seabrook Sidings 4B
SEABURN (Metro) 45B
Seacroft LC (AOCL+B-X) 26D
SEAHAM 45B
Seaham Harbour 45B
Seal Sands 45A
Seal Sands Biofuel Refinery 45A
Seal Sands Branch Jn 45A
Seal Sands LC (AOCL) 45A
Seal Sands Road LC (AOCL) 45A
Seal Sands Storage LC 45A
SEAMER 39E
Seamer SB (SR, YS) 39E
Seamer South Jn 39C
Seamer West Jn 39E
SEATON CAREW 45A
Seaton Carew Jn 45A
(Seaton Delaval) 23C
Seaton Snook Jn 45A
Seaton-on-Tees 45A
Seawheel Sidings 31B
Second Drove LC (AHBC-X) 13C
(Sedgefield) 20C
Seghill North LC (AHBC) 23C
SELBY 38A
Selby Canal Jn 38A
Selby Canal Viaduct 18A
Selby Dam Viaduct 18B
Selby Mine Sidings 40A
Selby Potter Group 38A
Selby Road LC (AHBC) 40D
Selby SB (S) 38A
Selby South Jn 38A
Selby Swing Bridge 38A
Selby West Jn 38A
(Sessay) 20A
SEVEN KINGS 5A
SEVEN SISTERS 10B
Seven Sisters Chord 10B
Seven Sisters Jn 10B
(Severus Jn) 19
Sewage Works Lane LC (UWG) (Sudbury) 5E
Sewerby LC (AHBC) 39B
Sewerston Lane LC (R/G-X) 25A
SHADWELL (DLR) 3A
Shadwell LC (UWC) 13B
Shady Lane LC (UWC) 42A
Shaftholme Jn 18A
Shaftholme Viaduct 18A
Shalfords LC (UWG) 5E
Shay Lane Viaduct 35B
Shearing No.2 LC (UWC) 8
(Sheepbridge) 27E
Sheepwash Viaduct 29A
SHEFFIELD 27E
Sheffield International Rail Freight Terminal 28
Sheffield North Jn 27E
Sheffield South Jn 27E
(Sheffield Victoria) 28
SHELFORD 11C
Shelford LC (CCTV) 11C
Shell Jn 47B
Shell Mex LC (Open) 31B
SHELLEY (Kirkless Light Rly) 34D
SHENFIELD 5B
Shenfield (Southend Line) Jn 5B
Shenfield Country End Jn 5B
Shenfield London End Jn 5B
Shenfield Stabling Sdgs 5B
Shepcote Lane East Jn 28
Shepcote Lane New Sidings 28
Shepcote Lane West Jn 28
SHEPLEY 34C
SHEPRETH 24C
Shepreth Branch Jn 11C
Shepreth LC (AHBC) 24C
Sherburn Jn 40A
SHERBURN-IN-ELMET 40A
Sherburn-in-Elmet LC (CCTV) 40A
SHERINGHAM 8
SHERINGHAM (North Norfolk Rly) 8
Sheringham East LC (open) 8
Shields Road Tunnel (Metro) 49
SHILDON 44B
Shildon (Prince of Wales) Tunnel 44B
Shildon SB (S) 44B
Ship Dock (Goole) 38A
SHIPLEY 41
Shipley East Jn 41
Shipley Scrapyard 41
Shipley South Jn 41
Shipley Tunnel 41
Shipley West Jn 41
SHIPPEA HILL 13A
Shippea Hill LC (MCB-OD) 13A
SHIREBROOK 29A
Shirebrook East Jn 29A
Shirebrook Jn SB (SJ) 29A
Shirebrook South Jn 29A
SHIREMOOR (Metro) 49
SHIREOAKS 30A
Shireoaks East Jn 30A
Shireoaks LC (CCTV) 30A
Shireoaks West Jn 30A
SHOEBURYNESS 3C
Shoeburyness Carriage Sidings (SN) 3C
Short Drove LC (UWC) 12C
Shrewsbury Road Bridge (Sheffield) 27E
Shrewsbury Road Carriage Sidings 27E
Shunter's Cabin GF (Thames Haven) 4B
Sibsey SB (S) 26D
Signal HR49 (Hull) 38C
SILKSTONE COMMON 34C
Silo Curve 1A
Silt Drove LC (UWC) 13C
SILVER STREET 10B
Simmon House LC (AHBC-X) 26D
Simon Storage East (Immingham) 31B
Simon Storage LC (UWB) (Immingham) 31B
Simon Storage North (Seal Sands) 45A
Simon Storage South (Seal Sands) 45A
Simon Storage West (Immingham) 31B
SIMONSIDE (Metro) 49
(Simpasture Jn) 44B
Simpsons LC (UWC) (Havenhouse) 26D
Simpsons LC (UWC) (Heckington) 25C
Sincil Bank LC (CCTV) 26B
Six Mile Bottom LC (AHBC) 11C
Sizewell LC (TMO) 9A
Sizewell Power Stn 9A
SKEGNESS 26D
Skegness Carriage Sidings 26D
Skegness SB (S) 26D
Skellow Jn 35A
SKELMANTHORPE (Kirkless Light Rly) 34D
Skelton Bridge 19
Skelton Bridge Jn 19
Skelton Jn 19
Skewbridge Tip LC (UWC) 26A
Skiff Inn LC (UWC) 21B
Skinningrove Works 48A
SKIPTON 42A
Skipton Middle Jn 42A
Skipton North Jn 42A
Skipton South Jn 42A
Skipton Up Sidings 42A
Slag Road (LC (TMO) 47B
SLAITHWAITE 37A
Slaithwaite Viaduct 37A
(Slater Quarry) 23B
SLEAFORD 25B
Sleaford East Jn 25B
Sleaford East LC (MCB) 25B
Sleaford East SB (SE) 25B
(Sleaford Jn (Boston)) 25C
Sleaford North Jn 25B
Sleaford North Jn LC (MCB-OD) 25B
Sleaford Sdgs GF (Boston) 25C
Sleaford Sidings (Boston) 25C
Sleaford South Jn 25B
Sleaford West Jn 25B
Sleaford West LC (MGW) 25B
Sleaford West SB (SW) 25B
SLEIGHTS 48C
Sleights LC (UWC) 26C
Slipe Lane LC (UWC) 11A
Sloley Church Lane LC (AHBC) 8
Sly Brother LC (MSL-X) 24D
Smeafield LC (CCTV) 23B
Smithfield Road LC (AHBC-X) 27B
(Snailwell Jn) 12C
Snailwell Sidings 12C
SNAITH 40B
Snaith & Pontefract Highway LC (AHBC-X) 40B
Snaith East LC (UWC) 40B
Snaith LC (AOCL+B) 40B
Snaith Road LC (AHBC) 40B
Snape LC (UWC) 9A
Snelland LC (AHBC-X) 27A
Snowdons LC (TMO) 9A
Soham Common LC (UWC) 12C
Soham Jn 12C
SOMERLEYTON 8
Somerleyton Swing Bridge 8
Somerleyton Swing Bridge SB (SB) 8
Sopers Farm Viaduct 24A
SOUTH ACTON 1A
South Acton Jn 1A
SOUTH BANK 47B
South Bank Coke Works 47B
South Bank Jn 47B
South Drain Viaduct 24D
South Drive LC (FP) (Metro) 49
South Drove LC (AHBC) 24D
SOUTH ELMSALL 35A
South Elmsall LC (UWC) 35A
South Farm No. 1 LC (UWC) 18A
South Farm No. 2 LC (UWC) 18A
South FLT (Felixstowe) 9A
SOUTH GOSFORTH (Metro) 49
South Gosforth Control Centre (Metro) 49
SOUTH HAMPSTEAD 1A
South Hampstead Tunnels 1A
SOUTH HYLTON (Metro) 45B
South Ings LC (UWC) 25B
South Kirkby Jn 35A
SOUTH MILFORD 40A
South Milford LC (FP) (R/G) 40A
South Scarle LC (AHBC) 26A
SOUTH SHIELDS (Metro) 49
SOUTH STATION (Southend Pier) 3D
SOUTH TOTTENHAM 10B
South Tottenham East Jn 10B
South Tottenham Jn SB (S) 10B
South Tottenham West Jn 10B
SOUTH TYNEDALE RAILWAY 43D
South West Sidings (Willesden) 1A
South Yorkshire Jns 17C
SOUTH YORKSHIRE SUPERTRAM 50
SOUTHBURY 10B
SOUTHEND AIRPORT 10A
SOUTHEND CENTRAL 3C
Southend Down Carriage Sidings 10A
SOUTHEND EAST 3C
SOUTHEND PIER RAILWAY 3D
Southend Royal Mail Terminal 10A
Southend Up Carriage Sidings 10A
SOUTHEND VICTORIA 10A
Southfarm Sidings 12A
Southfield Lane LC (UWC) 40B
Southfields LC (UWC) 38A
SOUTHMINSTER 10A
Southminster GF 10A
Southminster Magnox Sidings 10A
SOWERBY BRIDGE 37A
Sowerby Bridge Tunnel 37A
Sowerby Viaduct 37A
Spa Street LC (UWC) 26B
SPALDING 24D
(Spalding North Jn) 24D
Spalding Road (A16) (TMO) 25C
(Spalding South Jn) 24D
Spalding Up Sidings 24D
Speeton LC (AHBC) 39C
Spellbrook LC (CCTV) 11A
Spencers LC(UWC) 20B
Spinks Lane LC (R/G-X) 13B
Spital Jn 16A
Spital LC (UWC) 43E
Spital Sidings 16A
Spittal LC (Gatebox) (R/G) 23B
SPOONER ROW 13B
Spooner Row LC (MCB-OD) 13B
Sportsfield LC (UWC) 35B
Spratts Water LC (UWC) 8
Spring Lodge LC (AHBC) 40C
Springbank North Jn 38C
Springbank South Jn 38C
Springs Jn 41
Springs Tunnel 41
SPRINGWELL (Bowes Rly) 46B
Springwell Lane LC (AHBC) 20B
Springwood Jn 37A
Spronces LC (AHBC-X) 13B

SS Chemicals LC (AOCL)	45A	Stubbs Walden South LC (CCTV)	40D
ST PETERS (Metro)	45B	Stubbs Waldens North LC (CCTV)	40C
STADIUM OF LIGHT (Metro)	45B	Substation LC (UWC)	1A
Staggs Siding	38A	Sudbrook Lane LC (AHBC-X)	25A
Stainforth East GF	32B	SUDBURY (Suffolk)	5E
Stainforth Jn	32B	Sudforth Lane LC (CCTV)	40B
Stainforth Road LC (AHBC)	18A	Sugar Factory GF	38A
Stainton LC (AHBC-X)	27A	Summer Lane	34B
STALLINGBOROUGH	31A	Sun Lane LC (UWC)	41
Stallingborough LC (MCB-OD)	31A	Sun Wharf LC (AOCL+B)	9A
STAMFORD HILL	10B	SUNDERLAND	45B
Stamford LC (CCTV)	23A	Sunderland North End Jn	45B
Standedge Tunnels	37A	Sunderland North Tunnel	45B
STANFORD-LE-HOPE	4B	Sunderland South Dock	45B
Stanford-Le-Hope LC (CCTV)	4B	Sunderland South End Jn	45B
STANHOPE (Weardale Rly)	44A	Sunderland South Tunnels	45B
Stanhope Dock (Goole)	38A	SUNNISIDE (Tanfield Rly)	44D
Stanningley Tunnel	41	Suton LC (AHBC-X)	13B
Stanningley Bypass	41	Swainsthorpe LC (AHBC-X)	6C
Stanningley Viaduct	41	Swaithe Viaduct	34B
Stannington LC (CCTV)	22B	Swallwell Jn	21B
STANSTED AIRPORT	11B	Swan Fleet Lane LC (UWC)	38A
STANSTED AIRPORT PEOPLE MOVER	4E	Swinden Quarry	42A
Stansted Airport Tunnel	11B	SWINDERBY	26A
Stansted East Jn	11B	Swinderby LC (MG)	26A
Stansted GF	11B	Swinderby Road LC (AHBC)	26A
STANSTED MOUNTFICHET	11B	Swinderby SB (S)	26A
Stansted North Jn	11B	Swinedyke LC (R/G)	30C
Stansted South Jn	11B	SWINESHEAD	25C
STAR LANE (DLR)	2C	Swineshead LC (AHBC)	25C
STARBECK	18C	Swing Bridge Jn	7A
Starbeck LC (MCB)	18C	Swingbridge Viaduct (Somerleyton)	8
(Starbeck North Jn)	18C	SWINTON (S. Yorks)	32A
Starbeck SB (SS)	18C	Swinton Jn North	32A
Station Road LC (UWC)	26D	Swinton Jn South	32A
Steetley Sidings 'A' GF	20C	Switches Farm LC (UWG)	42A
STEETON & SILSDEN	42A	(Sykes Jn)	26C
Stepney Green Jn	2D	Sykes Lane LC (MCB-OD)	26C
STEVENAGE	15B		
(Stevenage Old Station)	15B	**T**	
Stifford Viaduct	3B	Tabrums Cross LC (UWC)	10A
(Stillington)	20C	Tallington Crossovers	16B
Stilton Fen Emergency Crossovers	15D	Tallington GFs	16B
Stilton Fen GSP	15D	Tallington LC (CCTV)	16B
Stocksbridge	29B	Tallington Sidings	16B
Stocksbridge Light Railway	29B	TANFIELD RAILWAY	44D
STOCKSFIELD	21C	Tankersley Tunnel	34B
STOCKSMOOR	34C	Tapton Jn	27E
Stocksmoor Jn	34C	Tattershall Road LC (AHBC)	25C
STOCKTON	44C	Taylors LC (UWC)	25A
Stockton Cut Jn	44C	Tees Bridge	44C
Stoddart Street Sdgs (Metro)	49	Tees Dock	47B
Stoke GSP	16B	Tees Dock Freightliner Terminal	47B
Stoke Jn	16B	Tees Dock Potash Terminal	47B
STOKE NEWINGTON	10B	Tees Dock Steel Terminal	47B
Stoke Newington Tunnel	10B	Tees Down Staging Sidings	46C
(Stoke SB)	16B	Tees No. 1 LC	46C
Stoke Summit	16B	Tees Riverside Intermodal Park	47A
Stoke Tunnel	16B	Tees SB (TY)	46C
Stokes Hall LC (UWC)	10A	Tees Up Yard	46C
Stonea LC (MCG)	13C	Tees Works Siding	47B
Stonea SB (S)	13C	Tees Yard	46C
Stonefield Farm No. 65 LC (UWC)	27A	TEES-SIDE AIRPORT	44C
Stonefield Farm No. 66 LC (UWC)	27A	Teesside EfW Plant	45A
Stones Sidings LC (UWC)	25C	(Temple Hirst)	18A
Stoneyhurst Road (Metro)	49	Temple Hirst Jn	18A
Stora GSP	4A	Temple Mills Depot (TI)	10B
Storrs Hill	37B	Temple Mills Depot Control Room SB (TM)	10B
Stourton Jn	36A	Temple Mills East Jn	2B
Stow Bardolph LC (CCTV)	12B	Temple Mills Lane Bridge	2B
Stow Park LC (CCTV) (Tillbridge Lane)	26C	Temple Mills West Jn	10B
Stowgate LC (AHBC-X)	24D	(Tempsford)	15C
Stowmaries No.1 LC (UWC)	10A	Tempsford LC (CCTV)	15C
STOWMARKET	6B	Tennyson Avenue LC (MCB)	12B
Stowmarket LC (MCB)	6B	Terrace Sidings (Lincoln)	26B
Stowmarket Stabling Point	6B	Tetheringrass Lane LC (UWC)	26C
Stracey LC (UWC)	8	Teversham LC (AHBC)	11C
Stranton Jn	45A	Thackley Tunnels	41
STRATFORD	2B	Thames Board Mills LC (MCB)	4A
Stratford (North London) SB (S)	2A	Thames Haven Jn	4B
Stratford Central Jn	2B	Thames Haven Yard	4B
Stratford Country End Crossovers	2B	Thames Oilport	4B
(Stratford Eastern Jn)	2B	Tharston Viaduct	6C
STRATFORD HIGH STREET (DLR)	2C	THE BOWES RAILWAY CO LTD	46B
STRATFORD INTERNATIONAL	2B	The Bridleway LC (UWC)	4B
Stratford International East Jn	2B	The Drove LC (UWC)	13A
Stratford International West Jn	2B	The Haggs LC (UWC)	32B
Stratford Low Level Tunnel	2B	THE MIDDEN HALT (Wells & Walsingham Rly)	7B
(Stratford Market)	2C	The Poplars LC (UWC)	44C
Stratford Market Depot (LUL)	2C	THEOBALDS GROVE	10B
Stratford Staff Halt (LUL)	2C	THETFORD	13A
Stratford Walk Bridge	2B	Third Drove LC (AHBC-X)	13C
Straws LC (UWC)	12C	THIRSK	20A
STREETHOUSE	35B	Thompsons LC (R/G) (Ranskill)	17A
Streethouse LC (CCTV)	35B	Thompsons LC (UWC) (Steeton & Silsden)	42A
Strensall LC (MCB)	19	Thonock Lane Farm LC (UWC)	30C
Strensall No. 1 LC (CCTV)	19	Thoresby Colliery	29A
Strensall No. 2 LC (CCTV)	19	Thoresby Colliery Jn SB (T)	29A
Strensall SB (S)	19	Thorn Lane LC	32B
Strensall Walbutts LC (UWC)	19	THORNABY	46C
Strumpshaw Fen LC (UWC)	8	Thornaby East Jn	46C
Strumpshaw LC (MG)	8	(Thornaby TMD (TE))	46C
Strumpshaw Occupation LC (UWC)	8		

Thornally No. 48 LC (UWC)	27A	Trent Jn (Scunthorpe)	33A
Thorne Jn	32B	Trent Sidings (Scunthorpe)	33A
Thorne Moorends LC (AHBC)	32B	Trent West Jn (Gainsborough)	26C
Thorne No. 1 LC (AHBC)	32B	TRIMLEY	9A
Thorne No. 2 LC (AHBC)	32B	Trimley No. 1 Gates LC (CCTV)	9A
THORNE NORTH	32B	Trinity Lane LC (MCG)	10B
THORNE SOUTH	32B	Trout Beck Bridge	39B
Thornfield House LC (UWC)	40B	TROWSE (disused)	7A
Thornhill LNW Jn	37B	Trowse (Lower) Jn	7A
Thornholme LC (UWC)	39B	Trowse (Swing Bridge) Jn	7A
THORNTON ABBEY	31B	Trowse Aggregates Terminal	7A
Thornton Gates LC (UWC)	39D	Trowse Swing Bridge	7A
THORPE BAY	3C	Trowse Swing Bridge SB (TB)	7A
Thorpe Bridge	7A	Tunstans LC (UWC)	44C
Thorpe Common LC (UWC)	38A	Tunstead Church Lane LC (UWG)	8
THORPE CULVERT	26D	Tunstead Market Street LC (AHBC)	8
Thorpe Culvert LC (MCB)	26D	TURKEY STREET	10B
Thorpe Culvert SB (TC)	26D	Turner Street Footbridge	27E
Thorpe Farm LC (UWC)	38A	Turners Lane Jn	35B
Thorpe Gates LC (MCB-OD)	40E	Tursdale Jn	20C
Thorpe Hall LC (MCB-OD)	40E	(Tuxford)	29A
Thorpe Jn	7A	Tuxford Emergency Crossovers	17A
Thorpe Lane No. 3 Gates LC (AHBC)	9A	Tuxford GSP	17A
Thorpe LC (AOCL)	18A	Tuxford No.1 GF	29A
Thorpe Le Fallows LC (UWC)	8	Tuxford No.2 GF	29A
Thorpe Marsh Jn	18A	Tuxford West Jn GF	29C
Thorpe Marsh Power Station G.F.	18A	Tuxford West Junction Sidings	29C
Thorpe Road LC (AHBC-X)	18A	Tweedmouth SB (TW)	23B
Thorpe Salvin Bridleway LC	30A	Tweedmouth Sidings	23B
Thorpe Yard	7A	Two Mile Bottom LC (AHBC-X)	13A
THORPE-LE-SOKEN	6A	Tye Green Jn	11B
Thorpe-le-Soken Jn	6A	Tyle Hall LC (UWC)	10A
Thorpe-on-the-Hill LC (AHBC-X)	26A	TYNE & WEAR METRO	49
Thorrington LC (CCTV)	6A	Tyne Coal Terminal	46A
(Three Counties)	15B	Tyne Dock	46A
Three Gates LC (UWC)	6A	TYNE DOCK (Metro)	49
Three Horse Shoes No. 1 (AHBC-X)	13C	Tyne Dock Bottom	46A
Three Horse Shoes No. 2 (AHBC-X)	13C	Tyne Dock International Freight Terminal	46A
Three Horse Shoes No. 3 (AHBC-X)	13C	Tyne Dock Tunnel (Metro)	49
Three Horse Shoes SB (THS)	13C	Tyne Green LC (UWC)	43E
Thrislington Quarry	20C	Tyne Yard	21B
Thrumpton LC (MCB)	30B	(Tyne Yard Box)	21B
Thrumpton SB (TN)	30B	Tyne Yard Engineer's Sidings	21B
Thrumpton West Jn	30B	Tyne Yard Exchange Sidings	21B
Thrybergh Jn	32A	Tyne Yard Maintenance Depot	21B
Thrybergh Jn LC (UWC)	32A	Tyne Yard Middle Cabin GF	21B
Thrybergh Steel Works	32A	Tyne Yard North Cabin GF	21B
THURNSCOE	32A	Tyne Yard South Cabin GF	21B
Thurrock Marine	4A	Tyne Yard Up Staging Sidings	21B
Thurrock Viaduct (HS1)	4A	Tyne Yard Virtual Quarry	21B
THURSTON	12D	TYNEMOUTH (Metro)	49
Thurston LC (Footpath) (R/G)	12D	Tyneside (IECC) (T)	22A
Thurstonland Tunnel	34C	Tyneside Central Freight Depot	22A
THUXTON (Mid-Norfolk Rly)	13B		
Thwaite Gates LC (CCTV)	39A	**U**	
Tickhill Viaduct	34A		
Tilbury Dock	4B	Ufford (36) LC (ABCL)	9A
(Tilbury East Jn)	4B	Ufford LC (UWC)	9A
Tilbury Exchange Sidings	4B	Ugley Lane LC (UWG)	11B
Tilbury Grain Terminal	4B	ULCEBY	31B
Tilbury IRFT	4B	Ulceby Chase Farm LC (MCB-OD)	31A
Tilbury Railport Jn (former Tilbury West Jn)	4B	Ulceby LC (MCB-OD)	31B
Tilbury RCT	4B	Ulceby North Jn	31B
Tilbury Riverside Sidings	4B	Ulceby South Jn	31B
TILBURY TOWN	4B	Ulgham Grange LC (CCTV)	22B
Tile Shed LC (AHBC-X)	46A	Ulgham Lane LC (CCTV)	22B
Tiled House Farm LC (AHBC)	12C	ULLESKELF	40A
Tindall Bank LC (UWC)	17B	UNIVERSITY (Metro)	45B
Tinsley Avesta LC (TMO)	28	Unstone Viaduct (River Drone)	27E
Tinsley East Jn	28	UPMINSTER	3B
Tinsley North Jn	28	Upminster (LUL) SB (FM)	3B
Tinsley Park	28	UPMINSTER BRIDGE (LUL)	3B
Tinsley Park Jn	28	Upminster East Jn	3B
Tinsley South Jn	28	Upminster GF	3B
Tinsleys LC (MCB-OD) (Campains Lane)	24D	Upminster IECC (UR/NL)	3B
Tioxide UK GF	31C	UPNEY (LUL)	3A
Tivetshall LC (AHBC-X)	6C	Upney Jn	3A
Tod Point Jn	47B	Upper Denton LC (AHBC-X)	43B
Tollerton	20A	Upper Denton West (UWC)	43B
(Tollerton Stn)	20A	UPPER HOLLOWAY	1A
Tollerton Up Sidings	20A	Upper Holloway SB (UH)	1A
Tolney Lane Viaduct	26A	Upperby Bridge Jn	43A
Tomlinsons LC (UWC)	26A	Upperby Jn	43A
Tong Park Viaduct	41	Upperby Yard GF	43A
Torworth LC (CCTV)	17A	UPTON PARK (LUL)	3A
Totley Tunnel	27E	Urlay Nook LC (MCB)	44C
Totley Tunnel East SB (TE)	27E		
TOTTENHAM COURT ROAD (Crossrail)	2D	**V**	
Tottenham Curve	10B		
TOTTENHAM HALE	10B	(Van den Burghs & Jurgens Sdgs)	4A
Tottenham North Curve Tunnels (1, 2 & 3)	1A	Vange Wharf LC (CCTV)	4B
Tottenham South Jn	10B	Vaseys LC (UWC)	20B
(Tottenham West Jn)	10B	Vellacotts Long Siding	4A
TOWER GATEWAY (DLR)	3A	Viaduct Maintenance LC (UWG)	11A
Town End Farm LC (UWC)	20B	Victoria Line Depot (LUL)	10B
Transit Quays (Immingham)	31B	Victoria Park	1B
Trees LC (CCTV)	11B	(Victoria Park Jn)	1B
Treeton	28	Victoria Road Covered Way	18C
Treeton Jn	28	Victoria Road LC (CCTV)	8
(Treeton North Jn)	28	Victoria Sdgs (Norwich)	7A
Trent East Jn (Gainsborough)	26C	Victoria Viaduct (Wicker Arches)	28
		Villa Farm LC (UWC)	39D
		Vine House Farm LC (UWC)	24D
		W	
		Wadhall Old Dam LC (UWC)	8

Engineers Line References

This listing is intended to show all the relevant operational ELRs that appear in this book, those that were live in the last edition but now closed, out of use or lifted and those that have carried over from the original network onto Heritage lines. More information can be found about these codes on the excellent website by Phil Deaves (see bibliography). The location of the start and finish boundary of each ELR can be found in the book from the map reference in the Location Index applicable to any of the locations named in the description. Some ELRs extend over several pages.

ABE	Allington Junction to Barkston East Junction Spur	CHM	Channelsea North Junction to High Meads Junction
ACD	Allington Chord	CHR	Chesterfield and Rotherham Line
ACK	Alnmouth to Alnwick Branch	CHS	Crigglestone Junction and Horbury Junction Link Line
ACW	Acton Canal Wharf to Willesden	CJC	Clapton Junction and Chingford Branch
ADH	Hull Alexandra Docks Branch	CJS	Carcroft Junction to Stainforth Junction Line
ALN	Haltwhistle - Alston Line	CNS	Carpenters Road North Junction to South Junction
ANL	Acton and Northolt Line	COC	Colchester and Clacton Line
ANS	Aldwarke North Junction to South Junction Link	COD	Cortonwood Colliery Branch
ATG	Turnham Green to Gunnersbury Junction	COV	Colne Valley Branch
AWL	Acton Wells Branch	CPM	Castleford and Pontefract Monkhill Line
AWP	Anlaby Road Junction to West Parade Junction Curve	CPS	Cottam Power Station Loop
BAH	Barnsley and Horbury Station Junction Line	CRC	Camden Road Junction to Camden Junction Line
BAR	Barton-On-Humber Branch	CRF	Camden Road to Finsbury Park Curve
BBW	Bradley Junction to Bradley Wood Junction Curve		(including King's Cross Goods)
BCB	Black Carr Junction to Bessacarr Junction Curve	CRS	Cromer and Sheringham Branch
BDH	Brent Curve Junction to Dudding Hill Junction	CST	Carpenters Road North Junction to Stratford Central
BDM	Bow Depot Midland		Junction West
BEC	Bevercotes Colliery Branch	CTH	Colne Junction to Hythe Junction Curve
BEW	Beighton Junction and Woodhouse Junction Branch	CTL	Calder Bridge Junction to Turners Lane Junction Curve
BFC	Bacon Factory Chord	CTP	Connington South Tip Sidings
BGE	Boldon West Curve	CWE	Clayton West Branch
BGK	Bethnal Green and King's Lynn Line	CWJ	Camden to Watford Junction Line (DC Electric Lines)
BHM	Barrow Hill Motive Power Depot	DAE	Darlington and Eastgate-In-Weardale Line
BHP	Boultham Junction to Pyewipe Junction Curve	DCF	Down Cambridge Flyover
BIB	Bingley Junction to Bradford Junction Curve	DDY	Decoy Down Yard
BKS	Brancliffe East Junction and Kirk Sandal Junction Line	DOC	King's Lynn Docks Branch
BLJ	Broughton Lane Junction to Shepcote Lane East	DOL	Doncaster and Leeds Line
	Junction Curve	DOW	Doncaster and Wrawby Junction Line
BNE	Benton North Junction to Earsdon Link Line	DRA	Drax Power Station Branch
BNW	Boldon New Curve	DRS	Dewsbury Railway Street Goods Yard Branch
BOH	Bowesfield Junction to Hartburn Junction Curve	DSN	Darlington and Saltburn Line
BOK	Broad Street and Old Kew Line via Hampstead	DUY	Decoy Up Yard
	(North London Line)	DWS	Dore West Junction to Dore Station Junction Curve
BRA	Braintree Branch	DWW	Dalston Kingsland Hackney Wick and
BRI	Brocklesby and Immingham Branch		North Woolwich Line
BTB	Barlow Tip Branch	ECM	East Coast Main Line
BTE	Barking Tilbury Line Junction East to Barking East	EGG	Eggborough Power Station Branch
	Junction Loop	EJM	Earsdon and Morpeth Line
BTJ	Brightside and Treeton Junction (via Tinsley) Line	ELL	East London Line
BWC	Bedlington Junction to Woodhorn Colliery Branch	ELN	Engine Shed Junction to Leeds North Junction Curve
BWO	Ashington Junction to Butterwell Junction	ELR	East Lincolnshire Railway
	(Butterwell Disposal Point)	EMP	Ely March and Peterborough Line
BWT Line	Barking Tilbury Line Junction West to Barking Tilbury Junction East Loop	ENT	Enfield Town Branch
BYE	Bury St Edmunds Yard	EPP	Epping Branch
CAW	Cricklewood to Acton Wells Line	ESK	East Suffolk Line
CBC	Carnforth Barrow and Carlisle Line	ETN	Ely to Norwich Line
CBI	Canal Tunnels	EWC	Ely West Curve
CCH	Cambridge Coldham Lane Junction and Haughley	FED	Felixstowe Docks Branch
	Junction Line	FEL	Felixstowe Branch
CDY	Chelmsford Freight Yard	FEP	Ferryhill Junction and Pelaw Line (Leamside Branch)
CER	Colchester Goods	FGW	Forest Gate Junction to Woodgrange Park Junction Curve
CFM	Church Fenton and Micklefield Line	FKW	Ferrybridge to Knottingley West Junction Curve
CFP	Canonbury to Finsbury Park Curve	FOM	Fletton to Orton Mere Branch
CGJ	Carlisle Grand Junction Line (WCML Crewe to Carlisle)	FSS	Fenchurch Street and Shoeburyness Line
		FWR	Rossington Colliery Branch (Doncaster)

FWW	Forncett Wymondham and Wells Line	LBE	Leeds and Bradford Exchange (now Interchange) Line
GDL	Goole Docks Line	LCJ	Loversall Junction to Flyover East Junction Curve
GFB	Gas Factory Junction to Bow Junction Curve	LCR	Loversall Carr Junction to Rossington Junction Curve
GLT	Green Lane Junction and Tyne Dock Line	LEC	London Euston to Crewe Line
GMS	Grantham Metals Sidings	LEH	Leeds and Harrogate Line
GOJ	Gospel Oak to Junction Road Junction Line	LEN	Longlands, Eaglescliffe and Newcastle Line
GRD	Greetland Junction to Dryclough Junction Curve	LLG	Low Level Goods
GRE	Graham Road Curve	LLP	Longlands Loop (Northallerton)
GRS	Grantham and Skegness Line	LLS	Lea Junction to Loughton Junction (now Temple Mills East Junction) Loop (Stratford)
GRW	Griffin Wharf Branch		
GUE	Guiseley Branch	LTN	Liverpool Street and Norwich Line
HAC	Harworth Colliery Branch	LVS	Liverpool Street, platforms 11-18
HAH	Haverton Hill Branch	MAC	Manchester and Cleethorpes Line
HAL	Haughley to Laxfield Branch	MAH	Manningtree and Harwich Line
HAU	Habrough Junction to Ulceby South Junction Curve	MAM	Maltby Colliery Branch
HAY	Harrogate and York Line	MAS	Manchester and Sheffield Line
HBS	Hull Bridlington and Seamer Line	MBW	Middlesbrough and Whitby Line
HCD	Holmes Chord	MCG	Maryport and Carlisle Goods Lines
HCS	Heaton Carriage Sidings	MCJ	Marylebone to Claydon L&NE Junction
HDB	Hertford Branch (Hertford Loop)	MCL	Midland City Line
HDT	Hackney Downs and Cheshunt (via Turkey Street) Line	MDL	Manchester Diggle and Leeds Line
HEB	Hertford East Branch	MEB	Moorgate Branch
HIM	High Marnham Branch	MEW	Methley Junction to Whitwood Junction Curve (Castleford)
HJB	Hexthorpe Junction to Bentley Junction Link Line (Doncaster Avoiding Line)		
		MGW	Milford Curve
HJM	Hepscott Junction to Morpeth Curve	MIT	Middleton Towers Branch (King's Lynn)
HJS	Hessle Road Junction to Saltend	MKB	Monk Bretton Branch
HLD	Hartlepool Docks Branch	MLN	Main Line (Paddington to Penzance via Bath)
HLK	High Level Bridge Junction to King Edward Bridge South Junction Line	MRB	Milner Royd Junction and Bradford Interchange Line
		MUP	March Up and Down Yards
HMC	Hatfield Main Colliery	MVL	Manchester Victoria and Huddersfield Line
HNB	Hendon Branch	MVN	Manchester Victoria and Normanton Line
HNC	Hambleton North Curve	MWJ	Marcheys House Junction to Winning Crossing Junction Curve
HOS	Holgate Junction to Skelton Line		
HOU	Hounslow Loop	MWL	March West Line
HPC	Hare Park Junction to Crofton West Junction Curve	MWN	Grimsby Dock Branch
HPQ	Harwich Parkeston Quay Goods Yard	NAJ	Neasden South to Aynho Junction
HPW	Harringay Park West Curve	NAY	Norwich and Yarmouth Line
HSC	Hambleton South Curve	NCW	Norwich Wensum Curve
HTM	Haywood Junction to Thorpe Junction (Shaftholme Flyover)	NEC	Newcastle and Carlisle Line
		NEK	Sunderland to South Hylton
HUE	Hunslet East Branch	NEN	Newburn Branch
HUL	Hull Line (Leeds to Hull)	NGD	Newcastle Goods Lines
HYM	Healey Mills Traction Maintenance Depot	NHM	Neville Hill Maintenance Depot Departure Sidings
ICS	Ilford Carriage Sidings	NJN	Neasden Junction Curve
ILK	Ilkley Branch	NKE	New Kew Junction to Kew East Junction Curve
INW	Immingham Dock North West Entrance Branch	NLF	Norwood Junction to Low Fell Junction Curve
IPD	Ipswich Docks Branch	NLI	North London Incline
IUP	Ipswich Upper Yard	NOB	Nottingham and Barnetby Line
JAW	Jarrow Branch	NOC	Normanton and Colton Junction Line
JCA	Joan Croft Junction to Applehurst Junction Curve	NOE	North Elmham Branch
JMM	Ferrybridge Power Station	NOG	Nottingham to Grantham Line
JRT	Junction Road Junction to Carlton Road Junction	NOL	Norwich Oulton Broad and Lowestoft Line
KBF	Kelloe Bank Foot Branch	NOP	Normanby Park Sidings Branch
KEB	King Edward Bridge East Junction to North Junction Line	NSE	Newark Crossing Curve
		NSM	Norwich City to Sheringham Branch
KES	Knottingley East Junction to South Junction Curve	NTE	North Curve (Manningtree North Junction to East Junction)
KGC	Kensal Green City Lines		
KGD	King George Dock Branch	NUJ	Nunnery Junction to Woodburn Junction Curve (Sheffield)
KGW	Kensal Green Junction to Willesden Low Level	NWE	Norton-On-Tees West Junction to East Junction Curve
KIL	Killingholme Branch		
KWS	Knottingley West Junction and Shaftholme Junction Line	OAJ	Oakenshaw Junction to Oakenshaw South Junction Curve
KWV	Keighley and Worth Valley Railway		

OSC	Oakenshaw to Crofton East Junction Branch
PBS	Pye Bridge to Shirebrook Line
PDL	Pelaw Down Link Line
PED	Penistone and Doncaster Line
PEF	Pontefract to Ferrybridge Curve
PEH	Penistone and Huddersfield Line
PGS	Palace Gates to Seven Sisters Line
PHC	Priory Yard Hull Central Goods
PHS	Peterborough Holding Sidings
PLG	Park Lane Junction to Greensfield Junction Chord (Newcastle)
PMJ	Peterborough to Manton Junction Line
POC	Port Clarence Branch
PSE	Pye to Shireoaks East Junction Line
PUL	Pelaw Up Link Line
PYE	Pyewipe Branch (Immingham)
RBY	Reedham Berney Arms and Yarmouth Line
RDG	Reading Line
REB	Redmire Branch
RLG	Rillington Junction to Grosmont Junction
RLY	Ripple Lane Yards
ROU	Romford and Upminster Branch
SAC	Settle and Carlisle Line
SAN	Santon Slag Sidings
SAR	South Acton to Richmond Line
SBF	Shipley and Bradford Forster Square Branch
SBR	Shepreth Branch
SCD	Scunthorpe Trent Junction to Dawes Lane Junction Branch
SCG	South Carlisle Goods Lines
SCW	Scarborough Gallows Close Goods
SDC	Stratford Central Junction West to Coppermill North Junction Loop
SEA	Dawdon Junction to Seabanks
SEC	Selby Canal Goods Curve
SEL	Shepcote Lane West Junction to Tinsley South Junction Curve
SES	Seal Sands Branch
SHB	Sheffield and Barnsley Line
SHG	Sherburn Curve
SHU	Shoeburyness Sidings
SHW	Shireoaks West Junction to Woodend Junction Curve
SIZ	Sizewell Power Station Branch
SJB	St James's Goods Junction to Bridge Junction
SJM	Swinton Junction to Mexborough Line
SKA	Skellow Junction to Adwick Junction Curve
SKI	Skipton to Ilkley Branch
SKL	Stocksbridge Light Railway
SKM	South Kirkby Junction to Moorthorpe Junction Curve
SKS	Skipton Middle Junction to Grassington/ Skipton & Swinden
SKW	Skipton and Wennington Line
SMJ	Swinton and Milford Junction Line
SNW	Sleaford North Junction to West Junction Loop
SOB	Soham Branch (Ely Dock Junction to Chippenham Junction)
SOT	Seaton-On-Tees Branch
SPC	St Pancras to Chesterfield Line
SPD	Spalding and Doncaster Line
SPW	Springbank Junction to Walton St Junction Curve
SSE	Sleaford South Junction to East Junction Curve

SSH	Scunthorpe Yard
SSK	Saltburn and Skinningrove Branch
SSL	Seven Sisters Loop
SSV	Shenfield and Southend Victoria Line
STB	St Botolphs Branch
STF	Norton On Tees South Junction to Ferryhill South Junction Branch
SUD	Sudbury Branch
SWP	Shirebrook Junction to Warsop Junction Curve
TAH	Tottenham and Hampstead Line
TCW	Temple Hirst Junction and Chaloner's Whin Junction via Selby Line
TDE	Tilbury Docks East Side
TEN	Cambridge Chord (Stansted East Junction to North Junction)
TEY	Tyne Yard
TFN	Trimley to Felixstowe North Freightliner Terminal Line
THG	Norwich Thorpe Goods and Carriage Sidings
THN	Thames Haven Branch
TJC	Tapton Junction (Chesterfield) to Colne
TJG	Thorne Junction to Gilberdyke Line
TLA	Third London Airport (Stansted Airport Link)
TLL	Tilbury Loop Line (Barking to Pitsea via Tilbury)
TNC	Treeton North Junction to Catcliffe Junction Curve
TOM	Thrapston to Orton Mere (Peterborough) Branch
TSE	South Tottenham East Junction to Tottenham South Junction
TSY	Tees Yard
TWN	Thorpe Le Soken and Walton On The Naze Line
TYB	Torksey Branch
TYC	Thoresby Colliery Branch
UCJ	Upperby Bridge Junction to Carlisle Caldew Junction
UDS	Up Decoy Sidings
ULR	Carlisle Upperby Junction to London Road Junction
UPG	Upminster and Grays Branch
WAG	Wakefield and Goole Line
WAW	Willesden to Acton Wells Line
WBC	West Burton Power Station Loops
WBH	Westgate Branch
WCI	Wilton ICI Branch
WCM	West Coast Main Line (north of Carlisle)
WEB	Werrington Branch
WEC	Westhorpe Colliery Line
WHC	Whitlingham Junction and Cromer Line
WHR	Whiskerhill Junction to Retford Curve
WIG	Wisbech Goods Branch
WIS	Wickford and Southminster Branch
WKC	Welbeck Colliery Branch
WLL	West London Line
WMB	Willesden Junction to Mitre Bridge Junction Curve
WMC	Wroxham to County School Line
WME	Woodburn Junction to Mexborough East Junction Line
WRG	Whitehall Road Goods Sidings
WSB	West Sleekburn and Blyth Branch
WWK	Wakefield Westgate Curve
WZS	Willesden Traction Maintenance Depot Sidings
XRC	Crossrail Central Section
XRS	Crossrail South Section
YDS	St Catherine's Junction to Decoy South Junction Curve
YMS	York Malton and Scarborough Line

Line of Route codes

Lines on the Network are given a Line of Route code (LOR) which may run over a number of ELRs. LORs have their origin in the codes used in the early 1990's in BR's Western Region. These were extended nationally by Railtrack in the late 90's as Possession Resource Information Database (PRIDE) codes and renamed LOR sometime after. More information can be found about these codes on the excellent website by Phil Deaves. The LOR description is the one generally used within the industry. To find an LOR in this book, take the location name from the list below and search for it in the Location Index.

Anglia LOR codes appearing in this book

EA1010	Liverpool Street to Seven Kings
EA1011	Seven Kings to Ipswich
EA1012	Ipswich to Trowse Jn
EA1013	Trowse Jn to Norwich
EA1020	Carpenters Road South Jn to Carpenters Road North Jn
EA1030	Forest Gate Jn to Woodgrange Park Jn
EA1040	Romford to Upminster
EA1050	Shenfield Jn to Southend Victoria
EA1060	Wickford Jn to Southminster
EA1070	Witham Jn to Braintree
EA1080	Marks Tey Jn to Sudbury
EA1090	Colchester Jn to Clacton
EA1100	East Gate Jn & Hythe Jn to Colchester Town
EA1110	Thorpe-le-Soken Jn to Walton-on-Naze
EA1120	Manningtree to Harwich Town
EA1130	Griffin Wharf Branch
EA1140	Ipswich Docks Branch
EA1150	Channelsea South Jn to Stratford Central Jn West
EA1160	Bethnal Green East Jn to Bishops Stortford
EA1161	Bishops Stortford to Ely North Jn
EA1162	Ely North Jn to Kings Lynn
EA1170	Hackney Downs North Jn to Enfield Town
EA1180	Reading Lane Jn to Navarino Road Jn (Graham Road Curve)
EA1190	Bury Street Jn to Cheshunt Jn
EA1200	Clapton Jn to Chingford
EA1210	Broxbourne Jn to Hertford East
EA1220	Stansted South & North Jns to Stansted Airport
EA1230	Royston to Shepreth Branch Jn
EA1270	Kings Lynn Jn to Middleton Towers
EA1280	Stratford Central Jn to Coppermill Jn
EA1290	Tottenham South Jn to South Tottenham East Jn
EA1300	South Tottenham West Jn to Seven Sisters Jn
EA1310	Camden Road West Jn to Richmond
EA1320	Camden Road West Jn to Stratford
EA1325	Highbury & Islington to New Cross/ New Cross Gate (ELL)
EA1330	South Acton Jn to Old & New Kew Jns
EA1340	Stratford Lea Jn to High Meads Jn
EA1350	Channelsea North Jn to Temple Mills East Jn
EA1360	Dudding Hill Jn to Acton West Jn
EA1370	Gospel Oak to Barking Tilbury Line Jn West
EA1380	Fenchurch Street to Shoeburyness
EA1390	Barking Tilbury Line Jn East to Pitsea Jn (via Tilbury)
EA1400	Gas Factory Jn to Bow Jn
EA1410	Upminster to West Thurrock Jn
EA1420	Thames Haven Jn to Thames Haven

EA1430	East Suffolk Jn to Oulton Broad North
EA1440	Westerfield Jn to Felixstowe Town
EA1450	Trimley to Port of Felixstowe North Quay Terminal
EA1460	Felixstowe Beach Jn to Felixstowe Beach
EA1470	Norwich Thorpe Jn to Lowestoft
EA1480	Whitlingham Jn to Cromer
EA1490	Cromer to Sheringham
EA1500	Brundall Jn to Yarmouth
EA1510	Reedham Jn to Yarmouth
EA1520	Saxmundham Jn to Sizewell
EA1530	Coldham Lane Jn to Haughley Jn
EA1540	Chippenham Jn to Ely Dock Jn
EA1550	Ely North Jn to Ely West Jn (Ely West Curve)
EA1560	Ely North Jn to Peterborough
EA1570	March (East & West Jns) to Wisbech
EA1580	Ely North Jn to Trowse Jn
EA1744	Bacon Factory Curve

London North Eastern LOR codes appearing in this book

LN101	King's Cross to Shaftholme Jn
LN105	Moorgate to Finsbury Park Jn
LN110	Canonbury West Jn to Finsbury Park Jn
LN115	Copenhagen Jn to Camden Road Central Jn
LN120	Wood Green North Jn to Langley Jn via Hertford
LN125	Hitchin, Cambridge Jn to Cambridge
LN126	Hitchin North Jn to Hitchin East Jn
LN135	Kings Dyke to Crescent Jn
LN147	Helpston Jn to Uffington
LN150	Flyover East Jn to Decoy North Jn
LN155	Flyover East Jn to Loversall Jn (Up Loversall Curve)
LN160	Loversall Carr Jn to Flyover West Jn
LN165	Harringay Park Jn to Harringay Jn
LN170	Werrington Jn to Flyover East Jn via Lincoln
LN175	Sleaford South Jn to Sleaford East Jn
LN180	Sleaford West Jn to Sleaford North Jn
LN185	Allington West Jn to Skegness
LN190	Allington East Jn to Allington North Jn
LN195	Grantham, Nottingham Branch Jn to Allington West Jn (Inclusive)
LN200	Wrawby Jn to Pelham Street Jn
LN205	Newark Flat Crossing (Inclusive) to West Holmes Jn
LN206	Staythorpe Crossing to West Holmes Curve
LN210	Newark Crossing Curve
LN215	Boultham Jn to Pyewipe Jn
LN220	Bessacarr Jn to Black Carr Jn
LN225*	Cleethorpes to Retford
LN230*	Retford Western Jn to Thrumpton West Jn
LN235	Rossington Colliery Branch
LN240*	Doncaster Bridge Jn to Saint James Jn

LN600	Shaftholme Jn to Reston GSP
LN618	Holgate Jn to Skelton Jn
LN620	King Edward Bridge East Jn to King Edward Bridge North Jn (East Curve)
LN622	Forth Branch
LN624	Northallerton, Castle Hills Jn to Castle Hills West GF
LN626	Northallerton High Jn to Northallerton East Jn
LN627	Northallerton Longlands Jn to Newcastle East via the Coast
LN628	South Hylton to Sunderland South Jn
LN629	Pelaw Metro Jn to Pelaw South Jn
LN630	Pelaw North Jn to Pelaw Metro Jn
LN631	Darlington South Jn to Eaglescliffe South Jn
LN632	Stockton Cut Jn to Saltburn
LN634	Guisborough Jn to Whitby
LN636	Beam Mill Jn to Slag Road (Lackenby)
LN638	Grangetown (Shell Jn) to Cleveland Freightliner
LN640	ICI Wilton Coal Terminal
LN642	Saltburn West Jn to Boulby Potash Mine
LN644	Hartburn Curve
LN646	Norton-on-Tees South to Ferryhill South Jn
LN648	Norton-on-Tees West to Norton-on-Tees East
LN652	Billingham-on-Tees to Seal Sands Storage
LN656	Seaton-on-Tees Branch
LN662	Ryhope Grange to Hendon
LN664	Boldon East Jn to Boldon North Jn
LN666	Boldon West Jn to Tyne Dock
LN670	Jarrow Branch
LN672	Wardley to Pelaw Jn
LN674	High Level Bridge Jn to Greensfield Jn (West Curve)
LN676	Park Lane Jn to King Edward Bridge South Jn
LN678	Darlington North Jn to Eastgate
LN682	King Edward Bridge South Jn to Carlisle North Jn
LN684	Low Fell Jn to Norwood Jn
LN694	Benton North Jn to Morpeth North Jn via Bedlington
LN696	Hepscott Jn to Morpeth Jn
LN700	Butterwell North Branch
LN702	Bedlington North to Lynemouth Alcan
LN706	West Sleekburn Jn to North Blyth
LN708	Winning Jn to Marchey's House Jn
LN720*	Doncaster Black Carr to Skelton Bridge
LN722*	Flyover East Jn to Decoy North Jn
LN724	Holgate Jn to Skelton Jn
LN726*	Gainsborough Lea Road to Flyover East Jn
LN728*	Wrawby Jn to Pelham Street Jn
LN730*	Staythorpe Crossing to West Holmes Curve
LN732*	Newark Crossing Curve
LN734*	Boultham Jn to Pyewipe Jn
LN736	Cleethorpes to Nunnery Main Line Jn via Retford
LN738	Great Coates No.1 to Union Dock
LN740	Grimsby, Marsh West Jn to Humber Road Jn
LN741	Habrough Jn to Ulceby South Jn
LN742	Killingholme to Brocklesby Jn
LN744	Ulceby North Jn to Barton on Humber
LN746	Cottam Power Station Branch
LN748	Retford Western Jn to Thrumpton West Jn
LN750	Woodburn Jn to Deepcar

LN752	Wrawby Jn to Marshgate Jn
LN754	Scunthorpe Foreign Ore Branch
LN756	Scunthorpe Trent Jn to Roxby
LN758	Brancliffe East Jn to Kirk Sandall Jn
LN760	Firbeck Jn to Haworth Colliery
LN762	St. Catherines Jn to Decoy South Jn (St. Catherines Curve)
LN764	Low Ellers Curve
LN766	Bentley Jn to Hexthorpe Jn (Doncaster Avoiding Line)
LN768	Mansfield Woodhouse to Shireoaks East Jn
LN772	Warsop Jn to Shirebrook Jn
LN782	Woodend Jn to Shireoaks East Jn
LN784	High Marnham to Shirebrook East Jn
LN786	Bevercotes Colliery Branch
LN788	Thoresby Colliery Branch
LN802	Welbeck Colliery Branch
LN804	Tapton Jn to Gascoigne Wood (Via Sheffield)
LN806	Tapton Jn to Masborough Jn
LN807	Dore South Jn to Dore West Jn
LN808	Dore Station Jn to Totley Tunnel East
LN809	Shepcote Lane West Jn to Tinsley Yard East End
LN810	Shepcote Lane West Jn to Tinsley South Jn
LN812	Shepcote Lane East Jn to Broughton Lane Jn
LN814	Tinsley North Jn to Sheffield Tram Transfer Line
LN815	Parkgate Jn to Sheffield Tram Parkgate Transfer Line
LN816	Beighton Jn to Woodhouse Jn
LN818	Holmes Chord
LN824	Moorthorpe Jn to South Kirkby Jn
LN826	Doncaster South Yorkshire Jn to Swinton Jn North
LN828	Mexborough Jn to Aldwarke Jn via Kilnhurst
LN830	Aldwarke Jn to Woodburn Jn
LN832	Doncaster Bridge Jn to St. James Jn
LN836	Doncaster, Marshgate Jn to Neville Hill East Jn
LN838	Leeds Armley Jn to Skelton Jn via Harrogate
LN840	Leeds Engine Shed Jn to Whitehall East Jn
LN842	Thorpe Marsh Jn to Adwick Jn
LN844	Applehurst Loop
LN846	Carcroft Jn to Skellow Jn
LN848	Hare Park Jn to Crofton West Jn
LN850	Wakefield Westgate South Jn to Wakefield Kirkgate
LN852	Holbeck Jn to Bradford Interchange
LN854	Hall Royd Jn to Skelton Jn
LN858	Milner Royd Jn to Bradford Mill Lane Jn
LN859	Greetland Jn to Dryclough Jn
LN860	Diggle Jn to Copley Hill East Jn
LN861	Bradley Jn to Bradley Wood Jn
LN862	Barnsley Station Jn to Huddersfield
LN864	Dewsbury Railway Street Branch
LN868	Wincobank Jn to Horbury Jn
LN870	Wakefield Turners Lane to Calder Bridge Jn
LN872	Altofts Jn to Leeds West Jn
LN874	Methley Jn to Whitwood Jn
LN875	Castleford West Jn to Pontefract West Jn
LN878	Sherburn Jn to Gascoigne Wood
LN880	York to Scarborough
LN882	Wakefield Kirkgate West Jn to Goole Potters Grange Jn
LN884	Oakenshaw South Jn to Oakenshaw Jn

LN886   Monk Bretton Loop to Crofton East Jn
LN888   Hadfield and Stainforth (Stainforth Jn) to
              Ferrybridge North Jn
LN889   Shaftholme Jn to Haywood Jn
LN892   Pontefract East Jn to Ferrybridge South Jn
LN894   Knottingley South Jn to Knottingley East Jn
LN896   Drax Power Station Branch
LN898   Neville Hill East Jn to Hull
LN899   Hessle East Jn to Hull Dairycoates
LN900   Neville Hill West Jn to Hunslet East
LN902   Micklefield Jn to Church Fenton North Jn
LN904   Hambleton South Jn to Hambleton West Jn
LN906   Hambleton East Jn to Hambleton North Jn
LN908   Selby West Jn to Canal Jn
LN910   Temple Hirst Jn to Selby South Jn
LN912   Thorne Jn to Gilberdyke Jn
LN914   Hull (Paragon) to Seamer West Jn
LN916   Hessle Road to Saltend
LN918   Springbank North Jn to Walton Street Jn
LN920   Anlaby Road Jn to West Parade North Jn
LN922   Whitehall West Jn to Hellifield South Jn
LN924   Apperley Jn to Ilkley
LN926   Dockfield Jn to Esholt Jn
LN928   Shipley East to Bradford Forster Square
LN930   Skipton Middle Jn to Rylstone
LN932   Shipley South Jn to Shipley West J

East Midlands LOR codes which appear all or in part in this book

LN3201   St. Pancras to Tapton Jn (Via Derby)
LN3210   Junction Road Jn to Carlton Road Jn
                (Tottenham Lines)
LN3213   Moorgate to Kentish Town
LN3214   Canal Tunnel Jn to Belle Isle Jn
LN3219   Cricklewood Curve Jn to Dudding Hill Jn
LN3222   Brent Curve Jn to Dudding Hill Jn
LN3273   Codnor Park Jn to Shirebrook Jn
LN3615   Helpston Jn to Syston South Jn
LN3625   Nottingham East Jn to Newark Flat Crossing
                (Exclusive)
LN 3635   Allington West Jn (Exclusive) to Netherfield Jn

London North Western (South) LOR codes which appear all or in part in this book

MD101   Euston to Armitage Junction (Exclusive)
MD120   Camden Junction to Watford Junction (DC Lines)
MD150   Kensal Green Jn to Willesden Suburban Jn
MD155   Kensal Green Jn to Harlesden Jn (City Lines)
MD160   Willesden High Level Jn to Mitre Bridge Jn
MD166   North Pole Junction to Wembley

MD167   Mitre Bridge Junction to Acton Wells Junction
                (South West lines)
MD701   Marylebone to Aynho Junction
MD715   Neasden South Junction to Harrow on the Hill

London North Western (North) LOR codes which appear all or in part in this book

NW4001   Preston Ribble Jn to Cove L.C.
NW4021   Upperby Jn to Rome Street Jn
NW4023   Upperby Jn to London Road Jn
NW4025   Currock Jn to Bog Jn
NW4033   Carnforth North Jn to Carlisle South Jn
                 (Via Barrow)
NW7001   Manchester Victoria West Jn to Hebden Bridge
NW7021   Miles Platting Jn to Marsden
NW9001   Dore West Jn to Edgeley Jn No.1
                 (Hope Valley Lines)
NW9901   Gargrave to Carlisle South Jn
NW9909   Corby Gates to Petteril Bridge Jn
NW9911   London Road Jn to Bog Jn
                     (Newcastle Goods Lines)

Scotland LOR codes which appear all or in part in this book

SC147   Berwick to Haymarket West Jn (via Waverley)

South East LOR codes which appear all or in part in this book

SO250   Battersea Pier Jn to Wembley

Wessex LOR codes which appear all or in part in this book

SW210   Clapham Junction to Reading
SW220   Latchmere Junction to Kensington Olympia
SW230   Barnes to Feltham Junction (via Hounslow)

Western LOR codes which appear all or in part in this book

GW103   Paddington to Uffington
GW110   Old Oak Common West to South Ruislip
                (Exclusive)
GW130   Acton Wells to Acton East

The following LOR code applies to an Anglia line but appears in Book 5

EA1327   Silwood Jn to Old Kent Road Jn

Note:

*A number of LOR codes appear in the list above which may appear in Network Rail documentation, particularly related to LNE Weekly Operating Notices. These are 'replicas' of the primary LOR, in full or in part, allocated solely for internal purposes. They do not have an authority in their own right and do not appear on the maps.

Bibliography

The Publisher is grateful for the access given by Network Rail to a significant range of internal documents, most particularly the Sectional Appendix, Weekly and Periodic Operating Notices, Signalling Notices and Isolation Diagrams. In addition, a large number of other references have been used, the most reliable of which are:

Railway Passenger Stations in Great Britain - A Chronology (4th Edition)
By Michael Quick
Railway & Canal Historical Society, Oxford OX2 0NP

Signalling Atlas and Signal Box Directory (3rd Edition)
By Peter Kay and David Allen
Signalling Record Society, Wallasey, CH45 4PZ

The Railway Data Series (20 volumes covering the British Isles)
By Michael Oakley
Sword Press, Sutton Coldfield, B73 5UL

The Railways of Great Britain - A Historical Atlas (3rd Edition)
By Colonel Michael H. Cobb
Patrick S. Cobb, Newbury, RG20 9LB

Minor Railways in the British Isles series (4 volumes of track plans)
By Peter Scott
Published by P Scott, Reading RG30 2DQ

Branch Line News
Published fortnightly by the Branch Line Society, Bristol BS34 8NP

Signalling Record
Published bi-monthly by Signalling Record Society, http://www.s-r-s.org.uk
(including the annual Signal Box Alterations Survey carried out by John McCrickard)

Midland Railway System Maps (6 volumes covering Midland Railway lines)
By John Gough & Peter Kay
Peter Kay, Teighnmouth TQ14 8DP

The 'Trackwatch' column from Modern Railways Magazine
2004-2011, by the late Gerald Jacobs
2011-2014, by Mike Bridge
2015 onwards, by Martyn Brailsford

British Rail National Route Codes; Catalogue of Route Sections at 1st January 1973
British Rail National Route Code Catalogue: List of Route Sections at 1st April 1986

Websites:
http://www.railwaycodes.org.uk/index.shtml: A site by Phil Deaves which details ELRs, past and present, LORs, Signal Box codes and a host of other useful information
http://www.limitofshunt.org.uk/: A site giving access to much older copies of Sectional Appendix and Signalling Notices
http://maps.nls.org.uk/: The National Library of Scotland which includes UK-wide old OS mapping at different scales
http://www.old-maps.co.uk/: Another source of old OS mapping
http://www.disused-stations.org.uk/: A source of information about station histories
http://www.whatdotheyknow.com/: A site collecting the results of FOI requests
http://www.google.co.uk/maps and Google Earth: Site and software providing aerial photography, often at a range of dates and over which detailed distance measurement can be made.